O— 6-13-01
R— 6-16-01

#32.95

Sgt.

GRIT

W—Dog Co. S'N
Never in Doub
Ray David
Cleared Hot

$12.48 w/SH

w/45m Bad
40 SLP.

NEVER
IN DOUBT

NEVER
IN DOUBT
REMEMBERING IWO JIMA

Edited by Lynn S. Kessler

with Edmond B. Bart

NAVAL INSTITUTE PRESS
Annapolis, Maryland

Library of Congress Cataloging-in-Publication Data
Never in doubt : remembering Iwo Jima / edited by Lynn S. Kessler with
    Edmond B. Bart.
        p.   cm.
    Oral histories.
    Includes bibliographical references.
    ISBN 1-55750-463-6 (alk. paper)
    1. Iwo Jima, Battle of, 1945—Personal narratives, American.
2. Oral history.   I. Kessler, Lynn.   II. Bart, Edmond B., 1955–   .
D767.99.I9N39 1999
940.54'26—dc21   98-47672

Printed in the United States of America on acid-free paper ⊗
06 05 04 03 02 01 00 99   9 8 7 6 5 4 3 2

Unless otherwise noted, photographs of individuals were provided by
the veterans themselves.

To Edmond S. Bartosiewicz

Weapons Company, 3d Battalion, 8th Marines, 2d Marine Division
Veteran of Guadalcanal, Tarawa, Saipan, Tinian, and Okinawa

Victory was never in doubt. . . . What was in doubt, was whether there would be any of us left to dedicate our cemetery at the end.

Maj. Gen. Graves B. Erskine, Commander,
3d Marine Division, at the dedication of the
3d Marine Division Cemetery on 14 March 1945

I looked back at that little island, and I said, Every day I live from now on will be a bonus.

Sgt. Alfred Cialfi, Company D, 2d Pioneer Battalion,
20th Marines, 4th Marine Division,
upon departing Iwo Jima, 15 March 1945

CONTENTS

FOREWORD

No Marine, sailor, soldier, or airman who set foot on Iwo Jima during the thirty-six days of fighting for that island will ever forget it—nor should anyone forget it. That bloody battle was one of the last chapters of hand-to-hand combat in World War II, and the U.S. victory on that island made it clear to the leaders in Japan that they no longer had any hope for victory over the United States.

The battle on Iwo Jima brought home the very clear message that it was the Marine "Grunt" at the team and squad level who epitomized what Marine Corps training and readiness was all about. Hundreds of young Marines found themselves face to face with enemy soldiers who had all pledged to kill ten Marines before taking their own lives, and the only weapons available to both opponents were the bayonet or the combat knife—it was kill or be killed. There were individual victors on both sides, but ultimately the Marines were victorious, and their difficult amphibious operation made another major contribution to ending the war in the Pacific.

It is never easy to get those who endured close combat—which is experienced by only a small percentage of warriors who are in eyeball range of the enemy—to talk about their personal experiences. They much prefer to talk about the bravery and the sacrifices of their foxhole buddies or their leaders. With the passage now of more than fifty years and a realization that not much time remains to tell their stories, a number of the Iwo Jima combatants have been persuaded to discuss their experiences.

These oral histories should be treasured because, God willing and if men of good will can gain the objective of peace on earth, these types of stories will never have to be repeated. Read them, and thank these men as you do so, because the veterans of Iwo Jima and all others who served in World War II, and those who stayed home and gave them magnificent material and moral support, are responsible for the freedoms which Americans enjoy today.

LAWRENCE F. SNOWDEN, Lieutenant General,
U.S. Marine Corps (Ret.)

Captain, Commanding Officer, Fox Company,
2d Battalion, 23d Marines, 4th Marine Division,
on landing on Iwo Jima, 19 February 1945

PREFACE AND ACKNOWLEDGMENTS

The interviews included in this book represent those obtained from a database of more than five hundred Iwo Jima veterans. Most stories were recorded face to face during the two-year interview portion of this project; others were sent in on tape, or were handwritten. In all cases, the veterans were generous with their time and memories, and I am truly grateful for their patience during the creation of this work.

This book also owes a great deal of its being to Lt. Col. Edmond B. Bart, USMCR, a friend, compatriot, confidant, and contemporary, and a pilot who flew an F-18 in Desert Storm. His father served with the 2d Marine Division at Guadalcanal, Tarawa, Saipan, Tinian, and Okinawa, and from him Ed gained a fascination and deep affection for anything Marine. Ed was also fortunate enough to accompany a group of Iwo Jima survivors back to the island for the fiftieth anniversary of the battle. Of this group, several belonged to the Iwo Jima Survivors Association of Newington, Connecticut, and Ed became an Associate Life Member and grew to know many of these men well. His affection for his father, and his respect for these veterans, led him to consider devising a way to give back, in some small manner, what all these men gave of themselves for the freedoms we now enjoy.

As a result, a book of *some* nature about Iwo Jima was Ed's idea, not mine. But Ed is a pilot, and at the time he first approached me with his idea in 1995, his writing *any* book was not at all likely. So we began a collaboration. Through Ed, I also met several members of the Iwo Jima Survivors Association who told me smidgens of their experiences on Iwo Jima, and Ed and I both realized that no one had ever published an oral history of the battle. Thus, a project was born.

Unfortunately, due to his father's declining health and other uncontrollable factors, Ed was unable to contribute to the extent that both of us had wished. But that does not make his contribution any less significant than mine. Without Ed's inspiration and his guiding knowledge of the battle itself and anything Marine, this book would never have existed. My first and best thanks, personally, must go to him.

Next, my best thanks, professionally, must go to all the members of the armed services who contributed their stories printed here, and also to those who contributed but unfortunately, due to space considerations, were not included. Special thanks are also extended to the Iwo Jima Survivors Association, who supported my efforts by allowing me access to their database of members, and by freely offering their advice, guidance, and several picnics; to the Marine photographer assigned to Gen. Holland M. Smith, Arthur J. Kiely Jr., who provided several of his photos taken during the Iwo Jima campaign; and also, to Charles W. Lindberg, the last survivor of the first flag-raising, for providing copies of his collection of Robert Campbell's and Louis R. Lowery's photos of that flag-raising.

Finally, my everlasting thanks must go to the 6,821 Marines, sailors, soldiers, and airmen who died at Iwo Jima. May this book honor their sacrifice.

MARINE UNIT DESIGNATIONS, TERMS, AND SLANG

Marines are proud of their unit designations, and justifiably so. Their fighting tradition is long and honorable, and they guard that tradition, and their unit's honor, quite jealously. Typically, a Marine refers to himself and his unit differently than does an Army soldier, and to the uninitiated confusion can arise. For example, an Army soldier might identify his unit as the 1st Battalion, 5th Artillery, 1st Infantry Division, but a Marine typically would identify his own as the 1st Battalion, 11th Marines, without reference to the parent division. First of all, Marine ground regiments, be they infantry, artillery, or engineer, are never identified by the military occupational specialty. They are all simply "Marines." And second, the occupational specialty, and the parent division of Marine regiments, are thus identified intrinsically by a regiment's number. In the above example, the Marine is an artilleryman of the 1st Marine Division, and even though the parent division remained unidentified, any other Marine would know which is the parent division automatically. Although I have not provided a table to identify the numbered units by occupational specialty, I have retained the traditional practice in identifying each Marine storyteller.

Many terms and slang used in this book are also peculiar to the Marines. Being a branch of the Navy, many of these terms have naval roots. Others are pure Marine Corps. Rather than footnote each appearance in the text, the following list should define most of those terms encountered.

AKA	Auxillary Cargo Transport, Attack
Amtracs	LVTs
APA	Auxillary Personnel Transport, Attack

BAR	Browning automatic rifle
Boondocker(s)	Ankle-height combat shoe
Bulkhead stare	Marine equivalent of the "thousand-yard stare"
CO	Commanding officer
Corpsman	Marine equivalent of Army medic
CP	Command post
Deck	Floor; sometimes the ground ("Hit the deck!")
DI	Drill instructor
DUKW	Amphibian truck used to transport light artillery
FMF-Pac	Fleet Marine Force, Pacific
FO	Forward observer
Gear	Marine equipment
Gung-ho	Borrowed from the Chinese by Colonel Carlson of the Raiders, meaning "work together"; later changed to describe any overzealous Marine
Gunny/gunny sergeant	Gunnery sergeant; refers to Army equivalent of sergeants first class and above
Higgins Boat	Landing craft for infantry and light vehicles (LCVP)
IFF	Identification Friend or Foe
K-bar	Marine fighting knife; not to be confused with a bayonet
KA	AKA
LCI	Landing Craft, Infantry
LCM	Landing Craft, Mechanized
LCVP	Landing Craft, Vehicle and Personnel (Higgins Boat)
Lock and load	Command to load personal weapon prior to combat
LSD	Landing Ship, Dock

LSM	Landing Ship, Medium
LST	Landing Ship, Troop
LVT	Landing Vehicle, Tracked (the "Buffalo")
LVT(A)	Landing Vehicle, Tracked (Armored)
M4A3	Late-war Sherman tank
Old salt	Career enlisted Marine; any enlisted Marine who is older and/or experienced (that is, "salty")
PA	APA
PI	Parris Island
RD4	Navy version of the C-47 twin-engine cargo aircraft
Scuttlebutt	Rumor
Tony	Japanese interceptor single-engine aircraft
Tractor	Amphibian tractor (LVT)
UDT	Underwater demolition team
Utilities	Marine combat dungarees
Zeke	Later variant of the famous "Zero," Japanese fighter aircraft

NEVER
IN DOUBT

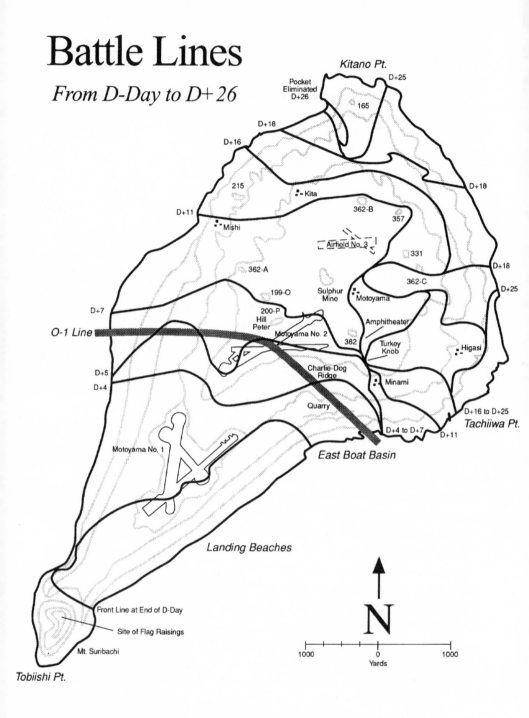

Battle Lines

From D-Day to D+26

Kitano Pt.

D+25

Pocket
Eliminated
D+26

165

D+18

D+16

215

Kita

362-B

357

D+11

Mishi

Airfield No. 3

331

D+18

362-A

199-O

Sulphur
Mine

Motoyama

362-C

D+18

D+25

200-P
Hill
Peter

Motoyama No. 2

382

Amphitheater

D+7

O-1 Line

Turkey
Knob

Higasi

D+5

D+4

Charlie-Dog
Ridge

Minami

Quarry

D+16 to D+25

Tachiiwa Pt.

D+4 to D+7

D+11

East Boat Basin

Motoyama No. 1

Landing Beaches

N

Front Line at End of D-Day

Site of Flag Raisings

Mt. Suribachi

1000   0   1000
Yards

Tobiishi Pt.

INTRODUCTION

There will be no detailed, day-by-day analysis of the battle for Iwo Jima here. That will be left to far superior books already in print. This book is intended to provide only an eyewitness report of personal events, impressions, and feelings about the battle for Iwo Jima, which imprinted itself sometimes indelibly, sometimes hazily, in the memories of these veterans. All of them were either enlisted or junior officers; their senior commanders are now long gone. Their oral narratives, as I recorded them, ran pretty much from the beginning of boot camp through the end of the battle, and on into the meaning that their experience has for them today. I have edited these stories for repetition and overlap, and I have corrected many inaccuracies with footnotes, but I have not always attempted to pursue absolute accuracy of facts, and therefore I will probably suffer the ire of the professional historian. So be it. The veterans told me their stories for the meaning these stories had for them, and for how their experiences have affected their lives since. They did not always have all the facts straight, but the meaning was always clear. Some were hesitant in telling the deep, visceral details of their experience, and I suspect this is because many of those details are still too painful to recall even today, more than fifty years after the end of the battle. Still, in my recording of these face-to-face interviews, some of these veterans broke into tears, yet none insisted that we not continue. Most insisted instead that they tell these stories not to glorify themselves, or glorify war, but to record the reality of the experience of the battle, partly because of their pride in participating, and mostly because they all want never to see a battle like Iwo Jima happen again.

For those familiar only with the name *Iwo Jima* and Joe Rosenthal's immortal photo of the flag-raising atop Mount Suribachi on D+4, a characterization of the battle is necessary. Typically, the Iwo Jima campaign is usually perceived as strictly a Marine Corps operation. It was not. Of course, the Marine element of the operation was the largest, and being a branch of the Navy the latter supported the former heavily with transport, gunfire, and air strikes, and medical facilities and personnel. But Army Air Corps bombers also participated in softening up the island, and its fighter squadrons called Iwo Jima home from early March though the end of the war. In fact, the whole justification for Iwo Jima's capture lay in its appeal as an air base. The Japanese had first used it as a warning station against our B-29 bomber raids on mainland Japan. Once forewarned, Japanese Zekes and Tonys had ample time to form up and greet our approaching bomber groups, and their effect was deadly enough to force the ditching of several B-29s far short of their Marianas Islands home bases. For the United States, Iwo Jima's proximity to Japan would allow long-range P-51s based there to escort the bombers all the way to Japan and back *and* cover them over their targets, while Iwo itself would provide an emergency strip for any B-29s too badly shot up to make it back to the Marianas. Naturally, maintenance and repair facilities had to be available on Iwo, which the Air Corps provided. And naturally, with Iwo being located on the edge of the Japanese aviation sphere of influence, and with the occasional sniper still active inside Iwo Jima's miles-long tunnel and cave complex, Army antiaircraft and ground units were also assigned to defend the island and airstrips. So what seemed to be a strictly Marine Corps and Navy operation was actually planned as an interservice venture far back in late 1943.

Planners expected the Japanese to be smashed beneath the naval and air bombardment and buried in their caves and bunkers, allowing the Marines to reach the 0-1 line halfway up the island by nightfall on D-Day, 19 February 1945. Marines who had seen action on Saipan—an island ten times the size of Iwo Jima—expected the campaign to last less than five days.

It would last thirty-six.

On D-day morning, units waited topside for the call to descend the nets into the Higgins boats, and watched the shelling and bombing of Iwo Jima. The top commander of all Marines in the Pacific, Lt. Gen. Holland M. Smith, also watched and paced his bridge on the *Eldorado*. He studied the circling LVTs through binoculars and chomped on his unlit cigar, asked himself how many Marines from Maj. Gen. Harry Schmidt's Fifth Amphibious Corps would die on the beaches because his Navy counterparts allowed only three days of preinvasion shelling instead of his requested ten. He worried that the bombing and shelling would have little effect on the concrete bunkers and caves of the Japanese emplacements.

He had reason to worry. Two days earlier, while a dozen gunboats deposited their UDT teams near shore to check for obstacles, Lieutenant General Kuribayashi, the Japanese commander, decided this little force was *the* invasion, and opened up with nearby shore batteries. Every gunboat was damaged or sunk, nearly two hundred men were killed or wounded.

When the men of the 4th and 5th Marine Divisions who had been circling in their LVTs finally hit the beaches, they reacted as they had been taught, or as they had learned through hard experience. General Kuribayashi's strategy was based on allowing the Marines to pile up on the deep volcanic sand of the beaches, then shell them into oblivion. But he did not succeed. He had waited too long. Too many Marines had landed, and their drive was too strong to stop. Many more would join them when the 3d Marine Division came ashore on D+2.

As the title implies, at no time was there any doubt of the outcome of the battle. Iwo Jima was far unlike, say, Tarawa, where the 2d Marine Division hung on to a bare strip of coral beach on Betio Island no longer than one thousand yards, and no deeper than one hundred, for thirty-six hours. Col. David Shoup, the commander on the beach at Tarawa, had occasional doubts then, as did Maj. Gen. Julian Smith, commander of the 2d Marine Division. But at Iwo, on D-day morning, only those Marines trying to climb up those volcanic terraces—Marines who slid back one step in the black sand for every two steps forward—had any doubt about the outcome, and then for only a few hours. Once the Marines had made some progress off the beach by afternoon, there would be no stopping them.

Most people unfamiliar with the battle believe that it ended when Suribachi was captured and the colors were raised at the rim of the dormant volcano. That was on D+4, or 23 February. Depending on your point of view, the battle would either continue for another twenty-one days, when the island was officially declared "secured" on 16 March, or until 26 March, when General Schmidt actually closed up the Fifth Amphibious Corps command post. Most people also believe that the flag-raising captured in Joe Rosenthal's photo was of the first, and only, flag-raising. It was actually the second. The story of the second flag-raising has been recounted in too many books and movies to bear another telling here. There is, however, a recounting of the first flag-raising, offered by Cpl. Charles Lindberg, the last surviving member of that event. Of the two, the first flag-raising is far more important. Without it there would not have been a second. It has never received the recognition it deserves.

Of the time subsequent to the capture of Suribachi, when the Marines started moving past Motoyama Number 1 airfield into the rest of the island and the final mop-up at Kitano Point, memories become unclear. Most Marines are sure of what happened, but not when. This is anecdotal of the rest of the battle, which was a series of repetitive actions. Iwo Jima above Motoyama Number 1 was one long expanse of ridges and volcanic outcroppings which concealed caves and spiderholes, and the divisions moved up the island roughly in line—the 5th on the left, the 3d in the center, and the 4th on the right. The Marines might move a few yards after jumping off during the morning's attack only to spend the rest of the day reducing a bunker or cave with flamethrowers and demolitions. Tanks, especially the flamethrowers—if they could get one—were valued more than any other weapon. All tanks were in high demand, but they could not maneuver in the tighter draws and ravines. So it was up to the infantryman, as always, day after day, to reduce the strongpoints of their defenders, whom the Marines never saw.

Physical features of the terrain began to look the same. Iwo Jima, being volcanic, was all sulfur and black rock, which the artillery and bombs had blasted and denuded of vegetation. Several veterans who have attended reunions on Iwo Jima in the last decade are amazed at how green the island looks now. Then it was barren. Not featureless, just barren. The features have names now: Charlie-Dog Ridge, Hills Oboe and Peter, Hill 382, Turkey Knob, the Amphitheater, the Meat Grinder. Then the veterans knew them only as "that damned place where we lost Lieutenant So-and-so." Even now, they could not pick those places out of memory on the numerous maps of Iwo Jima which have appeared in books on the battle since the end of the war.

At the end of the battle—"the end" meaning when they were "ordered off" the island, not necessarily the end of the fighting—they were all glad to leave, of course. They were also sad that they left behind those who died, sad that they did not yet know what happened to those who were wounded and flown out or who sailed off with one of the hospital ships. And they were sad because they also left a part of themselves on that island that they would never recover. But there was a tradeoff. There was a loss of innocence, but a gain of experience; a loss of doubt, and a gain of certainty and respect for country and duty; a loss of friends and comrades, but a gain of the future.

These Iwo Jima veterans, most now in their seventies some fifty years after the battle, regard each other with a deep respect and honor, regardless of each veteran's unit background. It may not always have been this way. Even now, most individuals probably secretly regard their own branch's involvement as the most significant, which would be only natural. It is called "unit pride," which every soldier, sailor, airman, and Marine has always had in abundance. The veterans allow it and tolerate it among themselves. They even encourage it. But every Iwo Jima veteran *always* acknowledges the sacrifice and participation of every other Iwo Jima veteran, regardless of branch. It is partly the passage of time that stimulates this, partly the notoriety of that battle in our half-century recognition of the Second World War. Mostly, there is simply a notion among the veterans that each participated in an event that tested and melded everything best about American honor, courage, determination, and sacrifice, and about themselves.

With the passing of fifty years, these feelings have not lessened. Perhaps they are even stronger, for these veterans are reaching the end of their lives, and they realize that there is not much time left to celebrate the memories of lost friends and share together the pride of a battle well won. Because of their victory at Iwo, 24,751 Army Air Corps crewmen would be saved instead of drowning with their ditched B-29s in the North and Central Pacific. Collectively, they brought the war closer to its conclusion, which, six months after the battle, would be its own cause for celebration. They also celebrate among themselves—Marine, Navy, Army and Air Corps, and Coast Guard alike—a sense of having participated not in just a battle, but an epoch.

1

RIFLEMEN, MACHINE GUNNERS, AND MORTARMEN

Poor, bloody infantry. *

In any armed force, the element that takes the greatest beating is the infantry. For the Marines this was especially true, since the doctrine of amphibious assault required that the landing force attack heavily fortified beaches head on, and push until the defending enemy infantry was overwhelmed. At Tarawa in November of 1943 this doctrine was first fully tested, and casualties were tremendous in the seventy-six-hour course of the battle. By February of 1945, the 3d and 4th Marine Divisions had been tempered by the experience of another half-dozen assaults in the Central and South Pacific and, alongside the new but heavily cadred 5th Marine Division, these units would assault the island of Iwo Jima.

This campaign would become known as the bloodiest battle in Marine Corps history. Out of about seventy-five thousand Marines and Navy personnel such as corpsmen who participated in the actual battle, 25,851 became casualties, a bit less than 35 percent.

Thirty-five percent.

Sounds like a lot. But that percentage does not tell the whole story. In most modern armed forces, the ratio of infantry to support personnel is one to nine. For Marine infantry, which provides its own immediate support primarily, the ratio is more likely one to five or less, since by Corps philosophy every Marine is a trained combat infantryman. Many support personnel, such as Motor Transport, often were selected to be replacements in line companies that had taken heavy casualties. Compound this by the fact that for a great deal

*Chapter title in John R. Elting, *Swords Around a Throne* (New York: Free Press, 1988).

9

of the battle, there was no safe "rear area." Everything was within range of the Japanese artillery, and no one was immune. In reality, strict infantry losses—that is, losses among those men who train only to fight in the line units—were closer to 80 percent.

The interviews in this section were gathered from some of those men who experienced these losses and survived. The three following stories from Sgt. Albert J. Ouellette, Pvt. Liberato G. Riccio, and PFC William A. Bain will provide a sense of the depth of those losses, and continuous sameness of the battle.

Sgt. Albert J. Ouellette
Squad Leader, Company L, 3d Battalion, 25th Marines, 4th Marine Division

I am very thankful for what I learned in boot camp, because it saved my life. When I enlisted I was going to fight for all those wonderful ideals we have in our history books. Freedom of speech, freedom of religion. But when I got overseas, I put all those fine ideals aside. I was fighting for one thing, to save my butt. After Saipan, I decided I was not going to be a hero anymore. I felt my mom would rather hug me than a medal. It was also at this time, after having seen all that carnage on that island, all those dead men, women, and children, I decided I had had my fill of war. I was no hero, but I did my duty, and I'm proud of that.

On our return to Maui after Saipan, I was asked to take first squad by the CO. I was told that if I did not take it, I might find myself taking orders from someone with the rank but no combat experience. This scared me to death.

There were three squads in a platoon. Everyone carried an M-1 rifle except for the BAR man. There were three functioning fire teams in each squad, each with a fire-team leader, a BAR man, an assistant BAR man who carried extra ammo for the BAR, and a rifleman. Bud took over 3d squad, the assault squad. The 1st and 2d squads were the same, and called the pin-up teams because they fired at the embrasures of pillboxes or caves. The assault squad moved in with the bazooka team, which consisted of a leader, a bazooka man and his assistant, who carried the ammo, and a rifleman. There was also a flamethrower team, which consisted o

man and his assistant, who carried extra

demolition team moved in last to set the c

three men. Besides the charges, they also

does. We also had two light machine guns

and heavy machine guns attached to the con

of 60mm mortars and four 81mm mortars fi

With this new setup some patrol leaders wou

trol of the whole squad, but I allowed my fire-

trol their own men. One day the general was g

my men advancing on an objective, and he said

to operate his squad that way. I would order my t

move their men out. How they did it was their p

they could see the terrain better from their locati

effect of one man popping up at the end of the sq

the other end, and then sometimes one in the mid ... enemy

didn't have the time to sight in on one man. The old way, it was a

steady stream of men popping up in a straight line, and the enemy

knew where his next target was going to be.

My company boarded LST 731, or 684 or 713, I don't know

which, on January 20 at Kahului. The following day we received our

operation orders. We were told that Iwo was bombed by land-based

bombers for sixty days, and the Navy blasted away at known enemy

emplacements. We also heard Tokyo Rose announce on the day

before the landings that a Marine landing on Iwo had been repulsed,

and that their bodies lay scorching in the sun. But the Japs mistook

the LCIs that supported the underwater demolition teams as the

landing force.* It was not comforting to learn that after all that

shelling and bombing their shore batteries could still hit our ships.

I went topside to watch the shelling. I spoke to this red-headed

fellow in our company who had a wife and two beautiful kids. I told

him that if I got killed, it wouldn't be any great loss. I had only my

---

*Ouellette is one day off. On 17 February the *Nevada, Idaho, Pensacola,* and
Tennessee provided covering support for the UDT reconnaissance operations con-
ducted by twelve LCI(G)s. Shore batteries opened up and hit the *Tennessee* and
Pensacola. Nine of the gunboats were also put out of action.

parents and a brother and sister. He turned to me and said, But, Al, you haven't, you haven't lived yet. The next day he was killed in action. I still can't help thinking about that wife and those kids.

On D-day, my LVT landed to the right of a beached Jap ship, and we started taking machine-gun fire from it. This was the first time we had the new LVTs with the ramp in the back, and we tried to contact the crew by phone to get them to drop the ramp, but to no avail. We pounded on the hull, telling them to drop the ramp, drop the ramp, but I don't know to this day if that machine-gun burst got the crew. My platoon leader was in the LVT and he said, Al, take them over the side. I felt like saying, After you, sir, but I just said to myself, Maybe somebody else might like a set of stripes.

I thought for sure as soon as I stuck my butt over the side, I'd be a dead man. But I was the leader, and I felt that if I were going to get killed, I might as well get it over with. I was up and over, and for some reason the machine gun stopped firing. I hoped all those new replacements would follow, and they did, and just then a guy to my left got hit by a shell from the Jap artillery. He just disappeared. All that was left was his dungaree jacket and rib cage.

Because of my experience at Saipan, I knew the beach was zeroed in. The firing all along the beach was murderous. To give you an idea what it was like, our medical team had landed with two doctors and forty corpsmen. Before the day was out, one doctor was killed when he lost both legs, and only two corpsmen were left. All the rest were dead or wounded. Bud, who had the assault squad, was wounded on landing. If he hadn't had his pistol on, he would have lost his leg. Even so, he lost a good chunk of it. So I headed toward where our men were attacking towards the airport, because I knew that if we got close to the Japs, we'd be safe from the artillery. They wouldn't want to hit their own men. My boys followed but the chain got broken when the BAR man got killed from the shelling. His assistant, Bready, dropped his weapon like he was supposed to and picked up the BAR. The place was a mass of confusion, men were being blown to pieces or wounded by the shrapnel, and running in that ash was like running in a wheat bin. But I got the squad together and we hooked up with Captain Headley, our CO, and we headed to our objective, which was to capture the high ground in the Quarry area.

When I got to the base of the Quarry, one of the men told me that a buddy of mine had bought it. I didn't go down to see him because I wanted to remember him when he was alive. And anyway, Colonel Chambers [Lt. Col. Justice M. Chambers, CO, 3d Battalion] had ordered us to get our goddamn butts up there and capture that high ground before the Japs got wise to us. Which we did, but at a cost. When the day was out, our battalion was down to 150 men, out of over nine hundred. My company was down to twenty-six. When we seized the Quarry, we took seventeen casualties. Twelve were my men. My platoon was now down to nine men, and all we had captured was less than a mile of area.

The next morning we could see the extent of our losses. For two miles, the debris was so thick that at only a few places could the landing craft get to the beach. Captain Headley went over to battalion to take over as executive officer. Lieutenant Ing became our new CO. That day we advanced two hundred yards. We couldn't see the Japs. They were all underground.

I took my squad down to get some ammo, and on the way back we took some small-arms fire from that damned Jap ship. We moved out on the double because one shot hit the case of rifle grenades I was carrying. After we got back and unpacked it, I found a bullet lodged in the head of a grenade, where it's filled with TNT. If that bullet had hit about three inches higher, in the primer, I'd have gotten my wings and harp.

On the third day, I lost one of my boys to a Jap rocket. It was about as big as a trash can, not too accurate but it could pack one hell of a wallop. It happened when we were in back of the front line. I saw this Jap officer come out of a cave with his men, and they started shooting our guys in the back. I was about to move in, but a tank opened up with its gun and that ended it. My guys were all standing around in the rain when the Japs fired the rocket. It landed about a quarter-mile away and all the men hit the deck. Everyone got up but one man. I pulled him into a foxhole and opened up his jacket to see where he was hit, and his guts fell out. I was so shocked that I flipped him back so the intestines went back inside and buttoned up his dungaree jacket. Now I have hunted and gutted animals, but I always felt that God made man a little better. This guy had a hole as big as a fist in his chest. He was also one of the nicest guys in the world.

The next couple of days was spent in reserve, where we received replacements and weapons and reorganized ourselves into platoons and combat units. We also found copies of the Japanese "Courageous Battle Vow," where every man swore to kill at least ten Americans. It took courage to push ahead against this unseen enemy beneath the rocks of this island, Japs who had survived two months of shelling, and to crawl ahead each day, count the losses, and get up the next day and do it all over again.

So we went ahead, and on the sixth day the 24th Marines captured Charlie-Dog Ridge and part of Motoyama Number 2. On the seventh, I got three replacements who jumped ship so they could get into combat. They had been unloading ammunition aboard ship, a relatively safe place from small-arms fire. My boys would have given anything to be unloading ammunition. They would have been the best ammunition "unloaderers" in the world. We had to move out, so one fellow, a Polish boy, I nicknamed "Ski." Another had red hair, so naturally he became "Red," and the third, a skinny boy, I called "Slim." As we moved up on the line, the Japs zeroed in and started to shell us. These new men, because of their lack of experience, didn't have the sixth sense to tell them these shells were incoming. It's something you can't teach, it has to be learned. Well, in less than five minutes two of the new guys were wounded. I turned to the last guy and said, Well, how do you like combat now? He said, I wish to hell I was unloading ammunition.

I brought my boys up on the line and told them to keep a sharp lookout for Japs. One of them, Hathaway, got the whole side of his face blown away by a sniper bullet, and if it had not ricocheted off his jawbone, it would have gone through his jugular. I sent over to Lt. Chick Long for help. He was the platoon leader, a mustang who came up through the ranks starting at Guadalcanal. Chick sent a guy who was once a fire-team leader in my squad, but was now a squad leader because of the casualties. Months back he had had his own squad, but he had gone over the hill in Pearl so the Old Man threw the book at him, took his squad away, and put him in mine. Although we were friends at one time, the idea of taking orders from a guy who was only an acting sergeant was repugnant to him. I told this guy to watch out for the sniper, that he had just gotten one of my men. Well, he had that attitude, "Don't tell me what to do." He just stood up and the sniper got him right through the heart. I felt badly about it, because he was married and had a couple of kids.

As we moved forward and set up for the night, one of my fire-team leaders, who was a former BAR man, and had always wanted my BAR when I was wounded, spotted the Nips setting up a machine gun. He let go with a rifle grenade, which hit the gunner right on the head and blew it off, and shrapnel got the other two. Now he didn't want the BAR anymore.

On D+8, we started the battle for the area known as the Meat Grinder, the chain of defenses that was made up of Hill 382, Turkey Knob, the Amphitheater, and Minami village. By D+9, we had gained two hundred yards. We found four buried tanks, three 75mm antiaircraft guns, twelve twin-mounted guns, four heavy machine guns, and numerous Nambu and Lewis-type guns. In addition there were twenty pillboxes and an uncounted number of caves, several tiers deep. Over the next four days, we moved only about four hundred yards. Engineers demolished the caves and built a road through the Quarry, but otherwise there was no change in our situation.

On D+13, a destroyer escort came by the shoreline. It turned on its PA system and announced it was going to ask the Japs to surrender, and if we saw any enemy gathering in groups with white flags we were not to open fire. The announcer came on saying, "Testing, testing, one, two, three," and repeated it. But then he started singing, "Come out, come out, wherever you are, and incidentally we're really not so bad, so come out, come out, wherever you are." Then the interpreter asked them to surrender, in Japanese. Well, after all our dying, it just broke us all up. But there was no surrender.

Our depleted company detached from 3/25 and combined with

the division reconnaissance company on D+14. We moved into a position to the left of the 2d Battalion. Our mission was to act as a containing force to prevent any movement of the enemy southward or westward out of the pocket around Minami village. We set up a strong defensive position by stringing barbed wire in two lines seventy-five feet apart with mines, trip flares, and booby traps between. Three 37mm guns were set up to fire canister rounds, and the avenue was covered by machine guns, 60mm and 80mm mortars and artillery. This attack went on for two days, in the caves and tunnels, and in the lines where the Japs broke through and hand-to-hand combat took place. After it was over, almost eight hundred Japs had been killed.

When I moved out, I thought we were going back for a rest, but it was not to be. We went almost back to where we were on the first day of the Meat Grinder. We were to relieve the 23d Marines, who would then come around and attack the Japs from the rear, driving them towards us. In fifteen days we had not been able to crack their defenses, and the Japs had been bypassed and surrounded in this pocket. Now the 23d Marines were dug in, and my company had to run and jump into their foxholes, and the 23d men would run out, and this under constant fire. It was a dangerous place, and had been for fifteen days, there were bodies of both Americans and Japanese that had been there that long. So my first man started to crawl and I yelled for him to run. He was damned lucky, bullets were kicking up the ground all around him. I got all my men in safe, the last two into a foxhole that I was going to head for, and this Jap was just waiting for some damned fool to come running across his sights. Now, I had had premonitions that something was going to happen on this operation, because I had gotten this Dear John letter aboard ship. Seems that this girl was writing to both me and this sailor, but I didn't know this, and she put the right letter in the wrong envelope. She killed two birds with one stone. So something was going to happen. Anyway, I started across at a dead run, saying a little prayer. I made my first mistake when I stopped saying the prayer. I made my second when I said to myself, This Jap can't hit the broad side of a barn, and my third when I said, I'm going to see the end of this operation, and when I leapt into the hole he caught me in midair. I fell into the hole and looked at my foot and the whole end of my boondocker was blown off by a dumdum and two of my toes were gone, but were held on by the tendon of the large toe. I thought maybe I should cut them off, but I put on a battle dressing and gave myself a shot of morphine. I felt guilty for leaving the squad, but I was really glad to get out of that hellhole.

I gave Ziganhagen the BAR he wanted so badly and all of my gear. I was wounded at one o'clock but they couldn't get me out because the firing was so hot, so I passed the word at eight o'clock that I was crawling out, hoping I wouldn't get shot in the process. I made it to the command post and Sergeant Steffan carried me to the aid station. On the trail, he put me down to check it was the right one, and there I was, without a weapon, right next to this six-foot-tall, 250-pound dead Jap. At least I hoped he was dead. I said, Steffan, if you don't come back I'll never forgive you. But he came back and I was taken to the division hospital where they operated on me and part of the large toe was reattached. From there I was flown to Guam on the first evacuation flight, and then on to Pearl, Oakland, Boston, and finally, Portsmouth, New Hampshire, via ambulance.

Time fades memories, and thank God for that, because war is the world's most brutal carnage. And for our small efforts, my own division suffered over eighteen thousand casualties. The Japanese on Saipan alone lost fifty-five thousand men, women, and children. We don't seem to have any trouble finding ways to destroy each other, but I just hope that the next generation can find a way to prevent wars. This is what the coming generations should know about.

Pvt. Liberato G. Riccio
Rifleman, Company C, 1st Battalion, 27th Marines, 5th Marine Division

We didn't find out until a number of days later that we were heading for Iwo. I didn't think anything of it, after they told us. To tell you the truth, I wasn't frightened. I guess I thought I was never going to get killed. They told us what to expect. They said it was like a pork chop, it would be over in seventy-two hours, and from there we're going to Chichi Jima, and then another. Of course, the way it happened everyone was surprised. They laid an egg, because it wasn't that easy.

When we were off Iwo, they called us up on the PA. You had to come up at certain intervals, and when they announced your outfit, you had to come up on deck, and get into the Higgins boats. It took a long time to hit the island. The coxswains would circle around, so the shells wouldn't hit us, but I saw a boat get hit. The damned thing went down right away. But I saw the Navy guys come out from nowhere and start fishing Marines out of the water. And I felt so goddamn proud of these guys I almost looked forward to getting bombed, that's how quickly they fished them out of the water. I said to myself, If that happens to me, I know I'm in safe hands.

When we were heading towards the beach, I was riding in with this Polish guy who hated Japs with a passion. And he wanted to kill Japs in the worst way because his brother was killed on Guadalcanal. That's all he talked about, killing Japs, killing Japs. And as we got closer to the shore, I got seasick. I wanted to throw up, but not on the guys in front of me, so I pushed up in front, and then the boat hit the beach. I was one of the first ones out. I ran up as far as I could, which wasn't very far, and puked. And after a few minutes I turned around, and this Polish kid who was beside me was dead. He got killed immediately. I don't know how long I stood there, looking at this kid. Then they told me to get the hell off my ass and move out.

We hit these terraces, like a step. You couldn't climb them. You took a step, you fell back two. So I had an idea. I said, Look, get on my back. And I stooped over, and had someone step on me so he could hoist himself up and reach the top. Then he could lift me up. I think at one time we had three guys trying to climb up this terrace at the same time.

Now, at this point, I don't remember a goddamn thing. How about that? My mind went blank. I don't know how many days went by. I could have done anything. The only thing I realized was when they raised the flag. There was a lot of commotion, a lot of guys were yelling. That's when I realized a couple of days went by. And even after that, I still lost track of time.

I still don't know for sure where I was at any point on the island, even when I read about it later and started retracing my steps. I sort of recognize certain locations, like when we were under a mortar attack. We tried to dig into the clay, but we couldn't go any deeper than one foot, that's how hard it was. So I just covered myself over, and believe it or not, I wasn't scared. I said, What the hell's wrong with you, why aren't you scared? I had no answer for myself. But in a short while, I heard someone yell, Corpsman, corpsman, from here, from there. Bombs were falling, and at that point, I started getting scared. I don't know how long it went on, maybe ten, fifteen minutes. Then it was over. We all got up and shook ourselves off and one of the Marines came up to me and said, Ric, you got some shit on your back. So I tore off my jacket and I had a whole gob of guts stuck on my jacket. Somebody got a direct hit. I threw the damned thing away.

I remember this time we were going down this track, and I'm a small guy, but I'm still carrying 130 pounds on my back, and two canisters of machine-gun bullets. And I got a .45 strapped to my shoulder. No idea where I got the damned thing. And in front of me a Jap springs up. His back is to me, and he doesn't see me, but I see him, of course. So what am I to do? I dropped the canisters and made a racket, and the Jap turns around, and I took out the .45 and I shot him three times. You say, how do you know, three times? The bullets hit him about the size of a baseball. Every time one hit, a little puff of smoke would appear. I knew he was dead. And I sat down and I started to cry. I never did anything like that before. To me, that was like an evil thing to do. But I couldn't stay there all day. I got up, and I went maybe twenty feet or so, and another Jap came up. He looked at me, I looked at him, I was scared, he ran into the rocks, and I kept going.

There was a sort of mountain over here, with a path going up like this. Off to the left was a big mountain with a big cave hole. I got to the top, and a shot rang out, and I got hit. Not seriously, though. The bullet hit my BAR pouches, and I felt it burning on my hip, and I thought, I'm dead. But someone came up and said, It's nothing, and put out the fire. Well, not a fire, but took care of it.

There was another place with a ridge, forming a gigantic oval. That's where I think my outfit took a big beating, the guys I went to boot camp with. From that point, they kind of disappeared from my life. On the left-hand side, at the base of it, there were caves going all around. And on the first night, we sent up flares to light up the whole area. You could see Japs running from one cave to another. They were so quick, you couldn't take a bead on them, and I'm the type of guy who didn't want to waste bullets. If I didn't have a target, I didn't shoot. Because I said to myself, I'm going to get my rifle dirty, the damned thing's not going to work, and I'm going to get myself killed. But that night, I killed three more Japs.

It wasn't as bad an experience as the first one. We had to stand watch, I think mine was the second watch. I looked off this little ridge, and you could see down maybe ten feet, fifteen feet, and there was three Japs down there. So I got myself three grenades, and I pulled two pins, and the other I left on the ledge. I dropped one off, then the other one, pulled the pin on the third, and dropped that off. In the meantime I woke the other guys up, too, and I looked over the ledge, and the three Japs weren't moving. I figured they were dead. I hoped they were dead, anyway. And the following morning, we looked off the ledge, and they were still down there. So I knew they were dead. Some guys saw that these Japs had watches on, so they went down and took their watches off. I would never do that.

I don't know if it was a day later, two days later, we had what we called a big push. We had to go through a big, wide area, and I ended up in this little area, and there was a wall which wasn't too thick because you could hear Japs dropping mortar rounds into the tube. You'd hear this click, and you knew there was a mortar coming at you. So after the first one, I saw where it came from, and it was kind of fun, because if it came towards me, I would go to a different spot. We all did it. Then I'd hear a "click," and look up and follow the mortar, and whatever direction it was going, you'd go the other way. Good thing they weren't dropping twenty at a time.

Now, at that point, a Jap ran across. There was another ridge on the other side, and I picked him off. Just like that. I'm not a good shot, but I knew I hit my target. Puff of smoke, two puffs of smoke, directly in the chest. I knew he was a goner. Then we sent over a flamethrower operator to flush out any others, and that was the end of them.

There is something that bothers me more than shooting anybody, and I've always wanted to tell somebody this. I don't know what I was doing there, whether I had direct orders to go down this alley-way or not, but there was just about enough room for me to fit in. I was running down, but not too fast because it was too narrow, and lying in front of me was a dead Jap. I knew at the speed I was going, I was going to hit him, step on him, and I didn't want to do that. So I tried to run faster, but my rifle hit one side of the wall and threw me off balance, and when I made the jump, I landed right on his chest. Know what the hell that sounded like? Smashed all his god-damned bones. That wasn't pleasant, and I don't care if he was a Jap or what. I still hear that crunching today. And I didn't kill him. He was long dead, dried out.

I remember the time when me and another Marine had to take this kid out on a stretcher. It really takes four guys to take a body out, but there was only two of us. Then out of nowhere comes a mor-tar, and the other guy was killed. The wounded guy got hit again, and he was dying. I didn't want to leave him. What got me was we talked a little bit, and I found out we liked the same things. I liked the sunsets. When I was a little kid I used to sit on top of the hill in the summertime, and I would stay there until it started to turn dark. And he liked sunsets, too. He reached up like this, and I grasped his hand with my left hand, and I held it. I squeezed it a few times and he responded. I knew he was alive. I waited a while, and did it again. Then he stopped. He was dead. And so now, whenever I write some-body a letter, I put on the envelope, "See you at sunset." That's about the time he died. He said what time is it, I said about sunset, he said, Good. So he died sort of pleasantly. He was a guy from down Georgia. That's all I wanted to know about him.

I don't even know his name. I don't want to know his name. When I entered the war, I made a promise to myself that I wouldn't get close to anybody. But you can depend upon me. If you ask me to guard your back, you can sleep easy tonight, because I will guard your back with my life. So no one was scared to leave me alone. I would do more than my share.

When I found out we were getting off the island,* they told us it was going to be our last night. So I went to the corpsman and said look, give me some pills to keep me awake, because I made it this far, I didn't want to die from some Jap creeping up on me and slicing my throat, so give me some pills. The goddamned fool gave me some aspirins. I took the aspirins and went to sleep right away. Next I knew, it was morning. And that was the end. We just straggled out, it wasn't a uniform manner, all the way back to Suribachi. When I got there, we hit the cemetery. As tragic as it is, it was pretty, white crosses and the archway. And I went around looking to find some of the guys who died. The only one I found was Benny Amarone. I can remember the words on some of the crosses. Some Marine came along and wrote on it, beautiful verse.

The mood on the boat back from Iwo was sad. I don't remember anyone laughing, or joking, cheering, none of that stuff. How could you? I don't know how you could ever laugh, knowing all these guys died. But we were safe.

I wish I could think of something gallant to say about the experience of serving at Iwo. I just hope it never happens again. If it does, I hope I'm not there. I don't think we've learned anything from it. Look at Vietnam. Those guys got the shit end of the stick, didn't they? I didn't realize it at the time. I kind of looked down my nose at them. "Quitters." It took me a number of years to realize these guys were serving just like I was. Now I go up to them at parades and memorials and I tell them, I apologize to you, you didn't deserve what you got. And look at all the wars we've had since then. And we're going to continue having wars. Shamefully. One after the other.

---

*5th Marine Division units began loading on 18 March and sailed for Hawaii on 27 March.

PFC William A. "Bill" Bain
Machine Gunner, Company B, 1st Battalion, 9th Marines, 3d Marine Division

Around Christmas of 1944, we didn't know that we would be going to Iwo, but we had pretty much surmised it. Every day we were getting reports of B-29s bombing the place, the fleet shelling the place, and it was plum between Saipan and Japan, and you couldn't detour those B-29s too much. The feeling was pretty much that Iwo was going to be hit, but obviously, we didn't know we were going to be involved in that until we were aboard ship.

When we did pull up to Iwo, word came up that anybody topside had to wear a helmet, because we were in close enough for the aircraft making strafing runs to drop shell casings on the ships. I saw a TBF making a strafing run which got hit and went down, and sometime later, up in the north end of the island, we came by that plane. And we knew it wasn't going to be a cakewalk because the Japanese had great intelligence somewhere, somehow. As all these things were happening, we were listening to Tokyo Rose on the ship's radio, and she's telling us about the units that are ashore. It gets your attention in a hurry. She certainly played good music, of the times and up to date, but she was getting information that was pretty damned factual.

Getting in to the island, that was typical Marine Corps, too. I don't remember what day we went in on, but I know that on D-Day word came down that we were officially going in, because we were originally considered reserve for the campaign. So earlier we had loaded the LCVP we were supposed to use with our air- and water-cooled machine guns and mortars and ammunition so we wouldn't have to take them down the nets, they were just going to drop the boats in. Well, about ten minutes before we were supposed to go, they announced that they were going to use only the boats already in the water, because there was such a mess on the beaches. So we had to very quickly unload everything we had loaded, and my job topside was lowering down the ammo and guns while somebody else in the boat guided them so we wouldn't lose them over the side. At that point, I was not happy, because they were hurry hurry hurry, and my hands were pretty raw by the time I got into the boat.

On the way in, probably maybe thirty yards off the beach, there was an LCVP backing off and the coxswain is giving it everything he can to get into deep water, because it had been hit, and it was sinking. The gunner was going over the side into the water, but the coxswain was sticking with it just as long as he could to get it to deep water so it wouldn't become an obstacle to the boats on the way in. Now, that gets your attention. You're about twenty-five yards from the beach, and the boat next to you is going down. You know *this is for real.*

When we finally got ashore, that was a big surprise to everybody, too. And I'm sure everybody has said as soon as you hit that volcanic sand, oh my God, what do you do now? You take two steps forward and slide back one. I can remember I was with a guy named Tommy Hantz. We used to call him "Der Gump," he looked like Andy Gump from the comics. Nobody ever used right names, everybody had a nickname. Of course, we've got our gear and as many cans of machine-gun ammo as we could carry, and we're not getting very far. Then a Caterpillar tractor came by trying to work its way up with a piece of sheet metal for a sled, so we decided it was just as easy for him to pull us up.

That night we were somewhere on the first airstrip, and sometime towards morning there was a great explosion. The Japs had hit one of our ammo dumps.* That also gets your attention. We worked our way up to the second airstrip, and that was a bit of a bloody mess. As we were trying to get across, there were five tanks also trying to get across the strip, and almost as quickly as they got up there they were knocked out. Tanks were great on one hand and terrible on the other. You knew that if there were tanks around, they were going to throw everything but the kitchen sink at you. But particularly in the north end of the island, flamethrower tanks were great when we were working those caves because they could really reach out.

We bypassed a lot of areas, so we had to keep a good watch out at night. I remember around the second airstrip one night—and they weren't supposed to do this—one of the corpsmen that we had could

---

*Probably that of the 25th Marines, 4th Marine Division, on the morning of D+2, 21 February.

really do a good job with the BAR, and he worked the BAR a good part of that night, keeping them off our backs. There was firing constantly. And I don't remember if it was at that point, or up around the sulfur mine, but I was on night watch, and the parachute shells and star shells kept things rather bright, but eerie, because they're descending and the shadows are strange. I sat in the foxhole with my .45 on my lap, and I thought I saw a hand coming over. I did the appropriate thing and let go with my .45, and I splattered a land crab all over the place. I mean, in the eerie light, there was something moving, and I guess I was pretty much aware of the sort of thing, because the guy I signed up with, Wes Baker, went right overseas to the Marshalls and a Jap crawled into a hole with him one night. Wes took care of the Jap appropriately, but the Jap, when he fired, severed the nerves in Wes's left arm. So I think a lot of things are by association, just reflex action.

We were pretty badly hurt on the second airstrip. As a matter of fact, we'd gotten across the strip, and then we were beaten back to the edge where there was an aircraft revetment. I had the gun and as I was pulling out, Lt. Jack Leims stopped me and took the gun and fired out of a little cover while I threw an empty cartridge belt out to a flamethrower man who had gotten hit. But by the time we pulled him in, he had expired. I think we were the last two out of there that day, and I wasn't very happy because we were taking off with a machine gun, and the Japs didn't like crew-served weapons people and tried to take us out as quickly as they could.

We were truly blessed with good officers. Leims was a good officer. Our company commander, Capt. Johnny Clapp, was a great guy. Our platoon leader in machine guns, name was Beade, had gotten a battlefield commission on Guam. Being a lieutenant in charge of machine guns doesn't necessarily call for longevity. I believe he lost his life on the second airstrip, and at the same time the squad leaders of the first and second squads both bought the farm. It didn't take long to get a promotion to gunner on Iwo.

Officers didn't live too long on Iwo, either. Leims was hit, but he wasn't evacuated. I think he was the only officer in Baker Company that survived the whole campaign. I could be wrong on that, but we were losing officers like crazy. At one point, for a couple of days, the division legal officer was our company commander. A nice guy, but legal officers aren't necessarily good infantry officers.

I got hit in my left leg at the airstrip. I was with a guy by the name of Ammie Lee. We were on one side of a hill, and the gun was on the other side, but close enough so you could heave cans of ammo over, and I felt something hit me in the leg. I said, Shit, Ammie, I think I'm hit, and I looked down and there was a piece of shrapnel, and I pulled it out and threw it away. Then I thought, Gee, I should have saved that, but I didn't. Ammie must have got hit at the same time, because he started to lose his eyesight, and he was evacuated. Later, they told me there was a little tiny piece of shrapnel in his back that was impinging on his spine, but he came out okay. I was never evacuated. Even then, they were bringing walking wounded back off the ships. All I did was put a battle dressing on it, and Corpsman Collins checked it to make sure it wasn't infected. I never went back to have it checked. That was kind of a luxury, to get away. And like I said, the life expectancy of a machine gunner was not very great, and experienced machine gunners were not too easy to find, so they didn't evacuate us much.

You've probably heard about the first night attack that the Marines pulled off on Iwo.* The 1st Battalion, 9th Marines won the toss, and we passed through the lines of the 21st Marines, then relieved them after dark. We dug in, then word came down to stand by, we were going to jump off in the attack, in the dark, without any preliminary naval or artillery bombardment. At that point, when the riflemen and machine gunners jumped off in the attack, the company was down to sixty-eight people, and some of these were replacements. And it proved very successful. We ended up about four hundred yards in front of the lines when the next night came, and in effect, we were cut off. We had good commanding ground. My gun was set up on

---

*On the night of 6 March, Gen. Graves B. Erskine, CO, 3d Marine Division, was ordered to jump off at 0730 the next morning, 7 March. But he believed the typical pattern of a preassault barrage, followed by the infantry attack, was proving unsuccessful in this sector, so he requested and was granted permission to jump off at 0500 without artillery preparation.

the right flank, but we really didn't think we were going to get out of there. It was almost one of those movie-type things where you were counting out the ammunition. That's what we did. We tried to figure out how much ammunition we had, how we should expend it, how many grenades we had. Eventually, word came that they were going to try to get us out. Between destroyer firing and keeping the place lighted with flares, and our own 60mm and 81mm mortars, they kept rounds in the air all night long over us. I got back only half to three-quarters of the way that night, and I ended up with a BAR and one clip of ammunition, and my .45 wouldn't work because it had taken a piece of shrapnel in the slide. It was a hairy night. Jack Leims was with us, then he went back to battalion, then he made it back to us, which was miraculous, to explain the predicament we were in. We were holding the commanding ground, but we had limited ammunition, and we were four hundred yards in front of the lines, not an enviable position to be in. As we were trying to get out, Leims carried out the platoon sergeant we called Rabbit, and Bob Pavlovich, who was unconscious, and dragged out Jimmy Ganopolous—every outfit always had a Greek—for four hundred yards. Leims got the Medal of Honor for that operation. But before we got to the point where we were on the way out, a rifleman by the name of Rentsch, who was also wounded, gave me his beautiful samurai sword. He said, Bring it back for me, will ya? I said sure, and I intended to, but it got to the point where it was every man for himself, and I flung that thing. And I never found out what happened to Rentsch, even to this day.

While we were moving out, we were on a sunken trail, and I was sitting on the side shoulder to shoulder with a guy named William Brown, and they were shelling us pretty badly. Then the word came down to move out, and I pushed him. He had gotten hit and died, didn't make a sound. Didn't even know he'd been hit.

The Japs were good warriors, no question about it, and they did a great job on Iwo. It was almost miraculous that we were able to take that island. Back in July of 1996, at a reunion in Philadelphia, Pat Anderson said to me, How many live Japs did you see? I said, Well, not too many. I did see one on the north end of the island. We had a good field of fire, and my assistant gunner spotted one who was trying to get through a sunken trail, and every time he tried to make a move, we cut loose. But very clearly, I can remember thinking at that point, I wonder how old he is? I wonder if he's married? He didn't stand a chance. He wasn't going to get away. If I didn't get him, somebody else would.

There was another time when I was with Punchy Fowler. I was the assistant gunner and we were going into position, moving up at dusk. We picked a good spot and Punchy put the tripod down and I put the gun in, and a shot rang out. Hit Punchy here, in the arm. I had a navy turtleneck sweater on, and I didn't know it then, but a bullet had gone through the neck of the sweater but didn't touch me. I grabbed the gun by instinct and fired where I thought the shot came from. It was one of these spider traps. I didn't see it, but a couple of riflemen said, when he was trying to pull that cover back over, I hit him in the hand. You didn't see them much. They were good.

We didn't always have all the things we needed, food, ammo, water. When we were working the caves, they would send a fire team, or two fire teams, and a machine gun out with the flamethrowers. This one time the flamethrower man said to me that he didn't have any matches left. No problem, I said. You just shoot it in, and I'll throw a grenade. And I did have enough sense to know there was going to be a backblast. So the first cave that we did that way, I'd gotten off to the side, but I really had no idea of the force of the backblast. Man, when that napalm ignited, *boom!* I thought I was clear enough, but the concussion was pretty great. I made sure I was way out of the way the next time.

I don't think any combat Marine will take umbrage with what I'm about to say, but some of the best Marines I ever knew were Navy corpsmen. Three of them I knew quite well. Emery Collins was our initial corpsman, then after a while he was starting to lose it. And a close friend of his, Doc Ray Crowder, who was at battalion at that point, convinced the battalion surgeon that Collins should go off the line and Crowder should replace him, and that's the way it worked out. We were up in the north end, and a fellow by the name of Stanley Parnell got laid open across the stomach with a piece of shrapnel and was out in front of our gun position. Doc went out, and time hangs. You're thinking, Doc, get the hell out of there, and you're firing. You didn't see too many Japs, because their cover and concealment was great, but they could see us. Parnell's lying out there, and his guts are literally outside of his body. Doc puts them back in, and the only thing that he had left in his kit were three safety pins. He put things in, put the safety pins in, and got Parnell out. Later, when we were back on Guam, Doc was in his squad tent and this guy came in and rather forcefully wanted to know if Doc Crowder was there. Doc says, Yeah, I'm Crowder. This guy lifts his shirt, drops his trousers, and says, See this, Crowder? Ya saved my life. Crowder became a missionary, spent eighteen years in Africa. The third was Jack Connolly, from the mortar platoon.

These corpsmen, they were incredible. I watched another one, I can't remember who it was, go out for one of the riflemen I knew, who had a million-dollar wound that could have gotten him off the island, and who was in a shellhole. This rifleman died of shock because he fought the corpsman off. It was just a flesh wound in the buttocks. But who knows how you're going to act when you get hit? Everybody reacts differently. It was a shame to see a man die when there was help.

One thing that I always thought was pretty much a shame was that when we had casualties, replacements coming in became casualties before you even got to know their names. These guys had only five or six months in the Marine Corps, but there wasn't any choice. I learned very quickly in the Marine Corps that if somebody gives me an order, it's in my best interests to follow it, whether I believe it or not. And I can remember a time when Der Gump had a gun set up not too far from us and he had gotten some replacements, and one morning one of these replacements stood up in his foxhole and shook his blanket. The guys knocked him down and said, Don't do that. Well, I don't know why, but he tried to do the same thing the next morning, and a sniper was waiting for him and nailed him. You hate to see people get killed uselessly.

The Seabees did create some problems every once in a while. They were all looking for souvenirs. And they'd get off and get pinned down and they'd send a rifle squad and a machine gun out to bring them back. When we were working on the caves, the Seabees were building some sort of area just down the trail, and at night we'd go out and put a Marine in each Seabee hole, and a Seabee would go in a Marine hole. One night, I was senior man on patrol, and my gun crew were all replacements. I was on from ten till midnight when Harold Goddard replaced me and shortly after, some Japs tried to come through the area, looking for water, we assumed. We had a firefight, and Goddard hit three of them. Two he had killed, but one we knew was still alive. He had a sucking wound in his chest. And I had passed the word, that night before it got dark, that if we had a firefight, nobody was to get out of their holes until I had made sure that the Japs were all dispatched properly. Well, I got out and let off one round with my .45, and man, the sound of that shot hadn't even died before these Seabees were out looking for souvenirs. They gave me fits.

Then, a couple of nights later, we were in the same place but we didn't get into a firefight, everything was quiet. We were on a trail, which the Seabees trucks would use, and we had just gotten back to our company area when a truck comes by with about twenty Japs inside, from a cave right across from where we were. They did not surrender to Marines, they surrendered to the Seabees. They had heard the story that the Marines would not take prisoners, and in order to be a Marine, you had to have shot your mother. We were a little ticked that day because all these Japs had been watching us all night, but when we leave, they surrender to the Seabees.

Late in the campaign, in the north of the island, I was with Bruno, working the caves. We had our gun set up on a trail and Bruno and I were in the hole together. We had wire strung with cans, and this night the cans started to rattle. We had stretched a poncho over the hole because it was raining, and I was on the gun. Bruno got a grenade, pulled the pin, then got the grenade tangled up in the poncho. We bailed out of the hole and the grenade went off inside. But that's just the way things go. He really was a character, a good Marine.

Getting off the island was sort of an attrition thing. I don't know who started to go off first by regiments, but they started moving the 4th and 5th Divisions out. We were the last Marine regiment to leave.* We were officially relieved of duty as the Army came in, but the ship we were supposed to leave on, the USS *Randall*, wasn't available the day we were supposed to leave, and our rations and everything had been cut off. And these Seabees were great. There was rivalry, of course, but we got along really well. The last night we were on Iwo, that was the first time I had slept in a tent. The Seabees fed us, gave us some clean clothes, they were just super guys.

Coming back to the States, we're on an attack transport, the USS *Baxter*. We'd been into Pearl and once again, we went by the *Arizona*. I don't care how many times you see it, it's always an emotional experience, especially for my generation. We came out and we were going around Diamond Head late in the afternoon, they were having Vespers on the fantail, and the sun was going down. There are no sunsets in the world like those you see out in the Pacific, and it was very spiritual. I really realized that I had survived and I was going home.

In contrast to the previous stories, the following two from PFC Bernard Dobbins and PFC Fred Schribert depict some scenes of both the absurd and the macabre that occur in every human situation.

PFC Bernard E. Dobbins
Machine Gunner, Company K, 3d Battalion, 23d Marines, 4th Marine Division

I pulled boot camp, then BAR school, and when we were shipped to the West Coast and Hawaii where we joined up with the 4th Division, I was put in the machine-gunners crew. In Maui we had heavy combat training, jungle, ship-to-shore, crawling through the brush, how to set up the machine gun, what the machine gun was supposed to do. It was rough work. Always on the run, the gun was heavy, and with your own stuff it was quite a load. You got your turn carrying

---

*The 9th Marines began loading transports from White Beach on 4 April. The 4th Division began loading on 14 March, the 5th on 18 March.

the gun, carrying the tripod, carrying the ammunition. I was number eight man in the squad. My job originally was to just lug ammunition to the gun. There was first gunner, and the second gunner would be lying right alongside, feeding the gun, and the rest of us would be pulling the ammunition up. You were generally behind the rifle companies all the time, shooting over their heads, until they hollered, That's enough, and then you would duck back under cover if you could find any, so the Japs wouldn't spot you. If they saw the gun set up, they threw everything at you, try to knock it out. We started out with eight men, but after we got on Iwo, we lost so many men so fast, you were up as some member of the gun crew right up close. Lots of times we ended up with just two or three. And that was a big crew.

You really didn't know how close we were to Iwo until the night before, then you could hear the big ships shelling. The next day, we went down the rope ladders over the side and into the Higgins boats. They'd run round and round in circles until they got the full third wave ready and then the whole bunch went in together. But that never really bothered me, even not knowing how to swim, except for the boat running aground before we got in close to shore.

It got pretty rough with the big ships shooting behind you, and the Japs dropping mortar shells and artillery all around you. And when the front of the Higgins boat dropped, everybody started to make a run for it. One of the guys said, Well, I'll see you back in the States, Dobby, I just got it. He never got off the boat. He got wounded before he ever hit the water and turned right around, went into the back of the boat and sat down. And that's when it really broke loose, just what war was like. The dead, the wounded lying all over the place and hollering for help, corpsmen trying to get to them, and you couldn't get to them, or you couldn't stop, you had to keep moving and look out for yourself.

We ducked down behind one of the sand terraces for a while, until somebody hollered, Let's go, and then we picked up and headed over towards the first airfield. I spent the first night right on the edge of the airfield. You'd get as much support as you could get around the gun, and then a lot of times, even though you were a machine gunner, you were a Marine, you were still a rifleman. And quite often, more times than not, I guess, I got sent out with rifle companies when they were short of help.

There were a couple of nights when somebody hollered for a machine gun and I was right there, I took over first gunner. But generally it got to the point that anybody who was close, that's who did the shooting and then got out of the way. Most of the time, I was back getting ammo, getting chow, or water, I wouldn't be close enough, somebody else took over the gun. Every once in a while you'd take turns and get sent out on the point at night, out quite a ways in front of the lines so that if anybody started sneaking in, you'd be able to spot them. They sent two out, and you stayed out there all night awake, just watching the horizon, listening. Sometimes they'd have some Japs that could speak good English, and they'd wait until dark and say there's a patrol coming in, and you'd holler, All clear. Then you'd wait until they broke out in the open and let them have it. You threw up these phosphorous grenades that would light up the area, and you'd get a good look at them. You knew your own crew, you knew how many was going to be there, you knew if there was a patrol out and they were coming back in that area. If they were yours, you brought them in. Twice that I know of we heard them say, Sergeant so-and-so, got a patrol coming in. And you'd swear it was an American that was talking, the English was just as clear as could be, no accent or nothing. Whether they ever made it back to their camp or not, nobody ever knew. But you'd generally find a bunch of them piled up afterwards when they tried to pull a stunt like that. Once in a while they'd try banzai charge, get all sakied up or whatever, and use sticks as spears, maybe a knife tied on, and they'd jab over the edge of the hole, hoping to get somebody, or they'd crawl up and drop a grenade in.

One night I was digging a foxhole, and there were a lot of sand crabs there. Really drive you wacky. There was one in my hole and I fished around and got it on my shovel and gave it a heave. Then somebody hollered "Grenade," and I looked over and two guys came flying out of their hole. No explosion. Pretty soon they crawled back in the hole and one guy says, If I catch the son of a bitch that threw that sand crab in here, I'll shoot him. But I didn't know nothing, didn't know where it came from.

We had a Rebel who couldn't read or write, but he could shoot anything you gave him. One day he found a bazooka, and he's lugging all this machine-gun stuff and that bazooka. The captain says, Throw that damned thing away, you got too much to haul now. He said, Oh, no, we might need it, Captain. The captain said, You ever shoot one of them? He said, Nope, but if you get somebody to stuff a shell into the other end of this thing, I'll get what I'm aiming at. He knocked out several bunkers after that.

I was sitting talking to a guy one time and he looks at me kind of funny and keeps saying, You feel all right, you feel all right? Yeah, I feel all right. Why? He reached over and touched me and said, Take your pack off. I swung my pack around in my lap and a piece of shrapnel had gone in by my shoulder and out by my canteen. I had underwear, socks, and shirts in there, and it looked like a bunch of rats got in and made a nest. Razor was cut in two, end was cut off my toothbrush. All that stuff I threw away afterwards. Always wished now that I had kept some of it for souvenirs. But you weren't thinking about souvenirs then, let alone fifty years later. I just thought if I can get off this place, I'll be happy. And I always felt the best when if some poor cuss was having a hard time, I could sit down and talk to him, try to get him over the hard spot so he wouldn't crack up completely.

We'd get replacements, and they'd always come in with a clean uniform, and Japs seemed to spot that right off quick. They'd hammer those guys, to break their morale, I suppose. One time we got this real heavyset kid, and he sat down next to us, puffing away, and he said, You guys need any help? We said, Yeah, we sure could use it. Then he looked and said, My god, I went through basic and advanced training with that guy that's going out on a stretcher. I said, That's because the Japs are going to be looking for you guys with the clean uniforms, they'll know you're replacements. They break your morale, you won't be any good to us. Oh yeah? he says, and he took his helmet off and poured water out of his canteen into his helmet and made a batch of mud and rubbed it all over his face and clothes and rolled around and said, There, I'm one of the old-timers now, they won't bother me.

One day another guy laid down behind a rock, and they always used to tell us not to wear your chin strap, because if there was a concussion close by, it might catch you by your helmet and snap your neck. Well, this kid always wore his strap. He stuck his head out around the corner of the rock and a sniper took a shot at him and caught him in the helmet, but on the glance. The bullet went in and followed between the liner and the outside, and he's lying out there in the open with both hands on his helmet, pushing it up, trying to get it off, but he's still got it hooked up. I often thought if that sniper that made that shot had sat there and watched that episode, he would have died laughing.

You saw some of the most foolish things sometimes, you just had to laugh at them. You lay digging a foxhole, and sometimes you would look over your shoulder and see the dirt puffing up where the machine gun was shooting right down your back, and your buddy's over behind a rock, taking it easy. You wanted to reach over and swat him with a shovel to get him digging.

I saw one guy sit down, taking a break one day, and he's got something under his arm. I jumped in the hole with him and I said, What do you got there? I looked and he's got a personnel mine. Got it right under his arm, and he's trying to get the core out of it to disarm it. He said, I'll get it, just wait a minute, I'll get it. I said, Don't you move, let me get out of here first. I told the sergeant there's a guy down there fooling with a land mine, he don't know what he's doing with it. He got down there and had him drop it before somebody really got hurt, namely him and anybody else that wandered close.

One day we were running across a field, and they started shelling and I fell down. I was just so tired, I fell to sleep, that was it. I woke up and there was two guys talking. They were about to put me on a stretcher, they thought I was dead. I heard one guy say, That poor bastard, he got it while he was running, never let go of anything. When I rolled over, they turned whiter than a sheet, packed up, and left. Finally I found my outfit and my squad leader says, Where the hell you been, Dobbins? I said, Out in the middle of that field. Doing what? I said, Sleeping, I just woke up. He said, The way they bombed that thing all day, you slept through that? I said, Right through it. I heard the first couple go off, and after that, I didn't know nothing. We lost over half our outfit that afternoon, right in that spot.

We had what we called the Tokyo Express come through every night. It was a big mortar that they'd run out and shoot. You'd see the tail of fire going up in the air, and as long as you could follow the fire, you were safe. But once the fire goes out, you better start ducking. And there was a bunch of old Jap trucks parked where we moved in, maybe a hundred feet behind. We dug in for the night when I'm watching the shell go off and the fire go out, and I ducked into my hole. It lit right into those old trucks, there was nothing left. The next morning, I hollered over to the two guys who were in the hole closer to the trucks, You all right? They said, Yeah, why shouldn't we be? Everything was quiet, no trouble at all. I said, You didn't hear the Express come through? He said, They didn't fire it last night. I said, Oh yeah? What about them old trucks that was sitting back there? They both turned around and looked and said, What happened to them? I said, The Express landed there last night. They'd both fell asleep, never even heard it.

And then you'd see guys walking along, getting ready to move out, and take one step and fall down. A shell had exploded, a leg would be missing, cut their arms off, slice their stomach open, and you'd see them walking, trying to hold their stomach in while they tried to get back to first aid. Those kinds of things, you just tried to put away.

It was rough, scared most of the time. Not knowing what to expect, being the first time I'd ever seen anything like that. But after that, I don't think I really had the feeling I was ever going to get hurt. I slipped getting off the ship on D-day and skinned both knees, but that was my own fault. That's the only scratch I got. And our corpsman would get close every once in a while and he'd paint my knees with iodine, turn them all red, but it didn't do anything. You get sand in there, and they would puff up all pusy, and if they got sore

you'd just pop them and go again. And about a day before we got off
the island he came over and said, C'mon, Dobbins, we got to get
down to the sick bay. I said, What for, I'm all right. He said, I'm going
to put you in for the Purple Heart, I've been treating your knees ever
since we got here. I said, Not me, not after the price that some of
these guys have paid for that Heart. You ain't getting me down there.
Some guys lost an arm, a leg, part of the face, and I slip and skin a
knee? Just for the hell of it, gain five points to get back to the States
a little quicker? I thought it was a poor way to go on, myself. Got to
show a little bit of honor somehow.

I got to be squad leader one time. The gunny sergeant said, Take
the gun and two or three guys with you, you're in charge of the gun
for a while. I said, I don't know anything about being a squad leader.
One thing about it, he said, was your first mistake will be your last.
Made you feel pretty good. And there was another guy supposed to
go with us that I went through boot camp with and he was always a
pain in the neck. He could do everything better than you, and you
were nothing but a dummy from the woods in Vermont, you didn't
know anything. Always had the right answers. So he started the same
old routine that day, up and hollering and waving his arms and
swearing, and pretty soon he's down on the ground screaming and
kicking. I said, What's the matter with you? He said, Get me a corpsman, I just got wounded. I said, "Good." I got him a corpsman and
left with the other two. A little while later the sergeant came around
to see how we were making out. He said, Didn't I give you three men
to go with you? I said, Yeah, that one who was doing all the mouth-
ing, he headed for sick bay. Sniper got him in the shoulder.

Later on that day, we were moving out and I told the guys where
to go, and one guy grabbed the gun, ran three steps, and stopped.
He said, I think I got hit. He came back and I said, Where you hit?
He said, Right in the fanny, I feel funny back there. You could see
his dungarees puff every time his heart beat. Sniper got him right
through the artery. I hollered for the corpsman not too far away, and
he was two or three minutes getting there, and by that time the guy's
eyes were going glassy. The corpsman said he was just wasting a shot

of morphine, but maybe it'll help. Even if he'd been shot on an operating table, you still couldn't have saved him. Something like that hits you hard.

There was a lieutenant that was with us in another foxhole who got a chunk blown out of his chest by a mortar round. This other kid jumped from his own hole to that one to help the wounded and he straddled the lieutenant. He took one look at him and turned around and he saw a couple of enlisted personnel who needed help instead, and left the lieutenant. The kid got hit afterwards and didn't make it back. And after it was all over and we had a ten-day leave back in Pearl, we went to the hospital to see the lieutenant. He said you know what that kid done to me? I said, Yeah, he told me. You picked on him ever since we left the States. Every time he turned around, you were on his back. When he jumped in and saw you with half your chest side blown out, he said, I don't think the son of a bitch is going to make it and I ain't going to be the one to help him. And that was the last time I ever saw that lieutenant.

One morning the executive officer came around and said, You guys line right up here and you head back towards the beach. And you pick up all the live ammunition you can find and put it in a pile so the bomb squad can come around and destroy it. We all walked right back to the beach and I don't think anybody picked up anything. When we got down there, he called us all into formation and said, Well, you didn't do it the first time, now you can all go back and do it again. But by that time an LST had come in and dropped her plank and said, All members of the 23d regiment come aboard, and we said, We'll see you, lieutenant, we're going home. You want to pick up duds, you go do it. We got this far without being blown to hell, we ain't going to try for another.

It's compelling, the way everybody fought so hard together. No matter who you were, if you were in a bind, there was somebody right there to give you a lift if they could. And there's quite a bond with the boys since. If you mention you were in the battle of Iwo and they were, why, it's a bond that can never break. And the guys who didn't make it back, they're the ones who should be remembered, and the ones who partially came back, who've been in homes, hospitals, the likes of that, who never did get back out on the streets as a young man, like the rest of us. They're just a marvelous bunch of guys to ever get tangled up with.

PFC Fred Schribert
60mm Mortarman, Company L, 3d Battalion, 25th Marines, 4th Marine Division

After boot camp I went to Cherry Point for about fourteen months pulling guard duty, with a bit as a prison chaser thrown in. And when we got shipped out of North Carolina, we were the replacements for the 4th Division that came back from Saipan, so they shipped us to Maui. How I got into 60mm mortars, I don't know. You could have been a flamethrower, I could have been a rifleman, right on down the line, mortarman, mortarman, rifleman, rifleman, mortar, mortar. It was luck of the draw.

Now, the 60mm mortar has a baseplate, which is sort of heavy, and which one guy would carry, and another would carry the tube. But having ten guys in the squad, we would switch off, so it wasn't bad. We got to fire a few rounds on maneuvers. A 60mm shell is not as big as an 81. To get the range, you had to look at a chart that came with it. If you want to fire so many yards, you let so many increments, so many packages of gunpowder, stay on your round. And in the middle was like a shotgun shell. There was a pin at the bottom of the mortar tube, and when you dropped the round in, it hit the pin and fired off and shot out. If you have your mortar at a good angle, you might leave on all the increments and shoot out about two hundred or three hundred yards. But if you had it almost straight up, you might take off almost every single increment you had on there and shoot fifty yards.

Up until the time we headed out, nobody knew where we were going. They said, We're going to an island called Iwo Jima. "Iwo Jima? Where the hell's Iwo Jima?" But it had been bombed sixty straight days by the Air Force. It's going to be a cakewalk, the Navy says we should take it in four days. Then we'll be held in reserve for the next invasion, which was going to be Okinawa. No problem at all.

So we're back on the LSTs again, seasick again. Life aboard was read, sleep, go up on deck, exercise, a lot of schooling with the scale map of Iwo. They'd tell you where we're going to land, what wave we're going to be in, and four days, no problem.

The day we landed, we got up about 4:30. One thing about the Navy—beans in the morning with coffee. But not this day. Steak and eggs, big breakfast. Best meal we had. After we ate, we went down in the hold and got aboard our LVTs. And as I was getting in, my hand grenade happened to fall when some guys were in there and they all nearly jumped out of their shoes. Of course, a grenade won't go off until you pull the pin, but when you see a hand grenade fall. . . .

Now, Jumpin' Joe Chambers decided that no one in our company should wear packs. And no blankets. And if we had no packs, we had no change of clothes. So from the time I left for the beaches, February 19, until March 26, I never changed my clothes. Now, not carrying a pack, I had on my cartridge belt two hand grenades, four magazines and one in my carbine, two canteens, first-aid pack, K-bar, and for some reason, a machete. I don't know why the hell they ever gave me a machete. Through the whole battle, I never let it go. And everybody had a wooden handle with a rope with knots, if we had to scale that high ground that they were telling us we had to take. And then there was the poncho. Everything on one belt.

We landed in the sixth wave, about 9:28 in the morning. That's one time I never got seasick. We went around in circles, then we got a signal and formed a big skirmish line, like a charge. And as we were heading in, I happened to put my hand in my pocket. A couple of days before that I was playing poker, and I lost everything I had except for one dime, and I took that dime out and I says, Good luck, and I threw it overboard.

Captain Headley was in my LVT with a radio. And he says, Men, I got good news. First, second, and third waves came in and there's not much firing except for small arms, not much artillery or mortars. Sure, because the Japs let the first four waves come in. Then when they had you on the beach, by the sixth wave, that's when it started coming down.

On the LVT we were on, I don't know how, but we landed on the beach and the front dropped. Usually the back dropped, but now the front dropped, because I remember we had 60mm mortar ammunition in crates that everybody had to carry, plus the six rounds that we carried in pouches over our shoulders, three in front and three in back. So as soon as you got off the boat you ran up the beach and dropped your crate of ammunition, but you kept the six rounds you carried.

I hit the beach and I saw this dead Marine, blood coming out, and I don't know what hit, but I saw this white smoke. I started putting on my gas mask, because I didn't know what the hell it was. I carried that gas mask all the way through the campaign, because that was a great place to put your souvenirs.

So that first day we were crawling, jumping from hole to hole, a lot of small-arms fire, and artillery and mortar fire hitting the beach, but you can't tell the difference. You're too scared. You keep running. But you don't think about getting killed. I never did. And the thing I had going for me was this was the first operation I ever had. I was never in combat before. The guys who were on Saipan and Tinian and knew what to expect were all a bundle of nerves.

So we're moving up, trying to get a better position. I took a step and I hear "ping." "Ping." The sand is jumping. What the hell was that? "Ping." "Hey, Schribert, they're shooting at ya!" Then you run like hell. And that's when I jumped in that big Navy shellhole and I saw my first Jap. This is right on the beach. And I thought he was dead. He had a sack over his head, he's half-buried in the sand. So I was going to shoot him, you know, he didn't have a head, but I figured what the hell. I tried to cock the bolt on my carbine and I couldn't pull the bolt back, it was so dirty from crawling on the beach. So I wasn't smart enough to pull out my knife, or take my machete. But then I just looked at him and said, Gee, my first Jap and he don't even have a head.

The first day, we had taken the high ground to the right, and as we were moving up, some wiseguy, I don't know who the hell ever did it, took a dead Jap that had no legs, no arms, just a helmet on, and put that stump right on a rock for you to see as you're coming up the trail.

You keep moving up, so many yards during the day, then we would set up our guns. We had two 60mm mortars in our platoon, which was like six guys to a squad. And you just stay there until you get any fire that they wanted. Sometimes you didn't fire too many rounds, sometimes you did. If the riflemen in the company got a better position, you would move up. If they didn't, you never moved. Sometimes we stayed in one place for days. So after we moved up, and we got together with the rest of our mortar company, we dug in for the night. We had three men in a foxhole, and each man would stand watch two hours, through the whole night. And I hated it because sometimes they'd take my carbine and move it in the foxhole, and then I couldn't find the goddamned thing. I hated that. I got pissed and I told them, Leave my carbine alone!

You know, I'm willing to bet that every night, every guy on that island was saying, "Our Father, who art in Heaven, Hallowed be Thy name. . . ." Every single night. I'll bet I wasn't the only one.

The first two days on Iwo, the only meals I had were candy bars. February 19 was a Hershey bar. February 20 was a Hershey bar. Then I got the runs. Boy, you don't know what it is to have the runs, to be in a foxhole, jump out and yank your pants down, and you no sooner jump back in, then you got to jump back out again. Then I saw the corpsman and he gave me some pills. Cured it right away.

I remember on the fourth day, about 5:30 in the morning, I was doing the two-hour watch and it started getting light. I got up and I stretched and one big artillery shell fell. And my helmet took off and went about twenty-five yards. Lucky I didn't have it buttoned. That thing took off and I thought for sure my head was in it. I found out a couple of years later that my buddy, Vance Waggoner, who was in the same platoon, got hit with the same shell, in the back. He's still alive today, living in Mechanicsburg, Pennsylvania. And my other two buddies in the hole with me, Paul O'Brien from Pittsburgh, and Frank Walker from Keyser, West Virginia, came through okay, too. We all still talk to each other about once a month.

There's an important story that happened just about this time. It starts back when we hit the beach, and I lost my watch. I never knew I lost it. A couple of days later, one of the men in my foxhole says, Look what I picked up on the beach. It was my wristwatch! I said, Where the hell did you find that? He said he picked it up on the beach. So he gave it to me. And at that time it was still running. Now, what we did when we were standing watch at night was I would let one guy take my wristwatch and he would wake the next guy up in two hours. And a few days later, this one guy, Millard Wiser, who was in our mortar platoon, came over to me and said, Hey, Schribert, I think I'm doing more than two hours, can I borrow your watch? I said, Sure. Millard Wiser was six-two, a good-looking guy, curly hair, husky. The only thing, when we went on ten-mile hikes, he used to take off his boondockers, and he used to walk barefooted. He was from Arkansas or Tennessee, someplace far out. So that night, when he had my wristwatch, we had infiltrators, and somebody threw a grenade in Wiser's foxhole. I don't know if he fell on it or whatever, but he took the full blast and saved two guys. He died instantly. One guy got shrapnel in his fanny, the other guy nothing. When the word spread around that Wiser got it, I said to the corpsman would he go get my watch? One thing I hated was looking at dead Marines. I didn't mind dead Japs. Even after that explosion, that watch was still running. Right now that watch is in the Bristol Armory, in Connecticut, in their museum. And you know, no one ever wrote up Wiser for that, falling on that grenade and saving those guys. He should have gotten the Medal of Honor. Other guys did. But I guess it's too late now. It's a sad case.

We had one job that I hated. Usually at night they had naval gunfire to light the front lines all night long. But every now and then our company would get the job of shooting those flares. That was terrible, because when you drop it in, you get a lot of sparks. When it's dark, they can see where the hell you are.

Anytime there was going to be an attack, they would let us know. We had about two hundred to three hundred rounds, and every mortar round comes with a pin, as a safety. And we took out all the pins. Which we weren't supposed to do. And during the attack, you don't just keep dropping rounds in the tube. You traverse it. There's a little handle you turn, and you drop it, traverse it, drop it, traverse it. A good mortar section can hit any target with three rounds. One over, one under, third round hits the target. At night we'd get calls for harassing fire. Just drop a couple of rounds down the tube to let them know you're here, you don't know where it's going.

We fired a lot of mortar rounds during the battle, and I can say honestly we never had one dud in the tube. If you drop a round in the tube and it don't come out, you better run like hell. That thing is going to go boom. Then if it doesn't come out, you get two volunteers, you know, you and you, whoever they pick. One guy loosens the clamp on the baseplate, the other guy picks up the tube. And while you're picking up the tube, the other guy puts his fingers over the end to catch the shell, hoping it don't go off.

Sometimes we'd have to go behind the lines to look for water, ammunition. So they would ask for volunteers, you know—Schribert, you, you, and you. The main thing you looked for was water, in cans. You dumped it out so the Japs couldn't have it. So we get our carbines and go out and one of my buddies goes into a cave. What the hell are you doing, I says. There could be Japs in there! So he pulls out a flag. Then my other buddy runs down and comes back with a big samurai sword. So of course Schribert goes down there, and I think, Boy, are we dopes, imagine if one Jap was there, or if the place was booby-trapped. I broke into a trunk, and I think it belonged to a Jap officer, because I had his pistol, I had his fountain pen, I had his dogtags, I had his combat ribbons, his wristwatch—even today, I still have his family pictures that I got from his wallet. But to this day I think, Boy, we were stupid. Marines are great for souvenir hunting. They're just like vultures. Soon as a Jap falls, down they come. One Marine had a souvenir that he carried with him through the front lines. It was a saddle. There was a Japanese major that was in the Olympics, so he must have brought his saddle along.

One of the worst sights I ever saw was the dead Marines, lined up in row after row, covered with ponchos. And you can see their hands, they're all black and blue and gray. Usually the ponchos cover their faces. And then when you see a truck pull up and you see two guys heave the dead Marines up on the truck for burial, what a sight. You can sit here, next to a Jap with his head blown off, his leg missing, and you're eating lunch. Doesn't bother you at all. But if you see a dead Marine . . . But you never think it's going to be you. Might be somebody else, but you're just hoping it ain't you.

I guess about the sixteenth or seventeenth day I had the watch one morning. They liked to send infiltrators out early in the morning, not so much to drop grenades but to look for food and water. So I had the Jap's pistol and some 8mm ammunition which I kept in my jacket and I see something crawling along. I yell out, Halt! What's the password? It's still a little dark yet, but I can see he's still crawling. So I take out my carbine, fifteen rounds, boom, boom, boom, boom. Took out my pistol, boom, boom, boom, boom, eight more rounds. Took my hand grenade, boooooom. He was dead, but I wouldn't go look at him.

The scariest day I ever had was in March. We got the word that we were going to go back aboard ship and head for Maui, but they needed some volunteers, you know, Schribert, you, you, and you, to go to the beach to look for Jap stragglers. Knowing we were going back the next day, and me, a mortarman! I think somebody gave me a BAR. I don't know how to fire a BAR! So we went down, and thank goodness, nobody was there. We went right to the water and boy, we were happy.

The next day we got to the beach and we were put aboard an LST. Then we transferred to an APA for the trip back to Maui. The first thing was getting rid of the clothes you'd had on for thirty days. We were stinking and bearded, but you didn't give it much thought. You didn't even think that anybody got killed, but you're alive. Not knowing who got killed is one thing, but a Marine getting killed and knowing him, that's when it's hard. We were lucky. We didn't have too many get killed in our mortar platoon. We lost Sergeant Higgs, but not too many men. We were fortunate. We had wounded, though. We started with 225 people in our company, we came back with fifty. We had a couple of battle fatigues, they'd just shake and cry.

*The following story from Sgt. William J. Smith is that of a career Marine.
Much of what he describes is simply "business as usual" for a combat infantryman.*

Sgt. William J. Smith
*First Platoon Guide, Company G, 2d Battalion,
23d Marines, 4th Marine Division*

I was a PFC and Brugger was a squad leader when we landed on
Saipan. I think I was assistant squad leader at that time. Brugger got
killed on the beach. Burnowski got killed at the same time, he was
the platoon guide. Doc Colombe was trying to work on Brugger and
they shot through his pack. So you got promotion kind of by process
of elimination. You got back, there would be something on the bul-
letin board that says the following men have been promoted to corporal. They didn't have warrants like they give you now. The longer
you were there, you seemed to get rank, if you had any know-how at
all. So when I hit Iwo, I was a platoon guide, which is kind of an aide
to the platoon sergeant, to see that you get your ammo and chow and
stuff up, whenever you can.

D-day morning, it was still dark. All you see is silhouettes, out-
lines. And then they piped down for all Marines to go down to the
tank deck, and you loaded into your respective tractor and drove
out the door. Riding in wasn't any different from any other landing
because you didn't know what was going to happen anyhow. You can't
anticipate because you don't know what's in there. It's just when
they say "lock and load" that you've got a pretty good idea that it's
getting close.

Soon as you hit the beach on Iwo, you went uphill. It was very
deep out there. My tractor stripped its gears trying to make it up,
and we had to abandon it. They let us get ashore before they started
shooting at us, the artillery was quite heavy.

Most of us were very disorganized. You got scattered. Some people
went one way from the tractor, some went the other. And it was next
to impossible to move. I probably spent the first night with Chase,

who had been commissioned and went to Easy Company, and a guy and his war dog, and the dog didn't make a sound all night. And then the next day we ended up near where the circle comes out of the first airfield.

Probably half a dozen of us were in this huge hole, and there was a mine down in there. They had just thrown corrugated metal over it, and it was quite huge. God, it must have been two foot square, with horns on it. Wasn't a land mine. A big old beach mine, I guess. And Kosek damned near landed on top of it when he came jumping in the hole.

Then Hegarty and Romanski and I went across the airfield to contact Baker Company. I came back across to tell Captain Grussendorf what the scoop was, and he said, What happened to your rifle? I said, Nothing, why? The butt had a hole blown through it, busted the oil and thong case and combination tool. I didn't feel a thing. Of course, going across the airport, I heard it go over and come down on the other side of me, but I didn't feel it.

The second day was the most intense artillery that I remember. And talking to the corpsman there, I told him that all my damned teeth hurt. He said, Well, that's from gritting them. There was so much inbound, you ground your teeth when the explosions went off.

We headed off towards Airport Number 2 on the third day, fourth day, whatever. It seemed, for some reason or other, we pulled out and we were on the high ground above the East Boat Basin. We were into Turkey Knob, Hill 382 area. One night we dug in, and we must have been near that damned sulfur mine,* I guess, because it was after dark and you took your entrenching tool and you removed a spade of dirt, and it would immediately fill up with fog so you couldn't tell what you were doing. And then I doubled and quartered my poncho and tried to lay still, but it was too damned hot.

---

*Actually, the sulfur mine was just west of Motoyama Village, a few hundred yards away from Smith's position, but that meant little. The odor of sulfur was everywhere. Iwo Jima had developed a reputation for this even as far back as 1673, when an Englishman named Gore visited Iwo Jima and renamed it Sulphur Island.

Usually we had two guys in the hole, so you got an hour's sleep, and an hour awake. One night, Hegarty woke me up, just at daylight, and there was a guy coming up behind us. And I didn't figure that Moose was asleep yet, so I said, Hey, Moose, wake up, there's a guy coming up behind us. He got his M-1, and I reached behind me because the weapons were in the corner, and I got the lieutenant's carbine instead of my M-1. We waited until he was alongside of us and we took care of him. And then when I went to clean my rifle, there was a piece of metal lodged between the gas port and the barrel, so had I fired it it probably would have sent the bolt back through my head. That was just luck.

At night, they didn't pull no banzais there. They weren't out wandering around so much as previously on Saipan. They just fought a defensive battle, there wasn't a hell of a lot of action at night, other than artillery or something going off. I mean, they weren't creeping around, trying to crawl into holes. At least, I didn't think so. Other islands, at night you'd hear them talking.

You didn't see Japanese above ground too much, although one time they got into the CP. It was early morning, about five o'clock, whatever, daylight, and a bunch of them broke into the CP. One made it up next to me, but he was about on his last leg, he had trouble breathing, he was all screwed up. So I finished him off. I don't think they could have done anything for him. Wasn't intentional or nothing, you know what I mean. We hardly took any prisoners, let's put it that way.

During the day, you'd throw satchel charges or grenades into the caves. You didn't assault them. We didn't go down in them. I didn't. Just blow them up. Those things went from one place to another. Probably go across the island underground.

It was hard to tell when the flag went up on Suribachi. They told us about it and we looked, but it was quite a distance, and it wasn't that large a flag. And we didn't do too much cheering. Hell, the day Hegarty got hit, every time we looked out the hole, a machine gun would throw dirt in our faces. We were stuck there for quite a while. Anytime he'd get any movement from our hole, he'd kick some dirt in on us. Hegarty got hit because he thought he had it timed. He went out the left side of the hole, and they got him in the leg.

There were a lot of casualties on the beach, seemed to eat up a lot of people I knew. A lot of us had been together three years, damned near. So you got to know some of them quite well. Not like when I went to Korea. That was a one-year thing, where you might know a guy for three months because he was leaving. We knew each other very well in World War II. We lost A. H. Martin, Bill Reed, MacNamara, Major Fought. I think he was at Battalion, he got killed. We heard him out there. We went out and got him the next morning. Spider Vaglia got killed there. But Martin was a tentmate, we were real close. I didn't see it, but somebody said a mortar hit him. And they had a huge damned mortar over there, the spigot mortar. *De-moralizing* when that thing went off. Went "cruuunnch" when it went off, big bugger.

Further up the island, Joe Bennett and I were sitting, probably as close as you and I, and a knee mortar landed right between the two of us, and it was a dud. They're not much bigger than a hand grenade, and I don't know what they'd do to you if they went off, but it just stuck there in the mud. We just looked at it and left. You have a tendency to want to leave a place when you're hit, get the hell away from it. I didn't get hit at all on Iwo. I got hit in Korea, so I know what it feels like to get hit and try to get away from it.

The closest call with artillery I remember was during the last day or two. It was eight o'clock and we were going to jump off, and they put artillery out in front of us. Boy, that was close, by God. I don't think it was more than twenty, thirty yards out in front of us. But nothing happened. You might get a short round once in a while, but otherwise it all went where it was supposed to go. It sure was close in.

We weren't very far from the water then, from the end of the island, the other beach. They pulled us back and we crapped out for a while, then they ordered us aboard an LST. We left the island on the eighteenth of March. And then we left Iwo on the *Rockbridge,* a Navy APA. I had two chow passes, I used to eat two meals a day to get even, catch up. And towards the end like that, all the people that you really knew for two or three years or so were gone, you didn't have too many old friends left. There was Kosek, Brown, and myself, in the platoon. There were very few old-timers by then. And you always had the feeling, Well, sonofabitch, I'm gonna get killed today and the war'll end tomorrow. That would really jerk you off. But everybody was just tired and kept to themselves, get something to eat, get clean, relax.

There's only one way, in those days, having what you had to take an island, and that was just go in and do it. Go straight in, there was no way of getting around it. Perhaps as many people were saved as were killed by taking the island and giving fighter support to the bombers, and letting the bombers land there. And that photograph did a lot for the Marine Corps.

The Marine Corps is just different, the way it's put together. People are just proud. If you watch history, you might see *The Forgotten War*. They'd pull out an Army regiment out over there in Korea and stick in a Marine battalion and they'd stop the enemy and go forward. And MacArthur was happy as shit when he got Marines, he didn't like to turn them loose. Most Marines don't care for MacArthur. Personally, I feel good about having been a Marine. There's no other branch of the service I would have cared to be in, and going in I didn't know a damned thing about the Marine Corps. It was training, and leadership, and they beat it into your brain down at PI. Sure changed you in a hurry.

2

COMMANDERS AND OFFICERS

Company-grade officers attained their rank in one of three ways. The "Mustangs" were former enlisted men promoted from the ranks due to their abilities and accomplishments. Others had graduated from college sometime before the war, or shortly after the beginning, and they enlisted on the promise that they could attend officers' school in their chosen service branch. The remainder were products of the Navy or Marine V-12 programs where officer candidates would finish their college education and study military training at the same time. Upon graduation, candidates would report to their respective service branches to complete their commitments.

Capt. Lawrence Snowden was of the second example; Lt. Angelo Bertelli was a product of the V-12 program. Snowden became a career officer who retired with the rank of lieutenant general; Bertelli left the Marines after the war to run a successful chain of liquor stores. Both men's stories are generally typical of the attitude and approach of career officers on one hand and citizen-soldier officers on the other. Like most Marine officers, both performed their duties well.

Capt. Lawrence Snowden
Commander, Company F, 2d Battalion, 23d Marines, 4th Marine Division

I went to officers' school, and then to Camp Lejeune, North Carolina, and joined the 23d Marine regiment, which at that time was part of the 3d Division. A couple months later I was a platoon leader in K Company, 3d Battalion, 23d Marines, but because a lot of officers were flowing into Camp Lejeune at that time to round out the 3d Division and in anticipation of the 4th Division buildup, each of

51

us at the platoon level were ordered to fill out rosters A and B, split our platoon into two parts. We didn't know which list we were going to be on, so we tried to make them very equal in manpower. Smart Marines, not-so-smart Marines, whatever. Two equal lists. It turned out that I was on the list that stayed as the 23d Marines. The other half moved a few tent rows away and became the 25th Marines. Together we constituted the bulk of the newly formed 4th Division.

We went back to our base camp again at Maui after Tinian for training. We had very good facilities, and we had a lot of regimental exercises in which we practiced turning movements, that is, we started heading west, then had to make a swing to the north to change direction. And that's a difficult move for a large-size military unit. It's the hardest movement there is, to make a ninety-degree turn. And not until we had left Pearl Harbor and headed for Iwo Jima were we told where we were going and permitted to open our sealed packages and maps and operational orders. We could see the scheme of maneuver which required us to land on the end of the island near Mount Suribachi and then swing right, do a ninety-degree turn and go up the island, work up to the other end. So now we knew what we had been doing and why we had been doing it.

When we were permitted to open the operational order packages and break out the intelligence data, which included the intelligence overlays, they had an awful lot of red defensive installations on them. Later we found out they didn't have nearly enough. There were nearly twice as many installations of heavy weapons and fortified positions. This was enough to make us understand that it would probably be much tougher than anything we had seen before. But we were young in spirit, and we were Marines. We knew we were going to win. We weren't very upset by that. We just expected it to be tougher. And we were encouraged at that time by the fact that our senior commanders had estimated it would take about ten days to wrap up Iwo Jima.

Transport life on the LSTs was a different life from the APAs and the AKAs. They had a lot more space. But on the LSTs, there were times when we had only two meals a day, and when you got out of the breakfast line, you got back in line for the afternoon meal. The ship was so small for the number of people that we carried. I had my company of 220 men, plus a platoon, plus the LVTs that would carry us ashore, plus a platoon of five Army LVT(A)s. And most guys, when they could, tried to sleep on the deck at night because it was so hot down below. They slept in the tractors and on the tank deck, wherever they could, trying to get a breath of fresh air, get some breathing space. But we spent our time during the day either studying our plans or talking about how we were going to work this operation ashore, or trying to stay physically fit or cleaning our weapons, which we cleaned and took apart and cleaned again and recleaned and took apart and cleaned again. That sounds like useless work but it wasn't because sea and salt air were very hard on weapons or any kind of metal. So with the heat and humidity aboard that ship, the weapons required constant care to assure that they would function when we arrived. I never found a problem with the morale among the Marines I associated with, never ever. I think I learned a lesson from my superiors in that troops that are busy doing something that is basically good for them, they stay motivated. We never had a problem about being crowded on ship. Marines above all others, I think, expected less than anybody else. They took some pride in being not too well taken care of. There's a spirit that comes from adversity. It breeds intimate social relationships. Social events don't do that. And every Marine who worked his many days across the Pacific on that LST was so glad to get off, they were willing to fight anybody. That's just the way life was then, and we didn't expect it to be any different.

In the first waves, you have to get embarked in those tractors on the LSTs very early, so it was about 1:30 in the morning we're up, trying to get some breakfast, then scrambling down to get into those LVTs. Now, you dropped off the ramp of those LSTs, and because the LVTs in those days were open, you just held your breath, waiting to see whether you dropped too far. If too much water came in, the LVT would go on down, and you went with it. And then we seemed to plow around in the water. First of all, it takes a long time to discharge all the LVTs, then you have to get formed up and while you're waiting for others to arrive, you circle and circle and circle. While the seas were not terribly rough, there was enough swell and there were a lot of sick Marines out there. You spent so long smelling those diesel fumes, circling, all the time naval gunfire's coming overhead. At one time we were directly underneath all those guns that were firing, and that's kind of a jarring experience.

Once we got up to the line of departure to head to the beach, the standard operating procedure was that everybody was down below the gunwales of the LVTs. One man was permitted to put his helmet and eyeballs up to see where they were going, and that was me, as company commander. So I was able to watch the movement. The other guys were down as they were ordered to be, and there was a lot of discipline. I was able to watch the gunfire we received from the island. And I'm sure you know the Japanese plan was to withhold the fire until a lot of us were ashore, and then open up with everything they had. There were a number of rounds received en route, because the line of departure was a couple of thousand yards offshore, and the tractors in those days moved at something like six miles an hour, that's pretty slow going. Obviously, you have some concern if you're in a slow-moving boat like that because to the gunners on shore you're a pretty easy target. But I didn't see any direct hits, not until we got very close to the beach.

Sands of Iwo Jima are different than any you might find at Daytona Beach, Atlantic City, wherever. Sand, generally, is pretty ragged, and it binds together because of the ragged parts that kind of fit together. You get good hard beaches like Daytona where you can drive on the beach, like a highway. The sand on Iwo Jima didn't have rough edges like that, and mixed with the soft volcanic ash, it was like walking in rice shells, one fellow described it. You put your foot down, pull it out, the sand would fill in the hole and you couldn't see where your foot had been. Our LVTs in most instances couldn't really make any progress in it. They would sit and spin the tracks. My own tractor got fifty yards in and spun sideways and we couldn't go. Now, if you've read about the Iwo Jima campaign, you know that the objective was reach an 0-1 line. We had hoped to ride up to that line in the LVTs and then dismount and take up a defensive line to get organized to move forward. But virtually none of the tractors made the 0-1 line. They simply couldn't navigate the soft sands. Most, like my own, just made a few yards, spun out, and stopped. So I gave the order to bail out over the side of the LVT and jump into the first bomb crater we could find.

I had kind of a disturbing incident in the first hole I jumped into. One of my men, a sergeant named Leonard Ash, who now lives in Daytona and I see him from time to time, was lying there with his leg very badly shattered. I thought he was going to lose his leg. He did what was expected, he said, Captain, you've got to help me. And I wanted to help him. And I had to do one of the things that was very hard for any young officer to do, but we were thoroughly trained that in our officer capacity we were not supposed to worry about one Marine. I had to say to him, Len, I'm going to get you a corps-man. He had already given himself a shot of morphine, and I yelled for a corpsman. One started for the hole, and I said, Len, I got to go, because my job is to worry about all the other Marines that were ashore. That was a very difficult moment in my life, when I had to leave Len when he was in such bad shape. And I really thought for many years after that that he really lost that leg, but he didn't. Only a few years ago he had his final operation on it.

All the bombing and the naval gunfire had worked that area, there was no vegetation left on the island, all blown away. The island was all gray and black sand. The vegetation that was left standing was very sparse, there was no cover and concealment as we had practiced in our training exercises. There wasn't anything to hide you. The only way was to get down below a rock that had been blown up, get down into a bomb crater and try to get your whole body down below the surface of the ground. Because of that volcanic ash you really couldn't dig a foxhole very quickly, you just moved the stuff aside until you could stretch out and hope that you had twelve inches of room if you had a ten-inch body. That way, if a mortar round hit, they went over you and not into you.

In those days, with as much ammunition as we produced, quality was not always first class. The very tragic result was that when I was up on the edge of the first airstrip, Motoyama Number 1, my foxhole was in a position where my eyeballs were just kind of looking over the runway. There were two fellows in the hole with me and about twenty yards away there was another foxhole which included a corpsman and a Marine, and a five-inch shell from one of our own ships landed right on the other side of that foxhole. There was a terrible blast and we immediately rushed over after we had recovered. But, to tell you how bad that volcanic ash and sand was, they were able to get the Marine out, but the corpsman was so deeply buried that he suffocated before we could get him out. In those days, all of us had experienced artillery rounds falling short, and we just thought that's the way things work in war. In recent decades, the concept of friendly fire has somehow evolved into a context of unprofessionalism. That's not it at all. You just have to recognize that no matter how much quality and consistency we put into ordnance, it isn't always consistent. We didn't get upset by that, it just happens. That's that.

I had a unique experience in that same position. It was about the third or fourth day that some Zeros had come down from Chichi Jima to attack the ships late in the afternoon. When they had made their diving attack and finished firing, they would turn back and then expend all their ordnance to improve the gas mileage or whatever. So several of them turned and made a run at the beach, firing their machine guns all the way. But old grunts, that is, myself and some of my men with combat experience, knew that in those days machine guns were generally fixed in position. And we knew there was a point beyond which that guy couldn't hit us, no matter how close he looked. So this one Zero came over our beach, straight toward us, and some machine-gun fire went on by, and then we stood up and watched. Well, this Zero passed no more than sixty or seventy feet over my head and I looked at him and he looked at me and I waved to him. And he looked at me, nodded his head and smiled, and went on.

On Iwo Jima we bounded in and out of the lines into a reserve status. But when you moved back you didn't go very far. In reserve, you really were not far out of any gunfire range, because it was all too close. And moving in and out so much meant that a lot of names like Charlie-Dog Ridge and Turkey Knob didn't mean much to us then. What you have to remember especially about the early days of

Iwo Jima is that there was virtually no tactical movement of units. Sure, at the upper level, battalions and regiments moved about some. But the fighting was done at the four-man fire-team level, and the twelve-man squad level. And with those fortified bunkers that had only a slot for a machine gun to fire from, the only way to neutralize them was by small team action in which two men fired at the port and tried to keep them covered, and two other men moved to the side to plant a satchel charge, drop a grenade, whatever. There was no opportunity to apply the principle of base fire establishment, maneuver element, and all that. The fighting was just all too close.

The Japanese had these big 362mm mortars, the spigot mortars. They looked like a trash can tumbling through the air. You could hear it going off the launcher, a screeching sound like it was just moaning and groaning to get off. And when you heard the launch, you'd look up. If we could see it, we'd point and measure the angle of descent, and it was over here or over there, we didn't worry about it. I don't really know whether I heard the screech or what, but I didn't know anything until boom, two of them hit close by. And I couldn't hear anything, I had shrapnel in my hand and the back of my neck, not too serious. But I was evacuated, and they hauled me down to the beach on a stretcher where I waited to get taken on board the hospital ship. I was not a smoker, but some guy offered me a cigarette and I took it. I smoked it, but it didn't make me feel any better so I said, I don't need that anymore, and I haven't smoked since. Later I was evacuated to the ship and it was an overnight run from there to Guam, to hospital 115, Fleet Hospital 115. By the time I got there, some of my hearing was back, and the shrapnel wounds were minor, so I said to the doctor the next morning that I wanted to go back to my unit on Iwo Jima. He said, I don't think they will allow any folks to go back, but I said, I want to try. Would you let me have a few hours away from the hospital? He said okay. So I went outside and flagged down a jeep and got a ride to the FMF-Pac Forward Headquarters. The colonel in charge had a son in my division and I knew him very well in my officer class. I said I wanted to go back, and he said no. Well, trying to be sneaky, I talked to him about his son, had he heard from him, and he said he was all right. I said, I really would like to go back, because these wounds don't amount to much, and I can hear fairly good. He finally said, Well, look, tomorrow we're sending the first airplane up there with some plasma and mail, and if you want to go down to that airfield to see if you can get in that airplane, I'll let you go. I went down there and the pilot said, If you're crazy enough to go back, you can go with me tomorrow morning. So then next morning I went down to that airfield and stretched out on the top of the mailbags with one thin Marine Corps blanket and froze to death, but I got back to Iwo Jima. The next day, I had been back with my company about four hours and I got another blast. And I couldn't hear. This time, though, I just went back to the regimental CP, and a couple of days later I got my hearing back and I rejoined the company.

Now, I didn't go back because I was a hero. The name of the game was I wanted to get back to my unit. Our units were our family, those are the guys I've been with for two and a half years, and I wasn't about to get cast off into a transient center and become a number on a board. Besides, all my worldly possessions were in my seabag, which was somewhere up there on Iwo Jima. And the thing that's important about these men who participated in the battle was that they really got down to the blood and guts of warfare on the battlefield. They were just hundreds of Marines who found themselves face to face with an enemy and with no weapon but his combat knife, his bayonet, rifle, pistol, whatever. It was just man to man, and you either killed or got killed. That's a dreadful experience and you'll never forget it in your lifetime, but the courage that these guys showed, and their top physical condition, let them sustain themselves. The battle was a matter of grunts going yards at a time, counting your losses and starting all over again the next day. It was won by the intestinal fortitude and physical stamina of hundreds of Marines who just wouldn't give up. If one fell, another one stepped in and took his place and moved on. There wasn't a man on that island who didn't want to go in the other direction, but it was never an option. And those are the kind of guys I'm so proud to have served with.

2d Lt. Angelo Bertelli
Liaison Officer, 21st Marines, 3d Marine Division

I was at the University of Notre Dame, and at that time the U.S. government instituted a program where you could stay in school for another semester, or possibly two semesters, if you joined what they called the V-12 program. It included the Marines, and also part of the Navy. This way I could get my degree before going to the war. This enabled me to stay on and play my last football season, although I didn't get a chance to finish. I played only six games, and I was very fortunate to get that far. But the V-12 program, as a part of the Marine Corps on campus, gave me that opportunity. And I guess the Marines were also part of my gung-ho, the spirit of Notre Dame, I always rooted for the Yankees, I always loved the Marine Corps. It was a combination of the rah-rah spirit of the Corps, and I was young and gung-ho and I was so happy for it.

I remember the experience of training as being very tough. I played my last football game against Navy, and the following week we were supposed to play Army, which was our biggest game of the year. The Army game was big for me also because my family lived in Massachusetts and they had an opportunity to come to Yankee Stadium to see me play. The morning after the Navy game, my time was up. The Marine Corps said, This is it, you've had your extra semester or two, you've had an opportunity to get close to your degree, we're taking you down to Parris Island. This is November of 1943. And it was very sad. They got us up at about five o'clock in the morning, they put us on a train in downtown South Bend, it was raw, it was cold, I kept thinking about the rest of the season that I was going to miss, I kept thinking about all of the friends I had made at the university. I didn't know what was in store for me down at Parris Island. I had heard all kinds of stories about PI, and about DIs, and I didn't know what to expect. But when I got down there, it turned out that my DI remembered my name from the college football situation, and at that time I was getting an awful lot of letters, fan letters, as such, because the Notre Dame football team was very popular. The DI broke me in immediately. Every time he called my name, he would

hand me one letter. And I would have to run around the entire platoon in this deep sand and in my boondockers and pick up one letter. Then I'd get back in place, and he'd call me again. And again.
And again. So that before the mail call was over, I was a very, very
tired young man. Of course, he used some strange words at that
time, telling me that "I'll teach you not to be a woman's man, you
damned college boy."

We were the first college group to go to Parris Island. The DIs
had had platoons before for years, but this was the first college
group to get down to Parris Island. The DIs were just waiting for us.
Of course, we had heard the stories, and we did our very best, and
I'm thankful for what I'd learned at PI. I learned that the DI was
doing what he did for a reason. The Marines were supposed to be
the very best, they were supposed to be able to take care of their
comrades in wartime and peacetime. I learned there was a camaraderie and a spirit of the Corps, and it was a hard lesson. It was a
completely new extreme, because the drill instructors were not very
nice, and for a reason. I always used to say that if I ran into my drill
instructor after the war, I'd probably clobber him. What happens?
I run into my drill instructor after the war and I keep buying him
drinks and we talk about the Marines all night long.

I remember the worst thing he did to me was when Notre Dame
played its last game, we lost on the very last play of the game. About
five of us who had been at Notre Dame were all in a Quonset hut
listening to this game on the radio. And when the game was over
and we'd lost, we came out of this hut and most of us were crying.
Tears in our eyes. And at the same time, someone came up to me and
handed me a telegram telling me I had won the Heisman Trophy.
Now I didn't know whether to cry or laugh or what. I was very
excited about it, so much so that when I had the opportunity to talk
to my DI, I said, Corporal Murphy, I have just won the Heisman
Trophy, I showed him the telegram, and I would soon be going to
New York to receive the Heisman Trophy, would he please take it easy
on my haircut? Well, Corporal Murphy just nods, and it comes time
for our haircuts and we're all sitting in the barber shop like cattle.

And everybody's getting the close crop and it comes my turn and Corporal Murphy gets up from his seat, walks over to the barber, and I figure he's telling the barber to take it easy, I'm going to New York to get the Heisman Trophy. But that's not what he told the barber. I had a complete baldy, so much so that I could have just killed him. But of course the Marine Corps came first and I didn't get to go to New York then. When I left Parris Island and went to Quantico, they let me go in between OCS and ROS, Officer Candidate School and Reserve Officer School. I had about a ten-day furlough. My hair was still a little short.

Quantico was worse than Parris Island. Parris Island was physical, and it wasn't the mental situation that Quantico was. Quantico was aerial photography, tough subject. Map reading, tough subject. And they tried to keep what they thought was the best, and if you didn't make it, you either went to Camp Lejeune or Camp Pendleton. OCS was an awful lot of study and concern about making sure you knew all of the subjects as best you could.

So we finished Reserve Officer School and we had a furlough, after which we went down to Camp Lejeune. And at that time Camp Lejeune was going to have a football team, but then they weren't going to have a football team. But to make a long story short, they put us into the first replacement draft, and we were shipped to California, from California we were put on a ship, the *Blumfontain,* and we headed toward Guam, which was the first campaign that I witnessed. There was a lot of anticipation about what was to come. And there was some humor. And we had a boxing program, believe it or not. We had Rocky Castellani, who was kind of a famous fighter, and a few others who were professionals. We would put on these boxing shows to entertain the troops. We also had a couple of what I would call vaudevillians. Not really big-time movie stars, but people who were in show business. And we would entertain after dinner in the evening, for an hour or so, with songs, sometime somebody would put on a sketch, and the boxing programs.

When I got to Guam, there was a telegram waiting from the commanding general at Lejeune, saying, Sorry we missed you, we decided to have a football team after all. Which I really didn't care about, I wasn't interested in playing service football to begin with.

Guam was just about over when I arrived. It was more of a mop-up situation. The Nips were still coming out of the woods and every day you'd hear a different story—there's four of them here, there's three of them there, but there was no real combat. Just cleanup. The Marines covered the entire island, and all we did was prepare for the next campaign. But in my case they used me at regimental and divisional headquarters running the division baseball team, the track team, and things like that because of my college football background. They had assigned me Pee Wee Reese of the Brooklyn Dodgers. He wasn't an officer, and he was a Navy man and I was a Marine, and here I am running the baseball team. And we would play the different teams that would travel the islands. We had days when we would play against Virgil Trucks of the Detroit Tigers, and Joe Ennis of the Philadelphia Phillies, Connie Ryan of the Braves, there were big leaguers all over the place. We had mostly GIs, but we would play against them, and Pee Wee and I ran that at the division level while I was still assigned to the 21st Marines. I was away from the platoon situation for a while, and my friends were either in a machine-gun company, or they had platoons already, because fundamentally every second lieutenant that comes out of Quantico is a platoon leader. But when the Iwo Jima campaign was coming about, we were all called in, regimental and division, and we all got a feeling that we were going someplace. They didn't show us any maps until we were on the ship going to Iwo, but we knew we were going on a campaign. At that time, they told me I would be a liaison officer. I didn't even know what the hell a liaison officer does. I still don't. I guess you carried messages from here to there, which could be very important at times, depending upon the message you were carrying, or who you're carrying it to.

I was aboard a ship on the way to Iwo. I don't know the name of it. It carried an awful lot of troops, but I couldn't tell you how many, or whether there was more than one division. We were briefed on the size of the island, and I remember so well that looking at it, I says, Oh, we'll be here only two or three days. They told us what we had for air, bombs, battleships, divisions of Marines, Seabees, everything. If you had put it all together and you were looking at this little island, you were saying, My God, we should take this in about four or five days and it should all be over. We found out later it wasn't that kind of a situation.

When we arrived at Iwo, we were so close, and there were so many battleships, and so much air power, it was like the Fourth of July a thousandfold. There was an awful lot of firepower. And when we started to go in on the second day, the weather wasn't too good. It was pretty rocky. There were these LCVPs that were bouncing the size of almost one story in the water, and everybody was sick, throwing up all over the place. But then we got back on the ship, and the next day, D+3, we did the same thing, only we went in.

I was still moving with the regimental headquarters. It was so bouncy, and everybody was so sick, and with the havoc on the beach, you've never seen anything like it. Congestion, confusion, tanks that had been bombed out, dead Marines. All I did was stay around with my regiment and wait to find out what I had to do. I was spending some time with the regimental doctor, people like that, just waiting for word from Colonel Withers [Col. Hartnoll J. Withers, CO, 21st Marines] about what he wanted me to do. The first night comes, and it's scary, noisy. I think maybe I slept. Not much, because even though there were patrols out there in front of the lines, you still didn't feel safe. There were mortars, machine guns, Christ, they were shooting everything all over the place. But I didn't get a chance to worry about it too much, because on D+4, first thing, I'm assigned to take over a platoon. The liaison part I never had a chance to participate in. The platoon probably had sixteen remaining original trained Marines. So there was all of this Parris Island, all of this Camp Lejeune, all of Pendleton and training on Guam that all of these platoons went through together, and then all of a sudden, first day, you lose all but sixteen. What's coming in is dribs and drabs, so this didn't help. What did help was I felt that I commanded some discipline from just having been coached by a great coach, having been disciplined and regimented as a football player, and having been through Parris Island and Quantico. I felt that I had enough discipline about me that the people who were under me were listening. Which made me feel good, but it also made me feel bad because I didn't know how many I was going to lose.

When I think of the day I took over the platoon, and these sixteen or so that had worked with this platoon all the way through, I remember how close some of them had become. And then all of a sudden they lost friends. They were disciplined, they would still listen, but they were down, I mean really concerned about friends that they had lost, and their own lives. I still remember the looks on their faces as I'm talking to them for the first time. It was like, Hey, I've already been though it, get me out of here, Lieutenant. But they accepted me, especially because as we started to get the fill-ins they had to help. They tried to tell the younger troops what they'd been through, what to expect.

We were always surrounded by other Marine platoons, other companies, and we had some kind of support. But I didn't witness any real hand-to-hand combat other than where we ran into a couple of situations with Japs who were dug in, and we would drop hand grenades into a dugout, and those hand grenades kept bouncing out. I never moved so fast in my life. The Japs were more or less sheltered, so you didn't know where the mortars were coming from. And the Japs that I saw at this time were undernourished, hadn't slept, but still not willing to surrender. There were ragged-looking individuals. And along those same lines, when we were making a movement, the thing that I felt saddest about was the smell of the dead, and the smell of the island, and the bloating of some of the dead. It was horrible.

Once we moved into the center of the island, past Charlie-Dog Ridge, the action was not very intense. It probably had been before we got there, because there were a lot of dead around. We were rotating in and out of the line a lot. Another sad duty we had at this time was to go out and pick up dead Marines and bring them back for burial. We knew that we were going to win, but there was an awful lot of casualties. We knew from the briefing we had on the ship how important this particular island was. In fact, to this day I cannot understand why we needed Okinawa, when this was close enough to Japan and we were that close to the end of the war.

Somewhere along the line, someone told us that we'd be leaving the island soon. The colonel that was in charge of my battalion had asked me at that time what I was going to do when I got back to Guam. I said I was most likely going back to run the division base-ball team. He said, I've been watching you, it would be good if you stayed down here and stayed with the platoon. I said, I don't think so, but I felt good that he thought I should stay.

Leaving on the transport, no one was singing songs anymore after dinner because they knew that what they had just witnessed was incredible. They were just waiting to get back to where they could rest and relax, and not worry about getting killed.

I didn't see the flag-raising on Suribachi, being with the 3d Division up here all the time. There were rumors about it, really. We felt that now that we have Suribachi, we wouldn't be another twenty days out here. And after I came back to the States, and because that was such a famous picture, everybody wanted to know if I had been anywhere near Suribachi. Just because you were on Iwo and you were a Marine, everything was Mount Suribachi.

Even today I still don't like to talk about it too much, but in recent years my wife, my children have come to realize what Iwo Jima was, and my grandchildren. It's not something you just talk about and say, Hey, honey, here's what happened on the second day at Iwo Jima. I still think back on people whose names I don't even remember. I do remember a close friend of mine who was leading a platoon who got hit in the heart, but he had a Bible in that pocket, and the Bible saved him. But it's all in the past, and it's very sad that we lost almost seven thousand Marines, but it was a part of our grow-ing up, I guess. At the time you didn't think about those things. All you knew was this was going to help save a few people the closer we got to Japan.

I hope no one forgets that many Marines died, and that there were twenty-five thousand casualties. If there's a legacy at all, it lets people know that the Marines are some hell of a group. There's something about Marines and the esprit de corps, the camaraderie, that people may chuckle at sometimes, but it certainly is no joke. I'm happy I was a Marine. I'm not knocking any other part of the service, but there was something about a Marine that to this day, when one Marine meets another, they have something to share, whether it's Iwo Jima or Pendleton or Parris Island. They all ended up as better men than when they went in.

3

THE LAST OF THE FIRST FLAG RAISERS

This story needs no introduction—almost. To most people, Joe Rosenthal's photo of the flag being raised over Mount Suribachi depicted the only event. It was actually the second. The first flag flew at 10:30 in the morning; the second unfurled at 2:30 in the afternoon. To this day, Cpl. Charles Lindberg and the other members of the first flag-raising—1st Lt. Harold Schrier, Platoon Sgt. Ernest Thomas, Sgt. Henry Hanson, PFC James Michels, and also Marine Corps photographer Sgt. Louis Lowery, who accompanied them to the top—have still not been acknowledged nationally for their accomplishment. Without their efforts, there would have been neither a second flag-raising nor an immortal Joe Rosenthal photo.

Cpl. Charles W. Lindberg
Flame Thrower, Company E, 2d Battalion, 28th Marines, 5th Marine Division
Last survivor of the first flag-raising on Iwo Jima

THE SECRETARY OF THE NAVY
WASHINGTON

The President of the United States takes pleasure in presenting
the SILVER STAR MEDAL to

CORPORAL CHARLES W. LINDBERG
UNITED STATES MARINE CORPS

for service as set forth in the following
CITATION:

For conspicuous gallantry and intrepidity while serving as a

Flame Thrower Operator of Company E, Twenty-eighth Marines, Fifth Marine Division, in action against enemy Japanese forces on Iwo Jima, Volcano Islands, from 19 February to 1 March 1945. Repeatedly exposing himself to hostile grenades and machine-gun fire in order that he might reach and neutralize enemy pill-boxes at the base of Mount Suribachi, Corporal Lindberg courageously approached within ten or fifteen yards of the emplacements before discharging his weapon, thereby assuring the annihilation of the enemy and the successful completion of his platoon's mission. As a member of the first combat patrol to scale Mount Suribachi, he courageously carried his flame thrower up the steep slopes and assisted in destroying the occupants of the many caves found in the rim of the volcano, some of which contained as many as seventy Japanese. While engaged in an attack on hostile cave positions on March 1, he fearlessly exposed himself to accurate enemy fire and was subsequently wounded and evacuated. By his determination in manning his weapon, despite its weight and the extreme heat developed in operation, Corporal Lindberg greatly assisted in securing his company's position. His courage and devotion to duty were in keeping with the highest traditions of the United States Naval Service.

For the President,

s/s John L. Sullivan

Secretary of the Navy

Before the war I was transporting automobiles from Detroit to Spokane, Washington. When war was declared and the factories closed and went to war production I was without a job. I was in Spokane at the time and, knowing I would be drafted in time, I decided to join the Marine Corps on January 8, 1942. I had always wanted to be a Marine, so I signed up for four years.

The boot camp at San Diego was hard. Since I had been a truck driver for many years I wasn't in the best shape. We only had five weeks of boot camp at that time. After boot camp I volunteered for 2d Raider Battalion, Carlson's Raiders,* and we trained at Jacques

---

*The Marines had developed two special-purpose units: the Paramarines and the Raiders. Raiders were similar to commandos in training and doctrine. Both were later incorporated into other divisions.

Farm, north of San Diego, for jungle warfare. Maj. James Roosevelt was the executive officer to Colonel Carlson, who was a real leader of men.

After Bougainville we returned to the States and I was assigned to the 5th Marine Division. I was made a corporal and given an assault squad which consisted of flamethrowers, bazookas, and demolitions. We trained at Camp Pendleton, where we had further training on volcanoes, caves, and the like. I carried a flamethrower and did lots of practicing on its use. But we had no idea where we were going until the *Honolulu Advertiser* came out with a picture of a plane bombing Mount Suribachi on Iwo Jima and it was a dead giveaway.

When we arrived off Iwo Jima on February 19, 1945, you could see Mount Suribachi, and it looked like a dust bowl. It was being shelled by ships and being bombed by planes. We found out this island had been shelled and bombed for seventy-two days around the clock. We thought it would only take about three days to take the island, but we were in for an awful surprise.

We landed in the ninth wave and the beach was all cluttered with equipment and the troops were pinned down. The Japs were mortaring up and down the beach and the casualties were high. The sand on the beach was very hard to maneuver in with large ridges to go over. It took us a long time to get off that beach, but when we did move up we cut Mount Suribachi off from the rest of the island. The 28th Marines was assigned to take Mount Suribachi and it took us to the evening of February 22 to get to the mountain and surround it. The going was very rough as we encountered pillboxes, caves, and bunkers. You would destroy one and start going ahead and they would be coming up behind you and by the time we reached the mountain our casualties were very high. That evening we learned that we were going to start climbing the mountain the next morning.

We really didn't know what to expect that night. They kept putting up flares to keep the island lit so we could watch. Nobody slept with all that stuff landing all night.

On the morning of the twenty-third, our platoon reported to Lt. Col. Chandler Johnson [CO, 2d Battalion, 28th Marines]. He handed a flag to Lt. Harold Schrier and said, If you get to the top, raise it. We started up the mountain expecting to come under heavy fire but surprisingly we met no resistance on the way up. It took us about three-quarters of an hour. At the top we put flankers on the ridge of the volcano and then Lieutenant Schrier said, Get the flag up. Two of our men found a long water pipe up there which had a bullet hole through the top of it in the right place to tie the flag on. After we had tied the flag on we carried it to the highest point we could find and we raised it at 10:30 A.M. The troops down below started to cheer and the ships' whistles sounded off-shore. It was a great patriotic feeling, this chill that runs through you. But then the Japanese started coming out of the caves and we had to move against them. We had the mountaintop secured by 1:30 P.M. Robert Goode, who was my assistant flamethrower operator, and myself left the mountaintop to reload our tanks in case we had a counterattack that evening. We wanted to be ready for them. It was at this time that Lieutenant Colonel Johnson ordered our flag replaced. He wanted it preserved, since it was the first American flag to fly over Japanese home territory in World War II. And he knew that Marines were notorious souvenir hunters, and he didn't want anyone getting that flag.

We returned to the mountaintop about 5 P.M. We didn't know our flag had been changed when we were gone. There were four hours between the second flag-raising. Ours had been replaced about 2:30 P.M.

We stayed on top of the mountain until the last day of February, when we moved to the north end of the island. I was wounded on March 1 at one o'clock in the afternoon on Hill 362, with a bullet through my right forearm. When I was shot it knocked me down and my arm turned numb. To me it was a million-dollar wound. Now I was leaving the island and on my way home.

I was evacuated from the island to Saipan, then I was moved to San Francisco and eventually to Great Lakes Naval Hospital in Illinois where I ended my hospital stay. I was treated very well. My last four months were spent as a guard of the Naval Brig in Charleston, South Carolina, the best duty I had in the Marine Corps.

My proudest moment of my time in the Marines was raising the

American flag on Iwo Jima. My feeling of being a Marine is I served with the finest, and I feel proud every day that I can tell somebody that.

Iwo Jima was one of the worst battles of World War II with the most casualties for such a small area. People should know years from now that freedom does not come cheap. We were caught bad at Pearl Harbor, and if we had been on our guard, things like Iwo never would have happened. It should be a good lesson, but it cost us a lot of men to learn that lesson. We should never have a letdown like that again.

First patrol to scale Mount Suribachi departs for the summit. Cpl. Charles W. Lindberg is the leading flame-thrower operator. *Louis R. Lowery photo from the Charles W. Lindberg collection*

Lt. Harold Schrier *(left)* and Cpl. Charles W. Lindberg *(foreground)* tie the first flag to be raised on Mount Suribachi to a scavenged iron pipe as Sgt. Ernest Thomas watches. *Louis R. Lowery photo from the Charles W. Lindberg collection*

Cpl. Charles W. Lindberg, today the last survivor of the first flag-raising on Iwo Jima, scans the rim of Mount Suribachi, 23 February 1945. *Louis R. Lowery photo from the Charles W. Lindberg collection*

Replacing the First Flag with a larger flag—
Feb.23,1945— about 2:30p.m.— 4 hours after
the first flag was raised.

The first flag raised above Mount Suribachi comes down at the same
time the second is raised, 23 February 1945. *Robert R. Campbell photo from
the Charles W. Lindberg collection*

Moments before the first flag was raised above Mount Suribachi, Cpl. Charles W. Lindberg stomps the ground at left. Pharmacist's Mate Second Class John H. Bradley—who observed the first flag-raising and participated in the second—stands with back to camera, and to the right, Ernest Thomas, Henry Hanson, and Lt. Harold Schrier. *Louis R. Lowery photo from the Charles W. Lindberg collection*

4
TANKERS

The Marine doctrine of amphibious assault was centered on a combined-arms effort. Infantry, of course, was the essential element, but theorists also stipulated that all arms accompany the infantry in the assault. Tank battalions, along with artillery and engineer regiments and amphibian tractor battalions, formed the core of the assault force. Tanks were included initially to deal with any enemy armored threat.

Throughout the Pacific war, however, Marines encountered few Japanese tanks. When they did, as at Saipan in 1944, Marine M4A2 Shermans outclassed the Japanese tanks and destroyed them almost as soon as they appeared. Marine tankers had far more to fear from the Japanese tank destroyer squads —the "suicide squads"—who rushed tanks and assaulted them with magnetic mines, satchel charges, or crudely fashioned lunge mines. Tanks always required heavy infantry protection as a result.

On Iwo Jima, as on most other Central Pacific islands, Marine infantry regarded armor as a mixed blessing. On one hand, a tank was a godsend whenever there was a bunker or pillbox to assault, especially when the tank carried a flamethrower in place of the 75mm gun. On the other, tanks were hated at almost all other times because they were magnets for enemy fire. Big targets draw attention, the absolute least desirable situation for an exposed infantryman. Nonetheless, tanks drawing fire were better in the end than no tanks at all.

In the following story, Cpl. James Carroll of the 5th Tank Battalion describes typical tank actions in his first and only World War II campaign.

Cpl. James Carroll
Gunner of "Goin' Home," C Company, 5th Tank Battalion

When we left Hawaii for Iwo Jima, we sailed under sealed orders. We didn't know where we were going, but we'd been training for months on the big island, and we knew that we'd be landing on one of the many islands there in the Pacific. After several days at sea, we were told we were going to land on Iwo Jima, which of course to us was an absolute blank. I don't think anybody in the world except the twenty-two thousand Japanese who were there even knew it existed.

Anybody can find in the textbooks that February 19 was the D-day for the landing of the ground-pounders and all the supporting units and everything else that goes along with the infantry. We got up well before dawn. The tanks in our company were embarked on a small amphibious vessel a little over a hundred feet long called an LSM— Landing Ship Medium. Smaller than an LST, larger than an LCVP, which was called the Higgins boat that landed the infantry. An LSM held one platoon of tanks and drew only three or four feet of water and could be driven right up on the beach and then pulled off by its own anchor. It was kind of a floating bathtub. It was hollow in the center, and that's where the tanks were parked. In the front was a set of bow doors which opened up, and then there was a ramp that was lowered and we drove down.

Being attached to the 28th Marines, we were to land on the extreme left* of the whole operation, sweep along with the 28th across the island, pivot and face south, and secure Mount Suribachi, and give the infantry an assist in any way we could. The tank we had was an M4A3, the Sherman. My position was gunner. The other members were Rusty Rutkowski from Chicago who was our loader; Duane H. "Dutch" Madsen, our tank commander, who sat just behind me; down below in the lower part of the hull was I. G. Stewart, from Indiana, a big farm kid, our bow gunner; and the driver was Don Pratt, a big, skinny, lazy Texan.

*The "extreme left" of the whole operation was Green Beach. Company C was ordered to land on Red-1, the assigned beach of the 28th Marines, one landing zone to the right.

As the bow doors opened and the ramp went down, it was time for the moment of truth. We had been training for a year on the big island of Hawaii, so we thought we had everything down pat, but we had plenty of butterflies wondering what we were going to run into, how we were going to survive, if we were going to survive.

The tank was buttoned up as we came down the ramp. A tank is kind of a blind beast when it's completely buttoned up. The crew depends on a series of periscopes to see what's going on outside, and while you can see at a distance, you really can't see close up. The periscopes could only be depressed a certain amount. My periscope was linked to the gun, and I had to keep the gun elevated so it wouldn't dip into the surf or sand. So I also had a limited field of vision. We were landing in about two feet of water, which was no problem, because we had a fording kit on our tank which would allow us to go in up to eight feet of water if we had to. All around on the beach were vehicles, equipment, some bodies, all scattered hither and yon, and in the edge of the surf, there was a jeep with a 37mm antitank gun hitched to the back end and pointing out towards the fleet. Standing in the surf, with his hand on the muzzle of the gun, was this guy who was too busy to be shooting anything but his bowels. He'd lost control. He had his trousers down, the water was washing up around his legs. I laughed, but I felt sorry for the guy. He's hanging on the muzzle of the gun and squatting down and everything in the world is shooting around him, but right now he's got only one thing in mind—to finish what he was doing and get the hell out of the surf. That was just a fleeting welcome to Iwo Jima.

We were in a column, and the Japanese had planned everything, so that any vehicles that left the beach had to follow a certain path. There was a shelf that you could walk up on to, but then it rose rather steeply to the plateau on the main part of the island. We had to wend our way up a path that the Japanese had built. Well, of course, you don't have to be a genius at antitank warfare to realize that something's gonna be waiting for you at the top of that road. Our executive officer, Melvin Hazaleus, an animal husbandry professor in civilian life, was in the lead tank, about six tanks ahead of my tank. Our company commander was an old China Marine by the name of

Edward "Swede" Nelson, a Mustang, and I don't know where his tank was. As soon as the column got up off the beach a little ways, there was this Japanese antitank gun that was zeroed in right on the spot where the first tank would come up off the beach. The thinnest, most vulnerable part of a tank is either the top or the very bottom. When you're coming up a hill, you're like a lizard showing its belly. When Hazaleus's tank pulled up there, the Japs fired one or two rounds but they didn't hit the bottom of the tank. They hit the place where the turret joins the hull, which jammed the turret, but more important, it was a big enough round so that caused a "backspalling" effect. That is, it didn't penetrate, but the shock from hitting the tank knocked some steel loose from the inside and flew around and wounded both Lieutenant Hazaleus and the gunner. Effectively, it stopped the column, because the driver was panicked, he didn't know what to do. Of course, the antitank psychology goes, if the whole column's stopped, you can pick off each tank one by one with whatever weapons you had, or maybe the crews of the tanks would panic and jump out, and you could shoot them as they came out of the hatches. So there we sat.

Over the radio, somebody said, Let's get someone out on the ground and see if we can find a way off this trail. I'm nineteen and indestructible, so I told Dutch, "Hell, I'll go!" Rusty Rutkowski—he thought I was nuts—opened his loader's hatch, and I slipped under the gun, climbed up out of the hatch, and I was exposed to all the world. When I was in the tank, I had a helmet and earphones on, and I couldn't hear the volume of fire. When I got out, and I heard all that firing going on, I was just about ready to jump back in. But I was already out, and Rusty had closed the hatch, so there was only one thing to do and that was jump down.

As I moved up alongside our tank and a couple of others, I could see how well planned the Japs had made this for any vehicle, not just tanks. On either side of the trail were deep pits, tank traps, and I looked down inside at the first one I came to, and here's half a dozen Marines squatted down in there, scared to death. I prowled around, asking dumb questions of the infantry, and they didn't know where the hell they were either. I determined that if we were careful, even though they had planned the thing pretty well, we could work our way off the terrain and between the tank traps and break out of this stalemate. So I went back and climbed up on my tank—why in the hell somebody didn't shoot me I'll never know—rapped on the side, and Rusty opened his hatch and let me in. I told Dutch what I'd found out and he radioed the info on back to the captain or whoever it was that requested someone to go out and have a look.

As we moved toward Suribachi in support of the infantry, they would point out targets to us either by getting out far enough from the tank so we could see them through the periscopes, or by calling up on the phone. On the back of the tank there was this little telephone box, believe it or not, with a handset and a cord that reeled in and reeled out. Anyone, if they had the balls, could get that phone out of the box, lay down in the sand, talk to us inside the tank, and tell us they had a target to the left or right or whatever. A lot of times, the wire would be cut, or the Japs shot the phone off, but it did function and was an assistance to the infantry. Sometimes they would pull us up close to a hole—and remember what I said about being blind inside a tank—and they'd be saying, "Shoot in that hole, goddamit!" and we wouldn't know what hole they were talking about. The place was full of holes. Only by firing and adjusting could we direct the fire. We were right up with the infantry after all. We had to be. That's the way the Marine Corps used tanks. There was no slashing runs like George Patton was making in Europe, because usually we were moving through terrain that was jungly or brushy, and if we couldn't depend on our infantry to help us see where the Japanese were, we would have gotten into a world of trouble. We depended on the infantry to "scratch our backs." If the Japanese sent an anti-tank team out, the infantry could pick them off. And if their fire hit us, it wouldn't bother us, it wouldn't penetrate the armor. It was good to know that our men were out there, keeping us safe from harm. Of course, they used to cuss us when we had a chance to talk to them. Nothing like a tank to draw fire. Everybody on the other side always wants to take a shot at a tank, no matter what, even though they know they can't knock a tank out with a rifle. They just couldn't resist shooting.

About the third or fourth day, we were sitting on line, one tank beside the other, firing away at various targets at the base of Suribachi, and up a little ways on the slope, when suddenly something hit us. There's always all kinds of firing going on, and when we tried to back the tank up, we knew the track had been broken. It could have been a mortar round, antitank round, no telling. We were dead in the water, couldn't move. Once your track is broken, you're effectively shut down until you get an opportunity to fix it. Normally it's the crew's function to repair their own track, but when you're under heavy fire like that, nobody expected us to get out there and fix the track. So we were told to abandon the tank. "Abandon the tank" means dismount the machine guns, take the Thompson submachine gun, disable the radio—which we didn't do—and then crawl out the escape hatch that's in the bottom of the tank just between the driver's legs. We went back behind the infantry lines and figured, Well, now what do we do? We were told that if the infantry were able to push forward far enough so our retriever could get up, it could pull our tank back far enough so we could put the track back on. In the meantime, it would probably be a day before that would happen. So we walked back to our company headquarters, and they had found a bulldozer and they dug a pit where they had put fifty-five-gallon drums of gasoline. As tanks in our company needed to be refueled —which wasn't very often, because most of the time we sat still during the day—they came by this pit, and our crew and some of the other Marines in the company would roll the fifty-five-gallon drums out, pick them up and rassle them up on the back of the tank where the fuel-filler opening was, put a flex hose on the bung of the drum and refuel the tank with all these rounds going off all around us. You wonder that there wasn't an explosion.

The infantry had finally gotten up far enough so that the retriever and the maintenance people could get the tank pulled back, and we could put the track back on. We were soon back in action, maybe one day we were dismounted. During that day, it was interesting, because this is the time that we were out on the ground just as the infantry was, we could see what a confusing situation everything was. Even though there were supposedly lines of infantry, Japs had been bypassed because some of the openings to their caves had been so well camouflaged that the infantry just went right on by them. There were snipers everywhere, a round could come from any direction, and you had to be on the alert all the time.

On the day that Dutch Madsen got hit, we were in column. By this time we had secured Suribachi and we had joined up with the other two companies and headed north on the left with our infantry. As we moved forward in column on this particular day, we weren't too alert, because with another tank in front of you, you're effectively masked as far as fire is concerned, except to the right or the left. All of a sudden I heard I. G. Stewart holler, Hey, there's a Jap coming out of a hole over here on the right! So I depressed the main gun as far as I could, and sure enough, we were far enough back from the next tank to see this Japanese that had come up from someplace of the right of the road. He was carrying a box with rope handles on it, an antitank explosive device. He was going to come out and immobilize the tank in front of us. So as he came out of the ground Stewart was able to move the bow machine gun far enough to start shooting at this guy. The Jap never even hesitated. He just kept on going up to the tank in front of us. Stewart must have hit him five times. I had depressed the main gun far enough to fire the coaxial, and I opened fire, too, but I was a little bit high. Stewart must have hit him a total of ten times, but the guy just kept staggering forward, trying to get up and push this box of explosives under the tank in front of us. Finally he did fall down on his face, and apparently one of the tracer rounds had ignited his clothing, because he started to burn. And about five minutes after that, something hit the top of our tank, big time, hit right on top of the tank commander's hatch. It exploded with such force that it actually blew the tank commander's hatch open, and dust and chips of steel flew around inside the turret. Neither myself nor Rutkowski were injured, outside of just being in shock, but I turned around and Dutch Madsen had slumped over and was bleeding through the nose. He hadn't been hit directly by any rounds. There wasn't any massive bleeding that I could see. I guess that the concussive effect of the round hitting on top of the tank commander's hatch had really dazed him. I said, "Dutch, can you move, what's wrong?" You know, it was so confusing, you say a lot of stuff that doesn't make much sense at the time. He couldn't answer. He was moving his head around, but obviously he wasn't in any shape to answer. Eventually we discovered that when the round hit, it had hit with such force that it had also broken the upper part of his left leg. So we had to get people up on the outside of the tank and down on the inside to help evacuate him out through the tank commander's hatch. He was still semiconscious when we got him out of there. Later, he was evacuated to one of the hospital ships offshore.

After we got him out of there the dilemma was, where did the round come from? Was there going to be a repeat? We sure as hell didn't want to sit there until they blew us completely away. So I started hollering at Pratt through the microphone that Madsen had been using, and I screamed at Pratt to back up. Pratt said, "How the hell can I back up? I can't see!" Because, you know, backing up a tank is like backing up a truck without mirrors. You got this thirty-seven-ton piece of junk that has to move, but you don't want to back up into a hole or into another tank. I don't remember how we did it, but we finally got out of the line and got back far enough to where we could regroup.

We found out later that Dutch had died aboard the hospital ship. We didn't know from what causes, they don't tell you. They just told you he had died.

Because of the intensity of the firing, and the activities, you're necessarily focused just on what's around you, and so we were not even aware of what was happening in the other two platoons in our company. Our battalion didn't take a lot of casualties, especially compared to the infantry. In our company, besides Dutch Madsen's death, I can't think of anybody else who was killed. It's amazing, when you realize that over six thousand Marines died there. We did have a chance one time to get out of the tank and walk around a bit where some other companies or maybe even another battalion, I think the 4th Battalion tanks were there. And in addition to those antitank guns that the Japanese had, the Japanese had buried, as an antivehicular device, these huge aerial bombs, two-thousand-pound bombs, nose up, with just enough sand over them, so that if a tank drove over, the bombs would blow it up. One of the sights I will never forget is when we came upon this hull of a tank. On a Sherman tank, I think we carried 104 rounds of 75mm ammunition. That's a lot of powder in there. Apparently these guys had run over one of those nose-up bombs, because not only did the bomb go off, but it detonated all hundred rounds or whatever had been left inside. It had blown the turret of the tank off to about thirty yards away—God knows how high it went—and amazingly, the driver of the tank had survived, but everybody else was killed.

Eventually, as we moved north and pushed up towards the end of the island, Holland M. Smith, our supreme commander, or whoever was running the show, had decided the resistance had been effectively reduced to the point where we could pull out, and this was about the twenty-sixth of March. The island had been secured, but that didn't mean all the Japanese had been killed. So as we left the island there was still plenty of Japanese, God knows how many were left. We loaded aboard troop ships and pulled away from the island with mixed feelings, as you can imagine.

5

ENGINEERS AND PIONEERS

Engineer and Pioneer regiments provided the hard labor for their respective divisions. Along with their attached battalions of Seabees, which repaired or constructed airfields and base positions, Engineers and Pioneers prepared demolitions and assaulted defensive points, and provided the heavier flamethrower support. Like all Marines, they trained and performed as riflemen, and on Iwo Jima they more often fulfilled this function than their military specialties.

PFCs Robert Lanehart and James Falcone, in the following stories, describe both functions.

PFC Robert G. Lanehart
Company B, 1st Battalion, 4th Engineers, 20th Marines, 4th Marine Division

I joined up with the 4th Division on the island of Maui after they returned from the Marshall Islands campaign. Maui was the 4th Division's base of operations for training. It was a tent camp, and we went into training for Saipan, which would be the next operation, but of course we didn't know that at the time. They never told you where you were going to hit. I trained with an engineer outfit, the 20th Regiment, which consisted of a battalion of pioneers, a battalion of engineers, and a battalion of Seabees. We trained in demolitions and flamethrowing, but basically you were still a rifleman. I was in Sergeant Pittman's squad. The company constituted about 160, 170 men.

When Saipan was over, we went back to Maui. Naturally we were all happy to get back, especially those of us who weren't wounded.

So we went back to training again for our next operation. I was trained on the flamethrower, which was a little rustic at the time. The first flamethrowers were ignited with a little tank of nitrogen on the gun itself. The later models had a phosphorous match in the front of the gun, which was more compact. They taught us how to mix the napalm, which is like a fine grain, and you add gasoline to it. We practiced a lot shooting fuel oil instead of napalm. You get a lot of smoke with fuel oil.

We boarded the troop transports again for the trip over to Iwo. I figured out that all the time I spent on transports in all the operations I was in amounted to more than twenty-five thousand miles. It was a nice cruise. You could lay out and get some sun. But if you didn't move when the swabbies were hosing down the decks you got wet, because they told you only one time. If you saw them with the hoses, you better move, they'd hose you down. We also had calisthenics so you wouldn't get too soft. Otherwise there wasn't too much to do aboard ship. If you were a reader, you read. If you were a card player, you played a lot of cards. You kept your weapons in good repair. I always enjoyed the Navy chow. Of course I was a young man, I wasn't too particular about food.

They also put us on work details, where we'd be carting food supplies from way down in the hold to the galley. And the Southern guys, the rebels from Mississippi, like my squad leader, got this idea. We were carting big cases, gallon cans of fruit cocktail. So anything that would ferment, we could make "jack"—you know, alcoholic. They called it "jack." We went by our sleeping quarters in the hold, they'd dump it. You could drink it if you dared.

We were supposed to hit in reserve, at one o'clock in the afternoon. As it turned out, we got in at about seven o'clock at night. We rendezvoused for hours and hours. You get in a circle with your LCVPs and you just keep going around until they're ready for you. That seems indefinite until you finally go in. And you would get seasick. All that jack we made, it didn't fully ferment and finish, but we had to get into the LCVPs to hit the beach, so a lot of the guys just gulped it down. And then when you get out in those LCVPs and you're going 'round and 'round and you're inhaling those diesel fumes, a lot of guys just stuck their heads over the gunwales and upchucked all that fruit cocktail. My squad leader was one of them.

And there are a lot of things going through your mind. You're naturally nervous, and afraid, even though you've been in combat before. You don't get that nonchalant about facing death. When the ramp went down on the LCVP, you just did your best to go forward. Some of the guys were hit when they came out. I was fortunate. Everything's bedlam, you've got to find the man that's leading you to follow him, do what you're supposed to do, and dig in. You'd like to think that everything's organized, but it's not. Everything is chaos.

Our first night on Iwo was pretty hectic. There's a lot of bodies lying around and that's another time when you didn't know if they were asleep or dead. The next morning, you're back to doing your chores. We were supposed to pick up mines, being engineers. We were supposed to know about mines. These kind of mines, they got a big horn on them, a lead horn, and they're heavy, I'd say at least thirty, forty pounds. Our detail was supposed to pick these mines up and put them altogether in another spot. It's hard work in that volcanic ash, because you're taking two steps forward and going back three. And right above us, on another position, the Japs would just look down on us, and they started to lob mortars in on top of us. We were sitting pigeons.

I was with my platoon leader, Lieutenant Piper, and Sergeant Burkhalder. I was right alongside of them, picking up the mines and lugging them about fifty yards away. And I'm here today because I decided that I would pick up two of them, one in each hand, so I fell back behind. About that time the Japs dropped a mortar right next to Sergeant Burkhalder and killed him and I thought Lieutenant Piper, too, but he lost his leg. I thought it was mortal, but years later I found out he wasn't killed. Just a few more steps and I would have been right there alongside of them. It's that close.

I had used a flamethrower only in training, so I didn't have the experience of fear wearing it in combat until my squad leader generously handed me one and told me, Lanehart, you are now a flamethrower man, probably because I was pretty large in size and could handle it. Flamethrowers are a good seventy pounds. It's a bit to lug around. I knew when you were shooting it you were going to be one of the main targets of the Japanese. But you don't very well refuse your squad leader. It was a job, you were going to do it.

Shortly after my squad leader issued me my flamethrower, and I was walking up, most of the guys were saying, "Go to it, get 'em," you know. But you might not have the same *esprit de corps* with that thing on your back, because you know you're a number one target for any Jap that sees you and gets a shot at you. I think they counted the lifespan of a flamethrower man in seconds, twenty seconds or something like that, when you're in combat. Which I can believe. You make a good target. You can't duck too well with a flamethrower on your back.

There was one time when I jumped in a hole and I was sitting down with the flamethrower on my back, and I got stuck. I couldn't get up again, with all the weight there. I was helpless. If a Jap had come at that time, I was done for, because I wasn't carrying a side-arm. I was supposed to have a .45 because you can't very well carry a rifle when you've got the flamethrower. But fortunately I finally managed to get out of the hole.

A lot of people ask me what it's like to actually burn somebody to death. I never actually saw anybody that I flamed. I might have seen them the next day, when I went by, but they don't all come running out aflame. The heat is terrific, they die right where they are. And you were shooting into caves and bunkers and holes, you couldn't see anything in there anyway. You have riflemen covering you, if somebody does come out. You need somebody to protect you. I had one close call. I had my canteen shot off my hip. But outside of that, I was very fortunate. Anybody was who didn't get hit.

Around Hill 382, we had gotten there when most of the frontline troops had finished. But all the Japanese and Marine bodies were still there and we could tell how intense the fighting was by the amount of bodies. Some of the guns they had were just shattered by explosions. And the smell of death, the sight of death was all over. The smell of the island was overwhelming. There was the sulfur, and of course the dead bodies. I always had the feeling that the Japanese smelled worse than dead Marines, I guess because of their diet. There was always the smell of death, you can't get away from it. And your clothing, too, you don't have any change of clothing unless they bring some up, which can't always be done. You're not worrying about what you look like or what you feel like. You're there to fight and win a war. So you can get fairly ripe yourself. It's just something you have to endure. But as long as you're in one piece, you're okay.

We knew we were finishing when there was no further to go and you got the word that the island was secure, you're going to go home, back to Hawaii. And you're always aware. You've got in the back of your mind that when they told us we'd be out in a week, and we knew that wasn't so the first day we hit the island. It had to be done the hard way, with good old Marine infantry, the grunts, and the flamethrowers. The flamethrower tanks couldn't get into places where the Japs were dug in so well. You had to send in a flamethrower man. I would much rather have seen the tanks do it. But the Marine Corps way was frontal assault, that was the only way you could do it. It was a hard job, and we left almost six thousand dead Marines there, and many more wounded.

We were very glad to see the end come. Each additional day you said to yourself, Maybe I'll get it today, but you try not to concentrate on that, you tried to concentrate on the job that had to be done. And when the day came when your squad leader told you that you were going to board ship, it sure was nice news. Kind of exhilarating.

PFC James Falcone
Pioneer, Company E, 3d Battalion, 19th Marines, 3d Marine Division

We were set to go on a new campaign. Scuttlebutt told us where we were going, and then on board ship we had the briefings about Iwo Jima. We were told we were reserve, we didn't even know if we were going to land or what, you know. And we got our equipment ready. On our machine guns, there were 250 rounds to a belt, and every fifth round was a tracer, so we were taking out the tracers so not to give our positions away.

On the first day of the invasion, while we were still in reserve, I remember being on deck and I could see the tanks roll over Moto-yama Number 1, and it looked like a spooky island to me. But we didn't start going in until the next day, when the 21st and 9th tried to go in, but came back to the ship. They were pretty well seasick and everything. My unit didn't go in until the day after. The coxswain was heading toward the beach, and you could see the fire, you know, the mortars and shells splashing around, and then for some reason he circles out fast and doesn't go in to the beach. And as he circled out, I'm looking out the back of the boat and I could see these mor-tars, plop, plop, plop, one-two-three right directly in line with the boat. They had a bead on us, and he swung the boat around again. He was a good coxswain. Then he got us up alongside of an LST. So we went up the cargo nets and get on deck, and then Condition Red goes on, and they close the darn ramp in the front and the thing backs out, we're out to sea again.

The next morning, we hit the beach. It's about five o'clock, and we're supposed to be on Yellow One and Yellow Two, where the 21st first went in. But I know we're down close to the volcano, I know we're on the wrong beach. So we got out and crawled around, but where were we going? We gotta go that way, so we headed down the beach, and the Japs had a vantage point, up in Suribachi. They'd wait, see some activity, and at an opportune moment they'd start shelling. It's shelling, we're crawling, and there's this fellow, McMann, we're kind of buddies on the same machine gun, he was the assistant gun-ner, I was the gunner, and I don't know where the riflemen and ammo carriers were, we were scattered all over. The Japs were shell-ing, and I got a little excited, and I had the tripod, plus my pack and everything, and I threw the tripod away. I don't know why, I just threw it, you know, and jumped into an area to cover myself. We made it up the beach a-ways, headed toward Yellow One, and I'm saying to myself, Jeez, you know, you gotta go back and get that tripod. McMann's got the gun, what if we had to use the gun? You're gonna be in trouble! So I says to McMann, Look, I'm going back. I don't know how far I crawled, but I went back and got that tripod. Then I felt better. I crawled back, and McMann's under a crane, a steam shovel or something. I get back to him and he says, "Oh my God, a shell hit the boom, and we're under the crane!" So we calmed down a bit, he had the gun, I had the tripod, we had all our stuff, and we started for that beach again. I don't know how long it took us to get there, two, three hours, maybe. I had no conception of time, and it took a while, because they'd start shelling the beach, and we'd lay low for a while. But we finally got back to our outfit and dug in.

We stayed there for the rest of the day. Then finally Corporal Young and Sergeant MacDonald, they had a job for us. We're supposed to get some supplies off a ship. And the way the pioneers would work it was we'd get the detail out there and we'd form a chain and hand off all the stuff on the ship, stack it on the beach. And maybe right away there'd be a tractor with a beach sled, drawn by cable, because you couldn't get a vehicle on those beaches, you'd go nowhere. They'd load the beach sleds and take off with the supplies. Some they'd even leave on the beaches. But the shellfire got a little more pronounced, so after that day we started unloading them at night. There'd be light in the ships, and we'd form the chain, but it was darker outside, and it was less of a problem that way, the Japs couldn't see what the heck you were doing.

So when there were ships to unload, we unloaded them, or if we had to go unload the sleds at the supply depot, we would. And if they need patrols, well, one time Sergeant MacDonald asked for patrols. He mentioned my name, then he said, Well, wait a minute, I'll get one of the newer guys. We had a lot of replacements, and he wanted to give them the experience of being out on patrol, mopping up, you know, the pockets of Japs. They don't get all of them. You were in more danger coming from the front lines to the rear rather than the other way around. I didn't get in on that, I was still working on the beach.

On Iwo, we were on the beach most of the time. On other campaigns, no, but on Iwo, we stayed on the beach. And also, our job was that in case there was an attack from the rear, we could defend, and that was the reason for all of our machine guns and everything, to protect the rear. At the end, we weren't shelled as much, because they were pushing the Japs farther back, and the farther they pushed them the easier it was on us. But they did key in on the equipment.

If there was unloading, they would blast it with mortars. And I remember being cold, and damp, and hungry. The sailors on the ships were nice, they'd feed us, give us eggs. That was a rare thing, to have a couple of eggs. And we'd get homesick, thinking about home, hoping that it would end so you could get out of there.

The word came that we were going back to Guam and getting off and they just one day packed up and loaded us up and we came back to Guam to the same area we had. In fact, I think our area was still set up, we went right back to our old tent and everything. Then I was told I would be going stateside on rotation, I had thirty months or so overseas, and I was designated to go home. Which I wasn't unhappy about.

6

REPLACEMENTS

Casualties in Marine divisions were made good by attached replacement drafts. For the Iwo Jima campaign, the 3d Marine Division relied upon the 28th and 34th Replacement Drafts, the 4th Marine Division upon the 24th and 30th, and the 5th Marine Division upon the 27th and 31st.

Replacement drafts were battalions that always consisted of fully trained Marines. Some Marines had been wounded in earlier campaigns but had not recovered soon enough to join their old outfits; some had just finished their advanced training only recently and were thrust into the replacement drafts to provide the necessary manpower availability for the inevitable casualties. Some, like PFC George G. Gentile, had completed the V-12 officer program, but because he was only five feet six he was considered to be lacking in "command presence" since by that point in the war there was an overabundance of taller officers. Gentile was assigned to the 30th Replacement Draft in time for Iwo Jima.

PFC George G. Gentile
Rifleman, 30th Replacement Draft and Company C,
1st Battalion, 25th Marines, 4th Marine Division

The 4th Division was put on a big pineapple plantation, one of four or five on the entire island that the government took over, for our base camp. We stayed and trained through November and early January of 1945 and then we boarded ship again, not knowing where we were going, with the whole 4th Division.

Aboard ship I met quite a few people I hadn't met before because now we were with the 4th Division. The friends you made aboard ship were so important to help you get through it all, otherwise you'd go stir-crazy after a while. There was another man, a Marine, and sometimes we'd get to the library at the same time, and we got to chatting one day and got very friendly. He happened to be an attorney, he had been through OCS, and he was short, too. And we were the same rank, PFC. His name was Izzy. Nice man, we got along very good. We read the same stuff, we were interested in the same things, and we spent a lot of time together aboard ship. I can remember reading Plato's *Republic*. It could be pretty dry if you weren't interested in that sort of thing. But we both got into it, discussing things that Plato said centuries ago that fit into situations today. And just a few days before we got to Iwo Jima, he asked me if I would witness his will. I said, Yeah, you know, I'd never even thought about making a will, I didn't have anything to leave anyway. So I witnessed it, and that was that.

The night before the landing we had a church service, and all the chaplains held their particular services and then they told us we would have breakfast at four A.M. We were served steak and eggs. That's the only time in the Marine Corps that I was ever served steak and eggs. And I got my gear on, and then they told us that my replacement battalion would not be going in that morning. So we actually had a great show as they all disembarked. We'd help with the guys' gear, making sure the straps were all tight and the blankets were on because we all went over the side on rope nets, with full packs and full gear. The dangerous part was that when you got down to the bottom of the net, if the timing wasn't right when you stepped from the net into the small boat and a wave moved the boat away, you could fall between the two boats and you could get crushed when the boats came back together again. We did lose men. When you got a full pack and you fall in, forget it, unless they could fish you out some way.

In the meantime, my job was to go down in the hold where there were fifty-five-gallon oil drums, which we were going to bring topside to send into the beach. It was fuel for the jeeps and the tanks and everything else. Another guy and I would be down below and the crane would drop the grappling hooks, which had four pairs of hooks that you would attach to the drums at the little rim, and they could take up four drums at once. And you know, you're underneath there, and the ship is swaying, the barrels are swinging back and forth, and we did this for a couple of days, down in that hold. It got so that I said, This is ridiculous, I want to go in. So I told them I'd help them unload one of the times we went in to the beach. We weren't supposed to go, but we did. I mean, there was no one there to watch us, they were busy doing other things. So we jumped into a small boat with the oil drums and went in. And then I said to myself, Well, that was crazy because if we ever got hit with the oil drums, we would have been dead anyway. But when you're young, you know, it's just one of those things.

Unloading on the beach, that was a real job, it was awful. We weren't prepared for all that volcanic sand. After a while the sand got in your shoes and everything, and we'd always take our leggings off, too, because the leggings got too warm. That's the first thing the guys did when they hit the beaches, take the leggings off. Same with the carbines. They'd throw away the carbines and pick up M-1s. Or if the guy was big, he might pick up a BAR. They were heavy. And there was a lot of fire on the beach, a lot of mortars dropping, we could see the dead and everything, they had some of the wounded on the beach. I was frightened. Especially when you saw the dead. You say to yourself, Hey, that could be me lying there, that's when you start to think. But then I got back to the ship, and I felt that I wanted to go back to the beach. I don't know what happens to you, but there's a certain thing that comes out of you, that you want to be helping them, and you don't feel like you're helping them by unloading fuel. But then the following day they said that the casualties got so high that we had to go in.

It was about a platoon from the replacement battalion when we went in. We landed on Blue Beach of the 4th Division, which I thought was fairly safe by now, since the 25th Marines had moved up a bit. And when I got there, we had to unload some stuff. I carried some K-rations up to the front line. There was a lot of sniper fire there, and the first thing the experienced guys would say was, Stay down, they knew where the fire was coming from. The K-rations came in cases, pretty heavy, about fifty or sixty pounds, and you got into the habit of carrying the K-rations on your shoulder on the side you thought the firing would come from to protect your head. I can always remember saying, Let's see, where would the fire be coming from? And I'd put the box on that particular shoulder to protect my head. You started to learn survival techniques real early. And the same with mortars. The first time you heard that whine, you didn't know enough to move even though you had the training. But after that first one, boy, you hit the ground before the mortar did or else you were dead. I could hit the ground awful fast. You learned things like that the first few hours on the beaches, the different sounds, the different smells, and you're just alert all the time to these things.

Meanwhile my friend the attorney was looking for me. He had become the company clerk, and it was about three o'clock in the afternoon at that time. Izzy said, You got a foxhole yet? I said I didn't even know what unit I was in, and he said, Okay, I've got a hole, you stay with me tonight. So I followed him and all this time he's carrying an attaché case full of the company records, and he showed where he had dug a hole underneath a disabled tank. I thought, This is fantastic, you know, what a great place to be, with the sand dug out from underneath the tracks, a little portable typewriter set up in there and everything. And we no sooner got in there and I was telling him what a great place this was when the mortars started to drop. Big mortars, like 80mm, and they got closer and closer and they didn't stop. They got so close that the sand would come in underneath the tank. And we started to get worried. I said, If they hit this tank and it's got fuel in it, we could really be in a bad spot. One was almost a direct hit, so we decided to get out of there. He grabbed his typewriter and attaché case and we started running down the beach where we had come from, and the mortars followed us. They actually followed right behind us, right down the beach. Looking back on this, after it all happened, I thought the Jap observer must have thought that we were setting up a command post, because Izzy had an attaché case when he went in there. They might have thought I was a general or something, you know? Why would they follow the two of us right down the beach with the mortars? It was really uncanny. They knew just how much to step it up, we called it. So I was going down the beach like a bouncing ball. Up, down, up, down, I'd hit the dirt when I heard the whine, then bang, up again, whine, down again, bang, up again, I must have done that twenty-five, thirty times. I didn't see where Izzy was, whether he was right beside me or behind me, and I finally got down where we were going and I looked around and didn't see Izzy at all. I figured he dug a hole somewhere else. I dug a hole down on the beach and then I got worried, I wondered if he had gone back to the tank. So I went back, like a nut. But with your training, you know, you never leave a buddy. But he wasn't there, so I went back to the beach and it was dark now. I tried to sleep but I really didn't, it was pretty bad. The Japs were dropping phosphorous bombs. That stuff really burns. And we were all afraid of a banzai attack. From our experience on other islands, you always worried about a banzai attack at night. The Japanese had changed their strategy on Iwo, but we didn't realize that then.

On the following morning, we got our orders to go up to the front lines, the casualties had been bad. As we were lining up, single file, one of the guys who knew me and Izzy said, Did you hear about Izzy? I said, No, what? And he said they found his dogtags. So he must have had a direct hit. That was real traumatic when he told me that, you know. But I think it was good that I was going up to the front lines when I heard about it. I didn't have time to think about it too much. And as you're going up there, you saw all the dead Japs, all the dead Americans, you're going up to where they had already been fighting. So in a way I think I was forced to forget what happened to Izzy because now I was worried about what's going to happen to me.

They move you up at night when they put you into your new position. The casualties had been so bad, there really wasn't enough replacements. They were spreading us out thin on the line. And having had OCS, having learned about strategy and how you set up positions, I could tell things were pretty bad. So the sergeant took me up to a position on the front line and he said, You have to hold it, and he showed me who was on my left, who was on my right and how far, what the password was. Where he put me, there were four dead Marines. One was still holding his BAR. Fortunately it was dark and you couldn't see very much. And I sat with them in their foxhole all night. In the front there was a ravine, I could tell by the way the sound was coming. There was moaning and groaning and I figured, Well, there were wounded down there, but you never knew whether or not it was a Jap playing tricks. Sometimes they would moan and groan and yell, Corpsman, corpsman, to get you to come down there, and then they'd do a job on you. So you just stayed put, that's all, and listened to it all night long. That had to be the longest night of my life.

In the morning, as the mists cleared, at first light, there was this apparition. I'm sitting there in the hole and a Marine comes by, walking, I'm sure he was shell-shocked, and I know he was an officer. He had his helmet off, he had a bulkhead stare, he walked right by me as if he didn't see me, no weapon on him, like a ghost coming out of the mist. Just like a zombie. Didn't say a word to me. Then I started thinking, Well, when are we going to get relieved here, when's the sergeant coming, and there wasn't a sound all along the line, we were so quiet. You begin to wonder, Am I the only one here? It was really frightening. Finally the sergeant did come over and he said, Okay, you can go back and we're going to bring up some K-rations, he wanted me to go help.

Afterwards we dug foxholes, and in the position I was in, it was really too rocky, I just used rocks for protection. We knew that the Japs had a pattern, and every day at certain hours they'd start a mortar attack where they thought your position was. And they attacked. It lasted all day, and it got to be so bad I lost all track of time. It seemed like an eternity. Didn't eat, didn't drink, didn't go to the john, just stayed in the hole. And finally we must have neutralized them, because we moved up and set up another line. They also brought more replacements in and I wasn't alone. We had two to the foxhole now, myself and a Southerner, with a drawl so thick I couldn't understand him. Now at least we could get a little sleep, two hours on, two hours off.

We moved up again and hit another ravine. The 4th Division sector was very rugged, a lot of ravines, a lot of rocks. When you hit a ravine, the Japs would have caves on the other side, and they would be looking at you from the caves. So we spent a lot of time firing at the caves with bazookas, flamethrowers, and grenades, if the other side wasn't too far. I used to love to throw grenades. I hardly ever used my rifle. A couple of times, the Japs started to come across the bottom of the ravine, and when we spotted them we would just have a grenade barrage. Usually it did the trick. One or two of them might get through and you'd have to finish them off individually. But you had to be on your toes all the time.

The Turkey Knob area, I think, I remember one thing. I think the officer was a little wacko. We had a machine gun on the top of a knoll, and a sniper got the machine gunner right in the head. And I was in line, which bothered me. So the officer called on another one of the men to go up and take the place of the machine gunner. The guy goes up, and he no sooner gets there and he gets a bullet right between the eyes. Three times the officer sent someone up, three guys got killed. Finally someone talked to the officer and someone crawled up and pulled the machine gun down to a different location. And I was standing there, he could have pointed at me, you know. So it's all luck. I could have been the one to get it.

But the Turkey Knob area was so difficult because of a ravine that ran through there, and one side there were all these caves, and you couldn't knock them out. You just couldn't get across to them. We had tank support, which was pretty good, but not air. We were working too close. One of the big morale boosters in the fighting was the air attacks, for us. When we saw our planes, strafing and bombing, it would really give you a boost. They'd come in with the rockets and actually pinpoint the caves. The guys would end up cheering, you'd think they were at a football game, you know. They'd see them make a hit and hooray, we'd wave to them.

It was about this time that they told us we were going to get a day to go back, change our socks and underwear, wash up out of our helmet, get some water, things like that. They sent us back in groups to a place where there was water and we washed up, they gave us a change of underwear and socks, and we had a different kind of ration. It was fantastic compared to what we had been having. I remember a can of bacon. It was so good. It was already cooked, it was canned, and you just heated it. We gobbled up that bacon like it was a real delicacy. It was a different ration from what we normally got, which was a piece of cheese, a hard cracker, some hard candies, maybe gum, and five cigarettes in a little pack. I liked the cheese, you lived on the cheese and crackers is what it amounted to.

One time I got put on a detail bringing up grenades. We had to have grenades, we were using them up like they were going out of style. And along the trail, back to the ammunition dump, there was a lot of sniper fire, so evidently the Japanese knew that was our supply line. That was one of the times I learned to carry a box on the sniper side. But that wouldn't help much if you were carrying grenades. You laugh now at some of the things you did.

We did that for half a day, brought up grenade supplies, food supplies, and it got to a point where everybody did everything, because there had been so many casualties. If they needed you for a machine gun, they would have put you up on a machine gun. That's where good training comes in. The Marine Corps taught us how to use every weapon. The only one they didn't teach me was the flamethrower. Evidently that was too specialized.

There were other strange things that happened. I can remember one incident where we were having quite a grenade battle, and we heard what we thought were sounds down there, the Japanese moving. So a couple of us decided that to see better we'd get out of the foxhole and look down into the ravine. There was a ledge that I was walking along, and I looked up and coming around the other way was a Jap. And we came up face to face. You know what happened? We both just stopped for a moment and looked at each other, then he turned around and went the other way, and I turned around and went the other way, and then I threw a grenade. We were so surprised to see each other face to face, your reaction time was just crazy.

Towards the end, it wasn't so bad. I guess they were running out of mortars. That was the most fearsome thing to me because there was nothing you could do about them. You don't know where they're coming from, you don't see them, you don't hear them until the last second, and if you're fast enough, you can drop. Still, you just can't defend yourself. But by then the Japanese were getting more desperate and starting banzai attacks at night. The ones that were alive were getting desperate for food. They told a story of a corpsman who heard someone calling for help, so he went off. Some of his guys watched him go off to where the sound came from and two or three Japs came out of a cave and dragged him inside and that was the last they saw of the corpsman. They wanted his uniform so they could put it on and go out at night and steal our food. We did kill some who had Marine uniforms on.

There were other things I saw which weren't too pretty. There was one fellow who started to go wacko, and he had a pouch hanging from his cartridge belt and a pair of pliers. The Japs, of course, were notorious for having gold teeth. When things got slow and quiet, he would go around extracting the teeth out of the Japs' mouths and put them in his pouch just as if it was an everyday thing. Men became animal-like. I can remember seeing guys throwing rocks at dead Japs, you know, Japs who had been lying around for days and were bloated full of gas. They'd throw a rock and pop them, "Pssst." We had seen and heard of worse atrocities by the Japanese on American prisoners. Atrocities on live Americans like beheading prisoners on Wake Island, the mutilation of bodies at other Pacific Island battles. It's kind of sad, when you look back at it, what happened to a human being, how fast you could change when survival was at stake.

They made us mop up on the way back to the ship. That was the most worrisome day I had, because there were still snipers. All I had to do was get hit on the way back to the ship on the last day, I thought. That was your big worry, and yet you had to go back to the caves and mop up, you know, take a grenade and throw it in and then check it out. The snipers were a different situation. They had manhole covers, and they would be down in a hole and just lift the cover a bit and fire and put the cover back down again. It was very hard to find them. And they used smokeless powder, so it was hard to spot them.

It was toward the end of the battle that we had a rare Japanese prisoner and we used him as an interpreter to call into the cave to get the other Japs to come out. We'd get him to say, They don't harm you, they don't hurt you, they treat me well, they feed me, they give me water. Sometimes they were successful. Sometimes you'd hear a big explosion in the tunnel. They killed themselves rather than come out. We never went in any caves. We threw in grenades or satchel charges. That's where the dogs were useful. If you had a dog team around, you let the dog go in the cave. They knew the difference if someone in there was dead or alive. If there was more than one entrance, the dog would find it and come out the other end, and come up and come around.

We were in a really great mood down at the beach, waiting to get off the island. The first thing we wanted was getting a good shower. We'd grown beards, which we weren't used to, because this was the Marine Corps, you had to be clean-shaven every day, and here's the first time in maybe three years that we hadn't been able to shave for three weeks. And of course you were dirty, too, and the dirt was in your beard, grubs and everything else in there. We just couldn't wait. And that was the best feeling, take a shower, clean up, and get a real meal. That was just like heaven. And the flag going up wasn't too visible to us in the 4th Division because we were so far from Suribachi, and at that time we were very occupied, we had our own problems over there. We had a tough time moving. We didn't realize the impact of the flag-raising until after we had mopped up. We got back to the beach and everybody was jubilant that we're getting the hell out of there. And on the beach there was a stack of newspapers flown in from Guam. I think it was the *New York Daily News*. And there on the front page was the picture of the flag-raising, and we all grabbed one and then we realized what kind of an impact this was making back in the States.

Going back to Maui was nothing like coming out. Except for once in a while when you'd think about the guys who didn't come back, and that would bother you, but it got so that it just wore off. When we arrived, they put on a fantastic parade, a big welcome party, for three days. Of course they had heard about the flag-raising, what we did there and we were all real heroes to them. The whole island was ours if we wanted it.

One thing this whole experience instilled in me was a sense of determination, of perseverance, not to be discouraged after you've been pushed around a day or two. I think the perfect example of how important it is to hang on was when those guys were on the beach the first couple of days, we could very easily have been pushed back into the sea. There was a very thin line of making a debacle out of it and what we did do, finally. I think it was only because of the determination and discipline that the Marine Corps instilled in the guys that made us hang on. And I like to think that that's what I still have.

Like George Gentile, PFC Ernest Moreau was also a replacement. He describes a friendship that was forged on Iwo Jima, and how that friendship and the battle conditions on Iwo Jima influenced both of their lives.

PFC Ernest E. Moreau
Rifleman, 24th Replacement Draft, 4th Marine Division

We were just a replacement draft, we didn't go in until the third or fourth day. All we kept hearing were reports on how bad it was. But we had wounded come aboard our APA and put them in sick bay. What got me was the burial at sea. They couldn't keep the bodies on ship, so they put them in tarps and dropped the bodies overboard. That gave you a funny feeling. I said to myself, I'd much rather die on land than be fishbait.

Watching that beach that first day, wondering how bad it was gonna be, it scared the hell outta ya, I can tell you that. And the worst part of it was going over the nets, down into the boats. I wasn't in the amtracs until I hit the beach, so we went to shore in an LCVP. There wasn't too much room when we came in on the beach. All you could see were dead Marines, some floating in the water. They had a hell of a time getting the LCVP in there because everything was all blocked off. When we landed, an officer came over and sent part of us to the amtracs, and God knows what the others did.

On that first night, I was with these other fellows who were old salts, and I'm a new recruit, this is my first campaign. And all of a sudden, they got word that the Japs were swimming around from Kitano Point to where we were. When we got the word, all of these old salts are just standing around, casually taking their time turning the amtracs around, and I kept saying to myself, What the hell's the matter with these guys, what's taking them so long? What happened, nobody knows. The Japs never showed up.

We sat down to eat our C-rations not long after that ammo dump had caught fire and blown up.* There were dead Marines all over the place. They came up with a dump truck to pick up the bodies. They'd put a body on a stretcher, take the stretcher and stack it in the truck, just like cordwood. This one dead Marine was just like a baked potato. Two men went to pick him up, and the bones came right out of the arms. Just like a chicken that's overdone. That really bothered the hell outta me. You look at the dead Japs and you say, Good, you sonofabitch. But you see a Marine, it bothers you.

Two days later, we were put in with a bunch of other people. They needed riflemen. There were about twenty guys standing there, and the officer said, I want some volunteers. Now, you know, in the Marine Corps they say, Never volunteer for anything. Then the officer said, You, you, you, and you, you either go on this mission, or you're going to get a court-martial. Naturally, the guys who were pointed out went. Fortunately for me, I wasn't picked, and I still don't know what the mission was, and I never saw those guys again.

There isn't anybody I know of in combat that's an atheist. You prayed. And there were priests who went around for confessions. Right after I finished, the Japs started shelling, and I didn't get a chance to say my penance. Naturally, we all jumped in any hole we could find. After it was all over, I spent about an hour going around, walking around, looking for that priest. Finally, I found him. I said, I went to confession, but I didn't do my penance, and I went to communion. He started to laugh like hell and he said, Son, if it makes you feel any better, say it now. I was a little teed off that the guy was laughing at me. But that's the way I was brought up, you know, that's the way you did it.

I became friends with this guy Tony Steltzer. He was a German Jew. We had dug a perimeter of two-man foxholes all the way around.

*On D+2, 21 February, the Japanese had scored a direct hit on the ammo dump of the 25th Marines.

We had dug our foxholes the best we could, but part of it was a sulfur bed. We laid there at night, and boy did we perspire. You don't get out at nighttime and walk around, you stay right where you're at. And down below the hill, we'd buried our canteens in the sulfur bed, so in the morning you could get up and go down and take the canteens out, and there would be boiling water. We'd use it for either hot chocolate or instant coffee. Anyway, this particular day, Tony and I got into an argument, because one day he would take the canteens down, the next day I would. He said it was him, I said, It was me, it's your turn to go. After about five minutes of this, he said, The hell with you, you get your own, I'll get my own. So we did. And while we were gone, the Japanese started shelling. A mortar shell landed right in our hole. We had requisitioned a lot of pineapple before we left Hawaii, and when we got back our stuff was strewn all over the place from that shell going in. If we hadn't had that argument, one of us would have been in that hole.

One night, Tony Steltzer, he snored like you wouldn't believe. His snoring bothered me more than the shells. You could tell an incoming shell, it would whistle. And because we were in this sulfur pit area, at night sometimes a fog would come in, like in London, with the warm ground and the cold drizzle. I poked my head up out of the hole, and I nudged Tony, and he'd wake up but go right back to sleep again, he was so darned loud. So I kept looking out of the hole, over the ridge, and all of a sudden, I saw this guy creeping. I kept looking at him, and I was so goddamned sure this guy was a Jap, I'd have bet my life on it. I picked up my rifle and I took aim, and I said, I'm gonna holler just once, and if that sonofabitch doesn't give me the right password I'm gonna nail him. I hollered, the guy said, Don't shoot, it's me, Tate. I'll never forget that name. He got over to the foxhole and I said, What in the hell were you doing out there, creeping around? He said, It's my watch. He came over to tell us it was our turn for the two-hour watch.

I used to take the rosaries and say so many Hail Marys for an hour. Tony's watch was broken, and I lost my watch. He said, How in the hell can you tell when your hour's up? I said, I say all the Hail Marys, so many in an hour. He said, Well, how do you say a Hail

Mary? And this is a German Jew, you know. So I told him. And I used to kid him. I'd say, Boy, if your mother and father could see you now, a German Jew with a pair of rosaries in your hand.

Now, being a replacement, I jumped around so much, it wasn't funny. They used us one day for one thing, another for another thing. I remember one night, we had just taken the airstrip, and the Japs had got wind that we were crossing. They started shelling the air-field. We were walking across, not running, because we didn't want to make too much noise, but when they started shelling we started running like hell again, as fast as my legs could carry me. I went head-first into a crater. I lost my rifle when I fell in, so I was without my weapon. It was pitch black, and I couldn't figure out what direc-tion the Japs were in, or what direction our troops were in. The only thing for me to do was to stay there till daybreak. And as daybreak started to come around, I saw what looked like a boulder on the side of the crater. When daybreak came, I looked at it. It was a Marine's head. No body around, nothing. Just a Marine's head. I got out of the hole and ran across the airstrip.

There are things you see like that, things that get grilled into you at boot camp, that do things to you. Once we came across this dead Jap once down at the beach. When you're dead, wherever you're hit just swells up like a balloon, and then it bursts, that's where it gets smelly. This guy evidently had been hit in the groin, and he looked like he had an erection. So five or six of us are lying there, with carbines and M-1s, and we're all shooting at that thing for target practice.

I picked up a lot of souvenirs off dead Japs, in foxholes, wherever. Some guys were going into the caves and getting hurt, so they made a summary court-martial if you got caught going into a cave. Once we found a Jap skull and took it back from the front lines. We knew this warrant officer quartermaster who was always in the back of the lines and never got a chance to get up front, and he said, If you guys bring me back a souvenir, I'll fix you up with K-rations. So we boiled the skull to kill all the maggots, and knocked all the gold teeth out. We brought it to the quartermaster and, wouldn't you know it, the guy's a dentist? Boy, he gave us rations for the rest of the campaign.

This one day, they knew the Japanese were in this cave, and this officer came up, we were standing there and listening to him. He talked on the megaphone for a good fifteen minutes, telling them to come out, that they'd be treated decently. Anyways, three of them came out. God know how many were in the cave. But there was this Marine standing there with a Thompson machine gun, he shot the three of them right off the bat. The lieutenant turned around and said, What the hell did ya do that for? You might as well blow the cave shut, nobody's gonna come out now. You just hated these people so much, you got that hard, hard feeling that you could do anything to them without it bothering you a single bit.

Before it gets dark, you kind of orient yourself to everything that's around. You know where the bushes and the trees are, or whatever there was. After it would get dark, and the flares weren't out yet, you'd look in an area, and you could almost see somebody there. It was just your imagination, but that's how you would feel. You would stare at a certain area, and you'd swear to God somebody was there. You knew the Japs were coming out of their holes, looking for food. You'd watch and watch and watch and say, That's a tree, or a stone. Then, after staring at that thing for five minutes, you're sure that's a Jap creeping around.

One night we went out with a sergeant. Again, we were new recruits with a couple of old-timers, and we went out this night, and when we came back in somebody screwed up on the password. When we came back, the Japs were shooting at us, and the *Marines* are shooting at us. The sergeant says, Jesus Christ, now we're fighting both sides. So we stayed there till daybreak, when the sergeant could show himself a little, the Marines stopped shooting.

Another day, the sergeant took us out on patrol. He said, Follow my path, don't wander away, just follow close as you can in my steps, because this area has been cleared of mines. And lo and behold, there was a dead Jap lying there, an officer, who had a sword on him, so this Marine wandered off to get the sword. When he did, he stepped on a land mine. Fortunately nobody got hurt, just him. The guy's hollering, Help me, help me, but the sergeant said, Don't anybody go to help him, stay put, someone will come and pick him up. They'll have to get a detail over to check for mines first. We felt real bad that that sonofagun was gonna leave him there. We felt like we should have stayed to protect him. But we didn't. We followed the sergeant, did our patrol, and came back.

One time we were standing near a cave, and this Jap came running out. They hit him with a flamethrower. What surprised me was he just kept right on running, totally in flames. I said to this corpsman standing next to me, Holy Christ, what a way to die. He said, That guy was dead the minute those flames hit him. It's just like when you cut a chicken's head off, the chicken jumps around. Well, that's what happens to the body. You're in the motion of running, and when you get hit with that flamethrower, your body just keeps right on going.

At another cave, they threw in a phosphorous grenade, and it didn't go off. This one guy went up to the mouth of the cave, and when he got there it went off. You could see the smoke coming from his flesh. So other Marines standing by ripped his clothes off, and the guy was standing there stark naked. They tried putting a blanket around him, but the minute the blanket would touch his body, he would scream blue murder. Three other Marines took the blanket and made like a pyramid around him that wouldn't touch him, and they walked him down to the aid station. They were going to make him go down naked, but just the sun beating down on him made the burns even worse.

There were all kinds of screwed-up things that happened, like when Tony and I were runners. We had an envelope to bring to Captain McCarthy, the one who won the Congressional Medal of Honor.* His headquarters was in a great big crater at the top of a hill, and there were five guys in that crater, but McCarthy wasn't there, and the message was for him directly. So we were sitting there, waiting, waiting, waiting, and finally I said to Tony, Let's get the hell out of here, we're not doing anybody any good here. I gave the envelope to the sergeant, and we headed on down the hill. We were sit-

*Joseph J. McCarthy, CO, Company G, 2d Battalion, 24th Marines. Captain McCarthy was awarded the Medal of Honor for his actions in successively eliminating four Japanese strongpoints on D+2, 21 February.

ting at the bottom, and all of a sudden I saw a corpsman coming down the hill with the sergeant that we had just spoken to. Right after we left, a mortar shell landed right smack in the middle of the crater. All the guys were killed but two. The sergeant had his arm around the corpsman, and I looked and he had jelly all over his back. I said to the corpsman, What the hell is that stuff? He said, That's the brains of somebody else. We were pretty well shook up. So the corpsman says, Here, you better take this, and he gave us a nip apiece of medical brandy.

The morning that I got hurt was the last day of the campaign. In fact, we were supposed to board ship at one o'clock in the afternoon, and we went out on patrol. I said to Tony that morning, Look, if anything happens to me, hang on to my stuff, will ya? He said, What are you talking about, we're going aboard ship this afternoon. So five of us took off, patrolling, going around the areas. The area we were in, it was full of caves. There must have been at least fifty, sixty caves, on the side of a big, big hill. And some goddamn Jap was up in a cave, and there were holes all over the place. We couldn't figure where the shots were coming from. The guy was a good shot, too. One guy jumped in a hole, and he had his knees sticking out. The Jap shot him in the knee. Shot another guy in the head. Out of five of us, four got hit. I was crouched, looking around, trying to locate the shots. While I'm bent there, I'm on my haunches, and I got like a bee sting in my foot. I realized I got shot. I looked down and says, Holy Christ, two inches more and he would have castrated me. So I laid flat on the ground. Everybody but the sergeant was hurt, and he said, Can you make it across the airstrip? I said, I think so. I started to get up, he says, Wait a minute, we're short of ammunition, gimme your rifle. I said, I'm not gonna walk around here with no rifle. He said, I'll follow you across the airstrip, and when you're on the other side, you'll know you're safe. I said okay. I gave him my rifle, and I took off.

I told them what happened when I got to the aid station, and they sent some men up there. From what I understand, they found the section that the Jap was in, and they used flamethrowers to get him. The minute I knew I was safe, though, my foot started killing me. It was sloshing around from blood inside the shoe. I waited for treatment, and while I was there, there was this young kid, looked like a baby. All he kept saying was he wanted his mother. "Mom, where are you? Mom?" From what I could see, it was a head wound. Hell, I wasn't much more than a kid myself.

From there, they sent me to Guam for two weeks, and then to Hawaii for five, and to a rehabilitation center, the Royal Hawaiian Hotel, for seven days, and then back to my outfit. When I got back, there was Tony Steltzer. I though the guy was gonna collapse when he saw me, he thought I was dead. We shook hands, got together, and I said, where's the stuff you were gonna keep? He says, Hell, that was too much stuff to carry, too many souvenirs, so I left them there. Well, came to find out he hadn't left them there. He had sold them aboard ship.

Anyway, for twenty-five years after, I never heard from Tony. And one day my wife and I were shopping, and we came back and I said, You're not gonna believe this, but I got a craving for a piece of pineapple pie. Now, for twenty-five years I never had a piece of pineapple in any shape or form or manner. I just didn't want to touch it, I was just sick of it. So you know what I did? I went to three different restaurants to find a piece of pineapple pie. We found one, and when we came back home, I told my wife about the incident in the foxhole on Iwo, with the pineapple being strewn all over the place. I had no more than put the key in the door and the telephone was ringing. The guy on the other end of the line says, "This is Tony Steltzer. Are you Ernie Moreau?" Well, after he called, we went to Florida to see him. We spent a few days there. He said, You go to church on Sunday? I said sure. He says, You want to go? I thought he was going to say we'll go to synagogue, whatever. His wife said no, he turned Catholic. He wouldn't miss Mass on Sunday even if he had to drag himself. I told my wife it must have been that experience with the rosaries. And then the coincidence of the pineapple pie, and within a half hour him calling on the phone!

But I guess we haven't learned anything from Iwo Jima. We're sticking our nose in all over the world again. Iwo Jima was a little different, that had to be taken. There were twenty-eight thousand flyers saved because of Iwo, otherwise they would have had to crash in the sea. But it took a lot of lives to take it. Still, I'm proud of my service in the Marines, and on Iwo Jima. I think they never should have given it back to the Japs. One time, we went on a tour to Hong Kong and we had to spend three days in Japan. I called the travel agency and told the girl, Look, I don't want to go to Japan. She said it's the only way to Hong Kong, there is a layover in Japan. Well, we took the trip, and when I landed in Japan, I'd see a guy my age, and I'd wonder if that was one of those sonsabitches that we fought, you know? I just was not comfortable being there. I liked every other part of the trip except going to Japan. While we were there, they were selling tours of Hiroshima. I said, What the hell do I want to go to Hiroshima for? Those people got exactly what they deserved. They should have blown this country right off the face of the earth. I'm sorry, but that's just the way I feel.

7

CHAPLAIN

Spiritual guidance has secured an important place in organized war-fare. For modern armies, chaplains provide a source of comfort, understanding, compassion, and a sense of divine greatness to a mission, not to mention a sense of divine forgiveness for actions that are inherently evil in Western man's interpretation of God's will. "Thou shalt not kill" was the Command-ment broken obviously, and willfully, by these God-fearing men. Chaplains provided a reconciliation for many Marines who would otherwise find killing completely abhorrent to their nature.

The Navy trained chaplains, as it did many other occupational specialties, for support of the Marines. Lt. Gage Hotaling explains how his duties affected the lives, and the deaths, of Marines on Iwo Jima.

Lt. (j.g.) Gage Hotaling, USNR
Chaplain, HQ Battalion. and HQ Company, 4th Marine Division

I was pastor of a church in Palmer, Massachusetts, the Second Bap-tist Church, when Pearl Harbor happened, and I saw about thirty of the young men and women of our church going into the service, Army, Navy, Marines, Coast Guard. For a couple of years, we had a Service Committee that sent out a monthly newsletter to each of these servicemen, and as I received letters back from them, I began to feel more and more the desire to go into the service, because they needed a pastor. And so in June of 1944 I went to the Naval District Headquarters in Boston and applied for the chaplaincy. I was accepted and went to Chaplains School in September of 1944. Chaplains School at that time was in the College of William and

Mary in Williamsburg, Virginia, and we had eight weeks of training. During that time, we were indoctrinated to the customs, history, and traditions of the U.S. Navy. We had one or two lectures on the Marines, and they would point to the big, rugged, husky fellows in the class and say, You're likely to get Marine duty. They would never point to me because I was one of the smaller men in the class. But the day we received our orders I was the only one who was ordered to report directly overseas to the Fleet Marine Force. When I asked what that meant, I was told that I would probably be assigned to one of the Marine divisions and would probably be in combat, perhaps within six or eight months.

During the six days that I was on Maui, I met our division chaplain, Harry Wood, and he told me that I was being carried with the division as an extra chaplain. When I asked him what he meant, he said that in the previous operations they didn't have a chaplain assigned to the cemetery, and when it was necessary to have committals for those who had been buried they had to search for a chaplain in one of the regiments, and it was not always an easy thing to find one. So he said, I want you, Gage, to be the chaplain at the 4th Division cemetery in the next combat. He may have known where we were to be, but I didn't, and most of the men had no idea where we were going either.

I was on an attack transport going to Iwo. We had all of the 3d Battalion, 23d Marines on board ship. We had some other units, but that was the largest unit we had. There were about forty officers on the ship, along with about one thousand to fifteen hundred enlisted men. My job, of course, was to get acquainted with as many of the officers and men as I could. And on Sundays, there were three Protestant chaplains—the ship's chaplain, and then two of us assigned to the Marines—and we took turns conducting Sunday service. After the second Sunday, when I preached, two or three men came to me after the service and said, Chaplain, did you know we were having a fellowship meeting every night on the open deck? And I said, No, but I'd like to join you. So they told me exactly where they were meeting, and that night I went and met about twenty-five or thirty Marines there. Most of them happened to be Southern Baptists who had gone to church and Sunday school and were the kind of Marines that sought out other men of their own denomination, and they would sing some of the choruses that they learned in Sunday school. And I've always liked to tell this story about the first night I was there, when one of the songs they sang was "Jesus Wants Me for a Sunbeam." And I said, Can you imagine Marines going into combat, singing that song on board ship?

I taught them a number of songs that I had learned, and they seemed to enjoy singing those, too. So our meeting that we held every night on the open deck was for prayer and sharing our thoughts, our hopes, our fears, our ambitions, and singing some of the old songs that gave us faith and courage and strength. Of the Marines that I met on board ship like that, I know at least one of them was killed on Iwo, and I buried him at the cemetery. Of the forty or fifty officers on board ship, at least ten of them were killed on Iwo, and I buried them.

We of course knew that D-day had been set for February 19, and on the day before, it was Sunday and we had two services so that all the men who wanted to attend church could do so. I preached at the second Protestant service in the afternoon. And knowing that some of the men who were there would probably never be hearing another sermon again, it was a real challenge to know what to say. I thought long and deeply about it, and came up with the idea of Saint Paul who went to Europe for the first time. And I said, "You men are going to make an amphibious landing and it's going to test your faith, and it's going to test your courage, as Saint Paul's faith and courage were tested in his amphibious landing. . . ."

On D-day, all of our 25th Marines went ashore that morning. I was a part of the Graves Registration Section, and we had been told we would probably go ashore on D+1 in order to set up the cemetery. The fighting was so terrific on D-day, casualties were being brought back to the ship to be taken care of by the doctors, and as we talked to some of them, we realized how terrific the fighting was ashore. So on D+1, we were told we would not be going ashore that day. Instead, we went ashore on D+2.

About 10:30 in the morning, we climbed down the cargo nets to the Higgins boat, and we were about six or seven miles off shore. There were twelve of us in our boat, all assigned to the Graves Registration Section. As we got into the control boat, which was probably a mile from shore, we were told to go in near an ammunition dump that was burning, pick up casualties, and bring them out.* We stacked all of our gear in one end of the boat, and once the coxswain landed we went ashore to look for the casualties. We couldn't seem to find them. And the next thing we knew, the coxswain of our boat had pulled out because he was afraid to stay there. Not only did he pull out, but he had all of our gear, all of the men's rifles, all of their backpacks, knapsacks, mess gear, everything, and went back to the ship.

There we were, on an enemy shore, with nothing but the clothes we had on our backs. At that point, of course, the shore was littered with all kinds of gear, so we decided to get off the shore as quickly as we could. And when we met our burial officer, Capt. Lewis Nutting, he showed us where the cemetery was to be. We went there and began digging foxholes, picked up some cans in the sand, opened them and ate a cold lunch.

While the men were digging foxholes, I decided that as a chaplain the best thing I could do for them was to go down to the beach and see if I could scrounge around and pick up some ponchos for the men, because otherwise it would be pretty cold to sleep that night without any kind of protection. For a couple of hours that afternoon I scrounged the beach and was able to get at least a poncho for every man, and in some cases one that he could sleep on and another that he could put over him.

The first night was pretty cold, and I remember shivering the first part of the night from cold, and then about two or three o'clock in the morning, when some Japanese planes came over and dropped some bombs on the airfield, which was not too far from our cemetery, I shivered the rest of the night from fright. Mighty glad to wake up in the morning.

That next day was rainy. In fact, it had rained ever since D-day.

*The ammo dump of the 25th Marines, 4th Marine Division, destroyed on the morning of D+2.

Again, there wasn't much I could do but go down and scrounge around for more ponchos, raincoats, shelter halves, anything I could get hold of to bring back to our men. And by the end of D+3, I think we had enough for every man in our outfit, which was anywhere between twenty-five and forty men. There were five officers, and of course the rest were enlisted, and their job was to go out and hunt for bodies, bring them in, and stack them near the cemetery. And as soon as we could get a bulldozer, the bulldozer would scoop a long trench, and then they would lay the bodies down, fifty in a row.

The first burials took place on D+5, which I think is remarkable when you think that we just went ashore on D+2, and by now we'd collected enough bodies and had a bulldozer to dig a trench. From that point on, the number of bodies collected were much more than we could handle in any one day. At one time, we had four hundred or five hundred bodies stacked up, waiting for burial. They asked me, as the chaplain, to make a count twice a day. That was a gruesome detail, just to go around and count bodies. They tell me the stench of bodies on other operations nearer the equator was terrific. Iwo, of course, was quite a bit north of the equator. We had cold nights, and so the stench of the bodies was not as great, but even so they were bad enough. I am not a smoker, but I found that the only way that I could go around and count bodies was to smoke one cigarette after another. So I've often told people smoking is good for only one thing—counting bodies. I was addicted to smoking for twenty-six days.

There were three or four men who would go through the pockets of the deceased and remove all of the personal effects, which would all be put into a ditty-bag with the man's name and serial number attached to it. I think we also had one or two medical corpsmen who were supposed to figure out the cause of death. In most cases, the death was shrapnel wounds. And in some cases the bodies were ripped apart so badly there was no question as to the cause of death. I helped some of the men remove the personal effects. There were some things that were taken out of the wallets, because we understood all the wallets were going back to the families. So if we found some pornographic literature, that was immediately removed so it would never go back to the families. There were pictures of Marines with gook girls and so on, in all kinds of poses, and those were always removed. The things that were sent back were wristwatches, rings, wallets with money, family pictures. And in many cases, this was a sad and tragic thing. You'd open a wallet, and there'd be a picture of a wife and child. That always made you feel bad. I have no idea now how many of the Marines were married. Of course, many of them were young fellows, seventeen, eighteen, nineteen years old, and probably were not married, but many of your officers and the older Marines that had been gunnery sergeants were.

Once we had bodies lined up, I would give a committal to each one, with Marines holding a flag over the body. And I said the same committal words to every Marine, because they were not buried as Protestants or Catholics or Jews. They were buried as Marines. We had no idea at the time of burial just what their religion was, other than what the dogtag might have said. But I didn't look at dogtags. And this is the committal I used: "You have gallantly given your life on foreign soil in order that others might live. Now, we commit your body to the ground, in the name of the Father, the Son, and the Holy Ghost. May your soul rest in eternal peace. Amen." And the largest number of burials we had in any one day was 247. But I kept a record in a little book of how many we had each day. The first day was 50; the next 100; next day was 105; then 95; then on February 28, we had 200; the next day was 100; the largest number, 247, was on March 2, and so on. The cemetery was dedicated on March 15. It was a general dedication to begin with. The general had a few remarks, the band played "The Marine Corps Hymn," they played "Rock of Ages." One of the chaplains gave the invocation, another had a few words, another one gave the benediction. Then after the actual memorial service, each of the three faiths had their own memorial services, Protestant, Catholic, and Jewish, and I took part in the Protestant. The last day I committed services was on March 17, because I packed up on March 18, and went to my ship, the *Jupiter.*

We left the island on the nineteenth, when my division chaplain told me to leave on the *Jupiter,* a cargo ship. I was right on the beach, waiting all day, and every time a little Higgins boat came in we'd say, Are you from the *Jupiter*? No, some other ship. Nobody came out from the *Jupiter* that day. So my last night ashore, I slept under an overturned amtrac. And the next day, a boat came in, and I said, Are you from the *Jupiter*? He said, Yeah, yeah. I said, Well, that's where I'm going! Can I get aboard? I went out there, and we didn't have too many Marines there. It was a cargo ship, and we had six officers and I don't know how many enlisted men, but nothing like the crowd we had coming out from Maui.

After the war, I became a member of the 4th Marine Division Association right away, and I attended a number of reunions, so that it gave me a feeling of comradeship with those that I had served with. And I have stayed with the Military Chaplains' Association through the years, I'm a life member of that. I belong to the Sons of Union Veterans of the Civil War, where I'm past commander, and present secretary-treasurer. I've stayed active with all of them. I've been Junior Vice-Commander of the State, and I'm Chaplain of the State, so we find comradeship in many different ways.

I don't know what we should have learned from the battle, because who knows what's going to be a hundred or a thousand years from now. But I think the thing which all of us will remember was the fact that it was the toughest battle the Marines ever fought, and the fact that the Marine Memorial in Washington has the six Iwo Jima Marines with the flag. Why did they pick that particular memorial, because that was going to be the memorial for all the two hundred years that the Marines have served? It just seems that that was the one thing that they wanted Marines and Americans to remember, which is that no matter where we go, or what enemy we face, our flag will be flying above us.

8

HEADQUARTERS AND SERVICE

Headquarters and Service companies and battalions were the nerve centers of all Marine ground divisions and regiments. They provided command, communications, intelligence, supply, and operations for their subordinates, and served as ad-hoc replacement units when needed. Their primary mission, in all cases, was serving the troops they led.

Platoon Sgt. James Boyle
Quartermaster, HQ, 2d Battalion, 21st Marines, 3d Marine Division

Now, there was a lot of scuttlebutt going on. You'd hear different things from different people. And scuttlebutt, you didn't know whether to believe it or not. People would say, Oh, we're going to go home after we leave Bougainville, which was a joke because we went to Guam. And of course they said, You're going home after Guam. I don't remember how we heard we were moving out. We were in training, and we were told we were going to be on standby for a battle that was coming up. We would not be in on the initial landing, but we were going to be there in reserve. Now this was my own company telling me this, my own headquarters. I had to go to a meeting with all the officers because I had charge of all the intelligence gear, all the flamethrowers, hospital corpsmen's kits, all this was my problem, getting this on shore, into combat. Before we went into combat everyone would get their own gear, but until then everything was under lock and key. There were cases as long as a piano, just about as high, full of flamethrower equipment, Navy equipment, wires, radios, a lot of stuff. It was rough getting it on and off the

LST. I didn't have to do that personally, the Navy did that. I just had to get it to the shore. They did all the loading. I had to check the hold, I spent a lot of my time below deck. I had to get one of the Navy men to unlock the quarters to get in to check this stuff. I had to make sure no one was getting at their personal equipment. No one could get their .45s until, say, the day before we were going to land.

Scuttlebutt was still saying we were going home, but something seemed to tell us that we weren't. There was too much going on, there was a big fleet of ships that were all moving. I guess we were told then that we were going to be in reserve for the Battle of Iwo Jima, which meant nothing to us. We had never heard of the name, nothing at all. They explained to us that we had to take this island because we were losing so many planes on their runs to Japan and back, they were running out of fuel, they were targets for the planes coming out of Iwo Jima. So we had to take this island.

I think my stomach told me we were just off Iwo. Every time I went into combat I got wicked heartburn where I wasn't able to eat anything. Tension, I think, built up inside. Looking at Iwo, it was something like I'd never seen before. Never seen nothing like this. Just boats all stacked up all over the beach, people running every which way, the Navy men on the bullhorn trying to get our boats in. The first time that we went off the ship, we rode 'round and 'round in the landing craft, must have been for a couple of hours. We never did go in that day. We were finally brought back to the ship and we had to climb back up and from then on we knew we were going in, that's what they told us. The Navy had all my equipment in boats, going in ahead of me, and they had to bring all that back, too, until we finally got in the following day.

We had heard that there were tremendous casualties on the beach. Everything was smashed up on the beach and there was no way of getting anything else in. I could see the island from my landing craft, a little bit. It was pretty hard to see up over the front of it, and actually I wasn't looking to see. I really didn't want to. You could hear the noise, it was horrendous. I was very nervous, I think all the guys were. There was very little talking, nobody hollering gung-ho or any of that stuff. I think a lot of them were saying a lot of prayers. To my knowledge, that's what I felt, I was very quiet. I know I did a lot of praying. I had the cross my mother had sent me, the religious cards and everything else, and I just hoped to get on ground. I said, Once I'm on ground, I'll be all right, I'll no longer have the pain in my chest or nothing. If I could just get my feet on the ground, where I could move. My biggest fear was in the little boats, that we were going to have a direct hit because they were all around us. But once I got in I was all right. Once you hit the beach, your training came into effect, you did what you had to do, and you didn't worry about anything, even though there was shooting all around you. And of course they landed us on a different beach because we couldn't get where we were supposed to go, and I'm running down this way, and everybody's running the other way, looking for my equipment, which I finally found, but it was just utter chaos.

After I found my gear, I had to check in with my headquarters and find out where they were going to need supplies. Headquarters was just a hole in the ground at that time. I had to wait for orders, be told what I had to bring up to the front lines. We had tremendous casualties. The three men I had working for me were killed or wounded. I never saw them after the first day. So I started out as a company quartermaster and ended up with the whole battalion because there was so many casualties. I had to use fellows who were coming back from the front lines who were demoralized—I don't want to use the word "shell-shocked"—but for a lot of them, it was their first combat and I guess it just got to them and they were wandering around. So they sent them back, put them on board ship for a day and then put them back on the island, and they would be used for handling supplies. I had to use these guys to carry equipment. Bazookas, mortar shells were the things in big demand. And BAR ammunition. So if I had ten guys, we would just carry everything. We'd have big blisters full of water, bandoleers, and as many mortar shells as we could carry, and go forward with that. There was no beaten path to get where we wanted to go. Walking in that black sand was like walking on a sheet of ice. You take one step and slide back. It just sunk underneath you. It took us much longer that it would have on normal ground. Because of the weight of the equipment, we were sinking in.

I don't know how many trips I made. I had an idea where the terrain was, where I was supposed to go, and they would just follow me in single line and hope that nobody got hit. I had a carbine, which I never got to use because there wasn't time to. And I carried a stiletto that I got from a Marine Raider on Guadalcanal. I still have it. I carried it all through the war.

So we would go up with this equipment, pick up the stretchers with the wounded, carry them back, and get ready for another trip up to another one of the rifle companies, and under fire all the time. But it's like I didn't know anybody was shooting at me, I knew what I had to do and you just went ahead and did it. That's where the training came in. And of course, being a little older than some of the other guys, already having two combats under my belt, that made a lot of difference. You accepted the fact that you might get killed, but that was it, you went ahead and did your job. I was fortunate. A lot of the fellows weren't. I mean, a lot of them got killed because they didn't stay under cover, do what they were supposed to do, and panicked.

My first night there was just utter hell. Constant noise, voices crying out for a corpsman, people running every which way on the beach, it was just utter chaos. Star shells were being fired. I don't think we slept much that first night. Didn't sleep at all. We had food, though, from the ships. Hot coffee, I think, was the biggest thing. The wounded though, carrying them back, all it seemed they wanted was a cigarette. I didn't smoke at that time, but I became a smoker on Iwo. It seemed to relieve your tension. A cigarette and a cup of coffee.

The quartermaster stayed basically on the beach, never moved up. I was on the beach proper for a least a full day. I never got to move forward with any of the troops. They might have moved in two hundred or three hundred yards for a bivouac area, but it meant going up day or night. We made night trips, too, which were kind of scary but, then again, you did what you were supposed to do.

I think it was my second day, or third day, I don't think we moved. I was right in back of the front lines and I don't think we moved that whole day. It might have moved fifty yards at the most, it was just impossible to get going. There was a lot of cursing and hollering, you know, Let's get out of this damn hole, let's go. It was just sheer frustration, because at least on the other two combats we did move, but on Iwo we were just stuck. Stuck until we got over that first airfield, going towards the second, and then we would move with them. It might be a hundred yards a day, it might be fifty, maybe two hundred. Whenever the battalion moved, I just tried to stay close to them.

We got up to airfield number 1, and all the fellows were dug in that terrace beneath the airfield proper. And I would leave all my equipment in that area, check in with the colonel or the captain to find out what they needed. They would radio back for me, they would give me a list and say they'd call it back so it would be ready when I got there. It was a constant thing, back and forth. I think I shut out the fact that I might get hit. I don't know why. I just seemed to be able to go and I never got tired. The adrenalin, I suppose, did that, but I never really seemed to have a fear of anything.

I remember I was on the second airfield when the Japs counterattacked one night. I was on my way up with equipment and it was just getting dark, and somebody yelled at me to get out of the way, there was a raid coming. And we just got to the side wherever we could and lay down and waited till it was all over. There was a lot of shooting, a lot of hollering, yelling. And when it was done, they said, Okay, you can go forward, and that's when we saw a lot of dead Japs. I never saw a live Jap in all the time I was running back and forth. I saw dead Japs, but I never saw a live one coming out of any place where he could get at me. I never fired a shot or nothing.

My headquarters and service company had a lot of casualties. A lot of battlefield sergeants became lieutenants. There was either fifteen or sixteen of us who came back that never got a scratch. There were a lot of attached units—we were over two hundred—between your intelligence, all your other groups. Other guys had it 100 percent worse than I did—the riflemen, the guys who were doing the actual fighting in the front lines, they were more the heroes than somebody way back on the shore. Which was bad, too.

On the men I carried back on the stretchers, there were all kinds of wounds. Some were missing legs. One fellow, his stomach was almost completely blown apart, some were hit in the head. The hospital corpsmen would fix up whatever they could and gave them morphine or something. We even carried dead ones back and didn't realize it. I carried my best friend back, didn't know it was him. He had had a direct hit, from what I was told. With the flamethrower on his back, he got hit directly and it just burned him all to pieces. I didn't know it was him until the following day when somebody told me who it was.

When we did get some lull time I moved my headquarters up, because the 3d had gotten quite a bit ahead of me. They brought up most of my equipment and I dug in a certain area, and that was when I first took a bath. All we did was scoop out a hole and put your outer helmet in there with water and it would heat up because of the sulfur. And I tried to write. I also heard the flag raising. Didn't see it. The word went around that they were on Suribachi. I don't know where I was at the time, I was too busy doing my job to notice. We heard a lot of hollering and yelling and everybody was pointing. I got a vague picture of the flag, that's all I saw. The horns on the ships were all going off and we figured, maybe the war's over, you know, which was not the truth.

I was on the island until the sixteenth of March, maybe the twenty-first. There was a lot of mop-up going on at the time, they were going forward all the time. At that point, toward the end, a lot of my work was trying to recover weapons, rifles, bayonets, helmets. Machine guns, I think I saw only one that we were able to bring back. Most of them were smashed. I remember doing that, in the lull moments, going out with some fellows and picking up a lot of the equipment, and stacking it up down towards the beach. Some was in good shape. We left the Japanese gear alone. I didn't touch anything Japanese. We had been warned, you know, booby traps and all. A lot of guys did, but I wasn't about to touch nothing.

We had to wait until the ships came in and they started taking all the equipment off the beach. I was one of the last off because I had to stay with the equipment. I remember getting on the small boat and leaving and then praying that that boat was going to make it to the ship before they blew us out of the water. I think a lot of guys felt the same way. They were still mopping up on the island, there were stray shots coming from different directions, you could see them landing in the water.

As far as I was concerned, Iwo was just another battle. The biggest thing to me was I was going home. They told us that when we left Iwo, as soon as we got back to our base, we were going to be on board ship to go home, within two days, and we were. And that was the greatest feeling of all, going on board with the other guys who were still there.

Platoon Sgt. Frank Juszli also was assigned to Headquarters, but his function was never quite as distinct as James Boyle's. Nonetheless, his interpretation of that function is typical of the fighting Marine's sense of duty on Iwo Jima.

Sgt. Frank L. Juszli
Platoon Sergeant, HQ Company G, 3d Battalion,
27th Marines, 5th Marine Division

When I went out the Fleet Marine Force, and got assigned immediately into G Company, I was in the role of a platoon sergeant. This role, and all the squad leaders who were sergeants, were guys who had not had combat. But somewhere along the line there was a hell of an influx of guys who had been in combat, the now-disbanded Paramarines and Raiders. These guys came into the 5th Division in big numbers, and to a large extent they supplanted the guys who were already there, in position, including me. This was hard to take because what the hell, we were pushed aside into other activities. In my case, I was a fifth wheel in the company. I was sort of in company headquarters, and I sat on my sheet. What were my duties? No specific duties. You had to bend to it.

We were up at three o'clock on the morning of the landing. We had steak and eggs for breakfast. It was nice, and everybody's laughing and joking about fattening us up for the kill and all that, the fatted calf, you know, bleating like a calf bleats, "baaaaaaa." We went down into the landing boats and circled, circled, and circled until we went up to the line of departure, passing under the guns of the ships that were actively shooting, which was probably the loudest damned noise I've ever heard.

This is very dull, you know. Just cruising around in these landing craft. You can't see much, the island's too far away, and you need something to do. I don't know how I came by it, but I had picked up a book. James M. Cain's *Serenade*. We got to the line of departure, moving alone, and there I am, reading this book. There was a particular raunchy passage in there, and I just stopped and said, What in the hell am I doing, reading this raunchy passage, going into combat? I threw the book overboard.

Our 3d Battalion of the 27th was regimental reserve. The 1st and 2d were the assault battalions. They landed at nine o'clock, their H-hour. Our landing was at eleven-thirty, twelve o'clock, something like that. By the time we landed, we were playing catch-up. The assault units had gone out and made a hell of a lot of progress getting off the beach and into the middle of the island. By the time we came on, the beaches were being pretty well pummeled by enemy artillery. When we landed, our goal was to get off that beach as fast as we could, and do some clean-up work, where the guys in the assault battalions had bypassed some of the active stuff.

I took my first hit then. I was hit five times and never drew blood. You began to wish for the million-dollar wound, you know? I wasn't on that island more than an hour, and a huge damned piece of shrapnel skipped off the edge of the depression I was in and dropped on my chest. I was on my back in the hole, and I looked at that damned thing and grabbed it, which was the first of many mistakes, and burned my fingertips and threw it aside. Dumb Marine.

We got into the line right at the base of the first airfield. It was here that "Manila John" Basilone, our Congressional Medal guy, was killed.* And the word just swept through the 3d Battalion. He was

*In October 1942, at the Tenaru River on Guadalcanal, Sgt. John Basilone—who had served in the Philippines prior to the outbreak of the war, hence the nickname "Manila John"—single-handedly wiped out a company of Japanese who had attacked his cutoff position. He held out alone with one machine gun and a Colt .45 until relieved at dawn. On Iwo Jima, Gunnery Sergeant Basilone led a machine-gun platoon of the 1st Battalion, 27th Marines, until mortally wounded by a mortar fragment on Red Beach 2.

just about where we were at that time, he was already killed. And he was a guy who didn't have come back. And this is where Louis Plain [Col. Louis Plain, XO, Regimental Headquarters, 27th Marines] got hit twice, in the same shoulder, and got evacuated. This is *first day* stuff, this left a hell of an impression on us.

Then we came under a mortar attack. On this airfield, just about everywhere you looked, the runway was built up, anywhere from two or three feet to thirty or forty feet, depending on the contours. I was on the edge, looking back, and it was our unit under attack. The Japs were using a square-tooth pattern, and I saw some of our own guys scrambling like hell. We hadn't dug in yet, and a couple of our guys got killed. Already, this day has been a very long day before we got dug in and squared away for the night.

A thing that became an important task for us was tying into the unit on our right. It just seems that the 3d Battalion was always the right-hand unit of the 5th Division, and we were tying into another division. At first it was the 4th, and very quickly after that the 3d Division got inserted. I was involved, in the early days, in that tying-in process, making sure the connections were there. We got tied in and settled down with the passwords and all, and at three o'clock the next morning the Japanese mustered an attack that was coming *right at us.* There was a hell of a call for illumination, which we got, and the naval gunfire really broke them up. There wasn't an awful lot of shooting on our part. These Japs, they were coming right down the runway, you know. That made the first twenty-four hours one hell of a twenty-four hours, there wasn't much rest.

Now, what the hell does a guy who's doing general duties in the company headquarters do during an actual attack? I reasoned that what the hell am I here for? My job was to get this thing over with, so I joined it, as a damned rifleman, in one of the line companies. Just hang out and shoot. No rank involved. We did a good job that day, went eight hundred yards, the full length of the airfield.

We did have tank support there, and this was a great feeling. I was close in with tanks around me, and pretty damned quickly mortars came in. But, you know, the mortars coming in, their job was not to destroy the tanks, but the protection to the tanks. Namely us. Immediately, what was the role here? Was the infantry protecting the tank, or the tank protecting the infantry? We pretty soon learned that tanks are not a very good thing to have around you. They tend to draw fire.

These sorts of things were not without a lot of humor. Every company had a company clown. Ours was involved in this attack. For the most part, the attack was do your firing while the other guys are running forward, and now it's your turn to run forward with their support. Some of the guys got picked off while they were in the process of running. And you learned very quickly what a hit looked like, if a guy was in motion, the way he went down. You could tell if a guy was going down deliberately, or going down hit. Our company comic, who was advancing on one of the runs, he went down. It looked like he'd been hit. Oh, jeez, that would be a hell of a loss. But when things settled down, we could hear him yelling, "Get me the hell outta here!" He had stepped into a used latrine, the little famil-iar Japanese triangular post sign had fallen off. He was up to his arm-pits in it. We pulled him out, and what do you do? All the changes of clothes, all our packs, we had dropped them. We weren't even carrying out blankets, our ponchos, none of that. There was nothing available, no way to get cleaned up. But we managed to find a dead Japanese sailor, and our guy—he was a little guy, cotton-topped, pot-bellied—we dressed him up in a Japanese sailor suit. And put him downwind.

We sat there while another unit passed through us. Hill 362A was a prominence that had a ridge in front of it, and taking that ridge was going to be the important thing, and that's where G Company, 3d Battalion, 27th Marines got the hell kicked out of it. That's where Bill Walsh got his Medal of Honor.* And where just about all of the NCOs in G Company got taken out of action.

We sat at the southern of the two runways. I don't know why, but somehow we were told to spread across that open area, in two or

---

*Gunnery Sgt. William G. Walsh, 3d Battalion, 27th Marines, was attacking a ridge approaching Hill 362A with his platoon when it was hit with fire from three sides. Rather than retreat, Walsh and his men charged ahead to the cover of a shell hole at the crest, where Walsh smothered the blast of a Japanese grenade with his body. He died that day, 27 February, D+8.

three waves, to get over to the other side of this first turnaround area, where there was this undeveloped gap. So we sprinted. I can recall the process of sprinting, in waves. I recognized a dead Marine who had broken out his wallet and was looking at family pictures. He was one of the guys in G Company. I don't know how many other guys we lost, but there was a decision made that we weren't going to go sprinting across runways anymore.

So now, how in the hell do you get past the second runway? The decision was made to go around the end. Units had been involved in the attack in front of us, and these units had advanced and left behind their own foxholes. As I was going around the end of this thing, a 37mm gun opens up, and he hit a few yards out from the position I was coming in on, and this was a signal to get down. So I dove into a prebuilt hole, a good one. And within an instant his second round had hit right beside this hole, but I was already in it. There was a hell of an explosion, I could have reached out and grabbed the shell. It cascaded a lot of dirt in on me, and I got flipped over right as the next round came in on the other side. I got flipped over again. Both of these hit on the same side, and there must have been concussion in it because I was out cold. I had no idea how long. But then I finally came around and shook off the dirt, I was alone. The 3d Battalion had moved forward, and I was a casualty back there, pretty well buried. I got up with a hell of a ringing sound in my head.

But my decision there was to catch up with my unit. I knew the general direction to head in, so I just headed that way, going in the usual style, which was run, hit the deck, zig-zig, hit the deck. Play catch-up. What I was looking for was a familiar face. I knew the general direction of the unit, and all I had to do to confirm this was see somebody I knew. But I wasn't recognizing anybody. And somewhere over on the left, on a ridge, a machine gun opened up. He's opening up on me. I hit the deck, and thank God there was an almost immediate response from the guys to suppress this, because now I knew where the units were.

People up there must have thought I was nuts. Here I am, working my way through this group that is now static, and I'm the only guy going forward. But the only thing in my head was I'm looking for a familiar face. I got on that damned ridge before 362A and made it just about right to the crest about the time it was getting dark, and our attack unit had just gone over the ridge when there was a lot of explosions happening, right up in front, from grenades, and for the second time that day I'm out cold. And through this whole thing, there's that ringing sound in my head, just overwhelming. I have no idea how long I was out. When I finally became aware again, I was in company headquarters. There was no shooting going on, everything was settled down. I suppose it happened from the practice that when a guy is out of it, confused, blank, whatever, you just tell him to report over to headquarters. No discussions, just point out headquarters, go report. That must be what happened to me. I got over there and it must have been a day or two before I was aware of what was going on. And from that point, I decided, no more am I going up to the lines. I'm sticking around the company, doing courier stuff. It came down to that. I was not going back to the line units, I'm gonna do whatever these headquarters guys tell me to do. I'm no longer unhappy to be out of the attack.

From there on out in the operation, it's just a series of isolated incidents. Like after 362, there was a swale where there was a Japanese unit that had held us up for a few days. A dozen filtered out and sat in a circle in front of us, and they're going through some mumbo-jumbo. May have been a prayer meeting, I don't know. We obliged them while they were out there, and we just opened up and cleaned them out. I was brought over as part of the company headquarters to observe the process. And I observed, but I didn't participate in wiping these guys out.

I remember a cook who had been pulled into the line. This cook was right beside me, and he got killed. Then I started to develop something of a pariah complex. Every place I go, something bad happens. Guys are getting knocked off all around me. What am I, a bad-luck omen? It really came to a head when we were in a lull, and I went back to battalion armor on the edge of the third airfield, looking for a familiar face. I found a guy, we chatted, had a cup of coffee, and I said, So long, and darted off. He was a perfect gentleman and stood up, sort of bade me farewell and a single shot rang out from the runway. He's dead. The pariah complex was really mounting.

As time goes on, units are getting really confused, all mixed up. Where the hell is headquarters, headquarters of what? Very late in the campaign, the three battalions of the 27th Marines and one battalion of the 26th got merged into a composite battalion, under the 3d Battalion, 27th Marines commander. And even with so many replacements coming in, those four battalions came up to only one battalion strength. Seventy-five percent out. You look for a familiar face, and most of what you see are replacements. You wonder about that bad-luck omen. What am I doing left standing?

There was a defining incident that happened in a lull up by the third airfield. It was part of this pariah thing. There were three of us, in a secure area. We were not on attack. We had our rifles slung on our shoulders. And the three of us were walking together, just chatting, when a shot rings out from an escarpment in front of us, and the guy in the middle goes down. The third guy hits the deck and fires into this Jap who's in the process of surrendering, and I surprised the hell out of myself, because here was the defining element. I went down to help the wounded guy. Completely exposed, you know, to the next shot. But that was the definition, *right there*, of what are you going to do after this is all over? I'm helping this guy that's down. Not long ago one of our residents fell out here in the lobby, and I happened to be nearby. I got down with him. Hey, what can I do, pal? And that defining element set me up into the teaching game, education. That's where I spent my career. I had gone from completely selfish acts to completely unselfish ones in a single rifle shot. Absolutely.

But somehow I got back into the line again, being led into the gorge by a major who was not with our unit. I was corralled into this thing. And now the old standard came back to save the day again. Somebody got up close to me and said, Here, take this message back to headquarters. So I was called out of there. I have no idea how that all came about, but I must have been spotted by one of those familiar faces and told to get the hell out.

I went directly from there to load up on a truck, to go down to the beach, because the 27th was now being withdrawn from all activity. Would you believe the old pariah thing still maintained itself? I'm already in the back of the truck, and a guy with a flamethrower —how he lasted through the whole thing as a flamethrower operator I don't know—but he puts his flamethrower up on the deck of the truck, puts one foot up on the step and I'm giving him a hand, and a shot ricochets out of the gorge and hits him in the leg. What the hell? While I'm helping the guy up? The guy laid down and cried. Broken leg and all that business.

But that defining element has guided my life ever since. There's no question about it. Every time I see somebody go down, every time there's an accident, I'm on it. And that tells me something about my own nature. I'm not gonna step away from it. Somebody's in trouble, I'm gonna help out. I just do not turn my back on it and say, What the hell, it's his fault. I could walk away from it, it's none of my damned business. But no, I'm in there providing the relief. When there's a need there, I'll be on it. And despite warnings, people who say you shouldn't do that, you'll get sued, you dumb bastard, I simply say, Sorry, it's part of me. It's been defined as part of me way back on Iwo Jima. Even in a condition where the next shot could have been at me, I still did it, I still helped that guy who got shot. It's a hell of a way to get a definition.

9

MOTOR TRANSPORT

Motor Transport carried ashore the heavier pieces of equipment—generators, radar machinery, medical equipment, anything a single Marine found too heavy to manhandle—in large trucks called six-bys. Once ashore, and once unloaded, their duty became to bring as far forward as possible any of the lighter supplies that the line units needed—ammo, grenades, mortar shells, food. And like combat Marines, men of Motor Transport shared many of the same risks.

PFC Samuel Girasuolo
Motor Transport, 8th Field Depot, 5th Amphibious Corps

We left Hawaii on board a Coast Guard LST. We didn't want to sleep below with all the diesel fumes, so we slept on deck where they had some Army Air Force radar gear with us. And we found out, being on guard duty in the hold, that there was some beer on pallets, Schlitz beer, all strapped in. So I came back and told all the guys, Hey, there's beer here. And they said, Beer? I said, Yeah, but it's warm, and they said, Let's get some! So we went down and stole some cans, took them up on the top deck and that's all you could see, just beer foam, because you know how warm beer is. And we threw the cans overboard and I swear the Japs could have followed us all through the Pacific just by the trail of beer cans. But then they found out about the missing beer, and instead of putting PFCs and privates on guard duty, they put corporals and sergeants on it. Of course, they started stealing the beer, getting everybody drunk, and so they put on sergeants and staff sergeants and master sergeants. Finally, they just put lieutenants on it, and we couldn't steal too much after that.

Some days later, we started hearing a lot of big guns from the battlewagons, shelling some island. And then in the morning you could just see the flashes off in the distance. And later, when the sun came up, you thought you were in the city with all these ships around, the LSTs, PAs, APAs, KAs, battlewagons, cruisers, one or two aircraft carriers.

We were going to go in on the second day, but somebody said we couldn't because the beaches were all congested with equipment. There was no real beach there, just this sulfur sand. I got in on the fourth day. The beaches were just so congested, there wasn't any place to go, and the radar we had would have been a hell of a target on land. And these big radar screens were all on big trucks with big tires, they couldn't get traction on the beaches. The tanks, all the heavy equipment was bogged down. They had bulldozers trying to pull equipment in, but even the bulldozers would get bogged down. You have to see the sulfur sand to know what I'm talking about. It's round, it doesn't bind together. Your foot goes right down, just like you're in popcorn.

Then they tried to get the 105s in, the big guns. When I got in the foxhole with a friend of mine, Raymond Bryzak, we were right alongside the airstrip, and we had these 105s shelling Mount Suribachi continuously. After a day or two of that, we got used to it, but not at first. We dug a foxhole, then filled sandbags and covered the hole over with ponchos, and at nighttime one of us would sleep and the other would stay awake, to keep guard with the rifle pointing towards the opening. And down near the beach, there was an ammunition dump that the Japs had infiltrated and blew up all the ammunition.* But we're up near the airfield and one night Ray came back from doing guard duty and said, Hey, Sam, I heard they're going to drop Jap paratroopers on us. What do you think we'll do? I said, We can't do nothing. There's men all around us, a foxhole here, one over there, one over there, all Marines, Seabees, too. I said, Shoot as many as you can, what else are you going to do? They didn't drop them, but it was a big thing. We feared it, but we didn't see it. It's a funny thing.

---

*Probably the 5th Marine Division ammo dump, which was struck by a Japanese incendiary shell at 2:15 A.M. on 28 February, D+9.

There were shells dropping and some holes would get hit. We found three guys that got hit, and we wrapped them all in burlap and took them down to the cemetery.

It was an awful sight. I'll never forget it, where these young kids were taken off the trucks and the burial group would take the fellow's dogtags and string one on the cross and the other they would keep for information. And the odor was terrible. They bury you by clearing an area out with bulldozers, make a long flat area, and lay them out side by side. But to see these young kids, it makes you sad, these eighteen-, nineteen-year-old kids.

It's a funny thing, but I don't think I was ever really scared. Except for the first day and first night, when we got on shore. Me and this kid, J. J. White, we slept under an amtrac that was knocked out, and we were scared. I don't know how we fell asleep. You hear all the fighting going on and you wonder, What the hell can you do? If a shell falls and it hits you, you're a goner, but if you think about it, you get more scared. But you kind of got frozen in that fact, what are you going to do? After a while, it just didn't bother me. And I'm not saying it because I'm something different, I remember only the first night.

We had a couple of snipers up around the airfield. There was this Jap that used to come out every day, and I'd hear the shots, and somebody said, Ah, that's Sniper Charlie up there, just let him shoot a few times, we'll get him. So I guess they must have laid for him, and one day he came out, and that was it. I didn't hear him no more.

We'd have to go down to the beach after they had a couple of roads open and passable after quite a few days. We'd have to go down and bring up supplies as far as we could to the people on the line. Ammunition, water, food, whatever. Motor transport did get the Navy Unit Citation for it. The Seabees got a citation for the same thing. The Seabees were a big help, they did a hell of a job. They used to make showers out of the sulfur beds. How they got the water out, I don't know. I never used it. I went down to the ship, got a five-gallon can of water and brought it back to the foxhole to give myself a sponge bath in the morning. On Iwo, there was very little vegetation, and the Japs had no water. They had to bring in their water from different islands, and I think it was getting to them. And the pounding from the bombs and the shells. So they'd go out at night and infiltrate, try to get something to eat. They were starving, and without water you can't live.

They brought in P-51s not long after they got the first airfield secured.* They were needed for escorting the B-29s to Tokyo and back. And about the twenty-fourth or twenty-fifth of March [actually 26 March], the Japs came up in formation early in the morning, about four or five o'clock, and everybody thought they were Marines. They were walking like Marines, and in the dark you can't tell. They were Japs pulling their last futile attempt. They got in where the Air Corps had their personnel, the pilots and mechanics, and they killed about thirty-eight or forty that belong to the P-51 group. They cut the tents and threw in hand grenades and shot anybody sleeping on cots. And our group was called in to drive them off. We killed as many as we could. There were about two hundred Japanese dead. No prisoners. And the next day, the island was officially secured.** It was just something we never expected, because we thought the island was pretty secure.

I got off on the eleventh of April. I had gotten hurt when I was driving a jeep back from someplace and I hit something and it flipped over. The thing was lying on me and I don't know how I crawled out. They took me down to the shore and took me on board an APA, and I spent the trip back to Hawaii in the sick bay.

I think the service time I did wasn't hard, not like the guys who were in the thick of things. We had some sniper fire, and of course there was that attack that one morning. But I didn't have it bad. You had a lot of heroes who threw themselves on hand grenades, take

*The first aircraft to use the captured airstrip were two light observation planes from VMO-4 based on the escort carrier *Wake Island,* on 26 February; sixteen more from that unit and VMO-5 arrived on 1 March. Advance elements of the VII Fighter Command arrived on 27 February, and twenty-eight Mustangs of the 47th Fighter Group arrived on 6 March. The first B-29, *Dinah Might,* landed on 4 March.

** The island was "officially" secured on 16 March, D+25; General Schmidt closed up the Fifth Amphibious Corps command post on the same day as the Japanese attack described above.

the explosive charge, to save their friends in the foxholes. You got twenty-seven Congressional Medals of Honor awarded in this battle, and you have to read some of the heroic things that these kids did to get that. Most of them is from throwing themselves on hand grenades to save you and me and our buddies in the foxhole. The first guy who sees that grenade would jump on it, or you would do it for me, and vice-versa. These were real heroic things that were done by young kids. We see kids today, seventeen, eighteen years old, and you say, Jesus, these are the kind of kids that help win a war. In our day, they were trained for it, and they became good warriors.

10

ARTILLERYMEN

Many Central Pacific campaigns consisted of assaults on small coral atolls, and once the Marines had landed and progressed a sufficient distance beyond the beaches, naval artillery fire became precarious and outright deadly to the Marines themselves. Amphibious doctrine applied by the Marines also dictated self-sufficiency. Consequently, an artillery regiment was indigenous to every infantry division, and they practiced assaults as frequently and as diligently as the infantry they supported.

Maj. Carl W. Hjerpe's battalion consisted of a mix of 75mm pack howitzers, which could be manhandled ashore, and the towed 105mm howitzers. Once in place, they rarely moved. In the following story, Major Hjerpe tells of his command experience on Iwo Jima and the peculiarities of artillery support.

Maj. Carl W. Hjerpe
CO, 2d Battalion, 13th Marines, 5th Marine Division

The auspicious job of commander of the 2d Battalion was awarded to me about two months before we left Hilo, in Hawaii, to go to Iwo Jima. We had a wonderful battalion commander who was a strict constructionist, a real by-the-book man who was never reticent to tell anybody what their shortcomings were. His name was Lt. Col. Ken Damke,* and the men in the outfit thought he was a real mountain of a man who ruled with an iron fist, and they thought the greatest thing that ever happened was when Carl Hjerpe became battalion

---

*Lt. Col. Kenyth A. Damke became XO, 13th Marines.

134

commander because they thought that life would be a little bit easier. And maybe it was, maybe it wasn't. But I had a great regard for Ken Damke, and a love for him to this day.

We left Saipan for Iwo Jima, and on the morning of February 19 it was the most beautiful day you could possible imagine. It was sunny, the sea was calm. Nobody really noticed because their minds were all on other things, of course. The night before I had had, as CO of this battalion, a visit from one of the underwater demolition people who had been ashore two days before. He indicated that the beach was sandy, but not too steep, and he thought that our DUKWs, into which we loaded our one-oh-five-millimeter artillery pieces, could drive up the beach and drive into position without any problem.

On the morning of the nineteenth, we were scheduled to get aboard a landing craft, an LCVP, and we were to go in with our thirty-one-man reconnaissance party, which included representatives from each of the three batteries, as well as our Bn-3 operations officer, our communications officer, and quite a few other people. We got aboard about seven o'clock in the morning, down the landing nets, and we started for shore, supposedly to join the thirteenth wave. The first wave would land at nine o'clock, and since they were scheduled for every five minutes, we figured around ten o'clock we would land. But there was a problem that developed aboard our boat in that some of the men developed a real severe case of diarrhea, so we had a number of them with their fannies hanging off the stern of the boat, idled to control themselves, and we gave that thing a little bit of time to defuse itself. George Moore, who was our operations officer, and I talked over the situation, talked to regiment on the radio, and finally we decided to just go in, so the net result was we actually went in on about the nineteenth wave. Which really didn't matter, because our job was a separate job which provided for us to go in, find our position, and then bring our guns in and set them up.

So we headed for the beach about ten o'clock. At about ten-thirty or so, we were there. I stood up at the gate, warning everybody to take it easy, go slow, so they wouldn't fall down, because the sea was pretty deep, and they had to wade though water that was up to their waists or maybe a little higher. Everybody got off the boat and up the beach safely except myself, and I went down on my face, so I got into the beach soaking wet.

We all highballed it for a point that was maybe two hundred feet inland, and we laid down there for a minute to catch our breath. I looked back at the sea, and I saw something that surprised the daylights out of me. As I looked, the boat that we had just come off of was trying to back off the beach, and it took a direct hit. It just seemed to blow all into smithereens. And a fellow who had been a member of my landing party and had been sitting at the stern of the boat told me later that when he saw that gate didn't go down properly, he slipped off the stern of the boat and almost drowned himself because he had a heavy fifty-pound pack, his rifle, and his ammunition belt, and fortunately, as we were all warned, his ammunition belt was left unhooked. He was down in the water quite deep, this stuff was all pulling him down, and he put his hands over his head and shed his rifle and all his gear. And as he came up, he saw the coxswain high in the air as the boat was blowing up.

I have some documentation of messages that were sent from me to our regimental commander that tell me more than I can remember, and the way it is formulated, it shows that I and our radio operator and our Bn-3 went up into our gun position, which was predetermined by our chart, and we couldn't really get to the position that was designated for our battalion. We were to support the 27th Marines, so rather than try to get to the designated position—which was in front of the existing front lines—we selected a place that was well to the rear to set up our guns, and everybody had to get busy and try to dig a command post in one of those great big sixteen-inch shell holes that were left there. We worked at this for a good three-quarters of an hour, and of course artillery shells began to fall all around us. Then I became concerned about the guns getting ashore, so I went back down the hill to the beach, and my memory is not too clear on this but I know I came across many, many wounded people and bodies between the position and the beach. Now the record shows that there were many messages between myself from the beach to regiment in an effort to decide which beach to land the battalion on. We had a choice of Red 1 or Red 2, and I had orders to select whichever one was best, depending upon the action. It looked as though Red Beach 1 was the best, so I called regiment and asked permission to land the battalion on Red Beach 1, which was granted, and issued the order. About half an hour later, I got a message from Fox Battery. "We're on Red Beach 2, awaiting instructions." So they were on the wrong beach.

Now, what happens from that point on is really vague in my mind, and I can only assume that I went back up to our gun position after contacting Fox Battery to be sure that they were going to make it up the hill okay, which they did. Although that could have been Dog Battery, I'm really not sure. So our first battery got up to the top of the hill and in position around two-thirty to three o'clock in the afternoon, and immediately we registered it through our fire direction center, and we were ready to fire and we notified regiment to that effect. Later, we had a little argument with the first battalion, because they claimed to be the first to shoot. What they did was set up a gun right away when they got on the beach and fired into Suribachi, and that gave them the title of the first to shoot. The last battery didn't get up there until two o'clock the next morning, because the beach was so jumbled up with massive problems of overturned LCVPs and stuck LSTs, the whole beach was just an absolute shambles.

At about two or three o'clock in the morning, there started a tremendous barrage of artillery right into our position. We had no idea where the shells were coming from, we didn't know whether they were artillery shells or mortar shells, but it was serious. It just happened to reach its peak just as I was out of the fire direction center, just looking around the area, just to see what was going on. I was looking up in the sky at the many, many flares released by the destroyers, which came down on little parachutes, all night long, to keep the area lighted up so we would know if there was any kind of a counterattack. When these shells started, I dove into the first open foxhole I could find, and shivered there for a long time with my radio operator. And after a while, Colonel Damke, the rough old Marine, came by my foxhole and almost stepped on my radio operator, who was lying on top of me. We jumped out of our hole then, and somebody beneath me said, "Thank you, Major." That was one of our Marine gunners, and there was somebody under him. It was funny, looking back on it, but it was absolutely frightening at the time.

The next morning, everybody was up at the crack of dawn. We were now all up in our positions, available and ready to fire any missions which came through either our forward observers or from our own regimental headquarters.

We stayed in this position for four days, and then on D+5 we had to move forward. Now, being in the artillery, we did not experience the problems of the infantry. We really had a much better life on Iwo Jima than most people, either the tanks, or transportation, or anybody, because we were put into a position, and that's where we stayed. On D+5 we moved up into our originally designated position. That day, we rebuilt a great big shellhole that was about a thousand yards ahead of our first position. We were out in the boondocks scrounging around, and we found some streetcar rails, of all things, which we could use for cover over our fire direction center. We had a lot of sandbags, which we loaded up and we built a real secure fortress, almost, a wonderful little fire direction center about fifteen by fifteen square. We had about three feet of earth on top of those rails, and outside we had a gasoline-driven air-conditioning unit which fed conditioned air down into our little center, and we had a blackout entrance so we could come and go as we wished.

About this time, we had a forward observer named Lt. Arvid Carlson. He was being reassigned from his battery to the front lines as a forward observer to relieve one of the fellows who was to be replaced, and we were standing and talking when he received a stray bullet from Suribachi that killed him. He just dropped down to the ground between George Moore and myself, right there at the top of the hill. He was the only officer that we lost in the entire operation. We were the battalion with the fewest casualties, and we don't know why that was. It just happened that way, I guess. Our casualties were about 11 percent, which was nothing like the 60 and 70 percent that the infantry regiments had.

We had all of our forward observers assigned to the various battalions of the 27th Marines, up in the front lines, moving right along with them, and our wire teams had regularly extended our lines to our own telephones, which were in the hands of our forward observers. We also had a small plane attached, which flew overhead, and a fellow by the name of Miller was the pilot for our plane, and we had an FO from our battalion in that plane. He told us that when he looked down on the island he could see where the front lines were, because there were thousands of people moving around all over the surface of the ground behind our lines, and in front he never ever saw a living human being. All the Japanese were holed up in their caves and tunnels all over the entire island.

About the sixth or seventh day, a shell struck the ammunition dump for the 5th Division, which was just ahead of our position, maybe five hundred yards. This happened in the middle of the night.* An incendiary shell from the Japanese hit the dump and it began to explode, and ammunition of all kinds ignited and was firing off in all directions, like Fourth of July fireworks. Our Marine bulldozers came over to shovel sand on to the fire, and it took maybe four or five hours to get the fire out. It was really a very exciting time.

In our outfit, we fired about eighty thousand rounds of ammunition while we were on the island. We were there for twenty-eight days, and as time went on, the days began to run together. After about D+15 or so, it really seemed, to the artillery people, no longer that exciting. And about that time, the first plane casualty landed on Iwo Jima [*Dinah Might,* on 4 March, D+13]. It was a great big Superfortress, and it landed right up on the Number 1 airstrip, which was right beside us. I went running up there to see what it was all about, to greet this guy. There was an airman who stuck his head out the open door of the plane and he said, "Boy, you guys should have been over Tokyo with us last night, was it hot!" And one of our people said to him, "You should have been here, buddy."

*Actually the tenth day, D+9, at 2:15 A.M.

Still, there was a lot of work to do up forward. We got a call to our battalion saying that we should send 10 percent of our enlisted personnel into the front lines because the casualties were so high. That was probably the worst job we had to do the entire time we were there. We had to designate who was going to go. So each section of ten men had to send one man per unit into the front lines. We sent probably forty-five people to the infantry units. Of that, there were three or four killed and ten or twelve wounded. I've talked to several of those men since then, and to a man they've told me that had they not had the privilege of boot camp, they would not have lived in the front lines. The Japs were firing at them from hidden positions all the time, they would emerge just enough so they could see to fire a shot, then they would duck back in again, whereas all of our people were out in the open.

The most extraordinary part of our stay on the island was the landing and getting the battalion into position to fire, and then the first five days until we moved into our big, beautiful, secure fire direction center. And we got to a point of about D+24 or 25 that the artillery was no longer of any use to the infantry because the island at the north end was a series of valleys and hills. The valleys were maybe fifty yards wide and the hills were fifty feet high, and in order for the artillery to do any good at all they had to drop high, arching rounds into the valleys. The range was so short that we just couldn't be of service. The weapons that we had were not suitable for that type of terrain. The only weapons that could get into those areas where the Japs had dug in were the flamethrowers. Our rounds would just hit the tops of the rocky outcroppings and bounce off. We were packed up and moved off to the water, and on the twenty-eighth day we boarded ship.

The greatest thing then was to be able to take a shower. And everybody felt that the Navy lived like kings, because they had showers. Also we had the most wonderful food. But we knew that we were going right back to the same camp that we had just left and settle back into our routine and everybody was anxious to hear from home about what they thought about the whole Iwo operation. We ourselves were tremendously relieved about the operation because we had no idea what we were getting into when we went out there. And then to find that we had a security that nobody else had. We had to go out into the field occasionally, but our outfit just didn't seem to get the casualties.

I couldn't possibly say enough about our manpower in the 2d Battalion. Although we didn't have a lot of casualties, we were right in the same fire that everybody else was, and for the first ten days or so, everybody was in the same jeopardy. It was just fortunate that we in the artillery didn't have to go up into the caves and dig out people piecemeal.

Pvt. Anthony Pastorello, in contrast to Major Hjerpe, tells of his experience as an enlisted member of an artillery crew.

Pvt. Anthony Pastorello
Loader, Mike Battery, 4th Battalion, 14th Marines, 4th Marine Division

Glory, yeah, the Marines were it, so I tried to get in 'em. Eh, it was all right. I mean, the Marshall Islands was a cinch. You just got in there with the guns, laid down there and waited. Then we went to Saipan and Tinian, it was a different story. We got shot back at.

We got back to Maui, it was all the same thing. Come back in, get ready for Iwo. We didn't hear much about it until we got on board ship. Then they started explaining it was built like a pork chop, different places. We sort of looked it over and said, makes sense.

The waiting was never good. You look in that DUKW and say, jeez. There wasn't very much above the water, you know? They got the one-oh-fives sitting in the DUKW, and I could just imagine going out, and going down. It did happen, I don't know who. Somebody went and just sunk.

From there on, we traveled in circles, through the ships, the battlewagons, the LSTs. And then they said go in, and we went in. It's not a nice feeling. You can imagine what you're thinking about. Is this my last one, or is there gonna be more? And those DUKWs, I was afraid with that gun sitting in the back. It's gonna go in and down. So you take your shoes off and everything, in case you have to swim. But when we hit, it was just dirt, sand. Like one guy says, they must have taken all the sand from around the world and dumped it on that island. You sink in about a foot deep. There, we got the hell knocked out of us.

From there on, we got our guns and set them up and started firing. You open 'em up, you got two trails and you sink 'em in the ground. You dig your two holes here, your two holes there, so your gun will sit in there. Then they line them up with the aiming stakes, set up the telephones, and then they start yakkin' away until we got lined up on our sights, and that was it. You got a loader, that was me, a guy setting the sights, you got a guy on the elevation, and you got two men to set the shells for timed fire or direct fire. Then they'd call out the kind of fire, they'd set it and give it to you. Boy, I'll tell ya, sometimes they get stuck in there and you gotta get out front. I could imagine that damned thing going off. We all had turns at it, but nothing ever happened. Most of the trouble was picking up those damned shells and carrying them up to the gun. But we were young, we did it. You did it or else you get your ass blown off.

We didn't travel too much on Iwo. We just swung the gun around and that was it. I just felt sorry for those infantry boys, they got the hell pounded out of them. Imagine going across an airfield, you got Mount Suribachi looking down, how the hell could they miss? No cover on an airfield.

You got to know your buddies pretty good. We all got along, no hesitation. New Yorkers, you know how New Yorkers are. We had a couple from the South. No fights, no nothin'. Argued, yeah. We all argued.

Getting off Iwo Jima, we hollered for joy. I think at that time, the Army came in, to take over. And we CSMOed, "close station march order," put the trails together, get your gun ready, hitch on to the truck, hop on, and go home. That's what we were waiting for.

So that's my big story. I'm happy, I'm home. I wouldn't want to go through it all over again, I'll tell ya that.

Communication from front-line troops to the artillery batteries was handled through a forward observer (FO). Most fire missions were called in by telephone over a wire strung from the battery communications center to the front lines—an antiquated method by today's standards, especially when the exposed wires were cut constantly by both enemy and friendly fire. In that event, missions could be called in by radio. With the technology in those days, most radios functioned best by line of sight, and radios with their power packs were heavy, ponderous pieces of equipment, apt to malfunction when wet or abused under combat conditions. The best option was simply to repair the wire.

Of all the duties of artillerymen, FO duty was the most dangerous.

PFC Robert W. Stewart
*Forward Observer, 4th and 5th Signal Battalion,
14th Marines, 4th Marine Division*

I was in the fourth wave. I was a little more apprehensive on this landing, because it was my fourth campaign. The first one, we didn't know what to expect, but we made it. The second one, we said, Well, the odds are a little smaller, but we made it. And then, when the third one came, everyone knew that there were no odds. But if you made that, and you got to the fourth one, you were on the minus side. The odds were stacked against you, you were really pushing it.

We were moving into position, trying to set up communication lines. But every time you'd get a line in, something would blow it out, and you'd either have to go up and repair it, or go up on radio, use radios instead of wire. We had guns set up, but we had lost a couple coming in. Two of the landing boats that had one-fifty-five howitzers got hit bad enough to sink, and the guns were lost. And the Japanese were shelling not only the beach, but the water surrounding the beaches.

I got called for FO duty, on the radio and telephone. When you're in an FO team, and they call for a mission—artillery, mortar, makes no difference—you feel that you're part of it, and you're doing something that's an absolute necessity. And when you're not calling for a mission, you're wondering, Did we do the last one right? Or did we do it wrong, and they're not going to use us anymore? The only thing you could think of was to be absolutely correct. When the officer calling the mission told you the shell, the powder charge, the direction, the elevation, whatever, you had to be absolutely correct, you had to repeat verbatim what he said. When you sent that message back to the guys with the GFT, they had to have precise numbers. If there was an error, the shell could land on you, or your own men. And we sure as hell called it close to our own men.

The calling-up part wasn't too bad. You'd get into a hole where you were going to be, you stayed there for so many hours, then you were relieved and you went back. I think the scary part was having to think about going back up the second time. The Japs were making so many direct hits on positions, and they had so many fortifications that there was no way you could get yourself into a position where you weren't within range of some kind of weapon. Hand weapon, shoulder weapon, artillery, mortar, it made no difference. And the Japanese had a mortar, and you know the story about everything but the kitchen sink. Well, this thing turned out to be the kitchen sink. It was huge. You could see it coming, but they couldn't control it. If it hit anything, it was on the other side of Suribachi. It seemed like it might sink that end of the island. I once saw a shell, a mortar shell, that landed on the edge of a foxhole. There were two guys in it that I recall. Stays in my mind. I tried to find out who they were, but I never found out.

I spent my time repairing lines, running messages, trying to keep down. I pulled a couple of lanyards just to make sure I got my hand in a little bit. One night they expected a heavy charge by the Japs, and all of us were sent forward to shore up the lines, reinforce what we had there, but nothing ever happened. There was sniper fire coming from pillboxes and bunkers, but no banzai charge.

We never got into mopping up the island. We had a lot of cleaning up to do for our equipment. All our communication lines had to be pulled in. Most of them were rolled up. Our phones, radios, things like that were all prepared to bring back to Hawaii. And there was a great feeling of, I don't know, accomplishment or relief. I guess it was more relief, because we were boarding ship to go back to Hawaii, and yet there are all these men left there, and so many who have left on hospital ships. It goes through your mind, even though we were all young men.

The FO's calls for fire missions went to a communications center in the Head-quarters and Service (H&S) battery of an artillery battalion. PFC Edwin P. Des Rosiers, who had already participated in three Central Pacific campaigns, ran the center for the 1st Battalion of the 14th Marines.

PFC Edwin P. Des Rosiers
H&S Battalion, 1st Battalion, 14th Marines, 4th Division

The Marines trained me as a switchboard operator. In field artillery, each battery has four guns. There are forward observers that are out with the infantry, and these observers need communication. You have radio, and you have telephone. If you're out there a mile, which was not hard to do, you'd have reels of wire that you ran out for field telephones. You turn the crank on the telephone, and it came back to a switchboard. When my phone rang, whatever they wanted, I connected them. Later I got to be known by my code name, "Fire-works Red."

We lived and trained on Maui, did amphibious landings there. We went out in the big fields where they used to keep the cattle and shoot our 75mm guns. And I can tell you, with our proficiency, you give us three rounds, three miles away, and we could kill a cow. Which we weren't supposed to do, because the government had to pay for them, but we'd get them by accident on purpose, okay? We had a good time with that.

Before we left Maui for Iwo, we went down to the harbor on a work party and we'd load the whole hold of our LST with clover-leaves. That's how our shells were packaged, three shells to a clover-leaf. We put about five feet of them in the bottom of the LST, and then put planks over them and drove the amphibious tractors in over them, and the tractors were loaded with our guns and whatever sup-plies you needed. If we had ever been hit on the way out, there would have been no need to look for anything because there were thousands and thousands of rounds in there. We had a submarine scare when we went by Eniwetok, shooting torpedoes at us, and there were destroyers all around, but nothing ever happened to us.

Now, this was my fourth invasion, and they brought out the map and said, This is what you're going to do, and I thought it couldn't be any worse than Tinian. No worse than Saipan. It was frightening, but, you know, in wartime you have a job to do, and the psychology and philosophy are different during wartime. There's something that's in you, so that no matter how bad it is, you just do it, okay? And we had done the Marshalls in a couple of days, Saipan in a month, Tinian took ten days, and these were comparatively big islands. So when they told us Iwo was only eight square miles, we said what the hell is that?

We were about three miles out on the day we landed on Iwo. Hundreds of ships were there, maybe thousands, I don't know. They're bombing it like crazy, and of course they stopped when we started going in. I was on the LST in an amphibious tractor with our gun and equipment when the big door came down on the LST, and away we go, but just then a huge wave swamped our tractor and it sank. We've got lifebelts on, and they pull us out of the water, we get back in another tractor, and away we go again. The seas were very rough on the day of the landing, it made it that much harder.

That was probably the first time we really got frightened about the landing at Iwo. Let me tell you, for the couple miles you had going in there, it was like raindrops, there were shells and bullets and stuff coming from the gooks. I never thought once that I was going to get killed. It's a funny thing, you always think it's going to be the other guy. It never bothered me.

I was on the fourth wave. They were going to let us just come right in, and then they were really going to give us the business, but even by the time we got in the shore was pretty well cluttered already. And we were wasted there, because there was nothing you could do. You got in twenty feet and there were terraces, and you couldn't move. You just ducked down and stayed there. The first day, nobody gained anything. We were right with the infantry, there was nothing you could do. But the next day we gradually got a little ground.

Like all war, it gets all messed up, you know, the wrong things are coming in, there's just no way to be perfect. The thing that got me the most was, it must have been the end of the second day, and they're bringing in Seabees to repair the airfield above us up on the left. I said, Boy, this is crazy, you couldn't bring in one vehicle on that sand. They had to bring in metal tracks, otherwise you bog right down. And some of these Seabees, they had never been in battle before, and at that time I had set up my switchboard in this concrete bunker that had been bombed but not completely destroyed. I dug a big hole in there, and when the Seabees came in, they didn't know what the hell to do. So this old fellow—he was about forty and I was only twenty-two so I called him old—I took him into my hole. He was a painter's mate from Chicago, going to work on the field. The next day I had to go out and lay wire, and I came back that night and there's the fellow in my hole. He had to go to the john, and he was too frightened to go out, so he did it in my hole. I said, You broke the sanctity of my house and I chased him out. I have never forgotten that. That guy must have died from fright that night.

At night we had shells coming around us all the time. They had great big things, huge things, and they'd blow up over you, they'd be flying all over. I remember one time, we had just gotten our jeep ashore, and this was several days later, because earlier jeeps just weren't any good there. I was standing next to this fellow named Libby. We were just standing and talking and all of a sudden, this great big piece of metal comes and takes Libby's head right off. And I began to think, maybe I have some special power, you know, being saved when these other guys are gone, and Libby's head is there, and the rest of him is over there. And these things happened a lot. These are lasting things, when you're standing face to face with a guy and he loses his head on you, you know.

The firing never stopped. There might be a couple of hours where you didn't have any, and maybe it was planned, maybe they wanted you to fall asleep a little, and they'd start in again, just to keep you going all night. Just as we did to them, you know, that's all a part of the battle.

When I wasn't on the switchboard, there was someone who

relieved me. Somebody was doing the job all the time, except when you didn't have any wires out, so of course you didn't need a switchboard. We didn't use it on Iwo for quite a while, so I carried ammo, I did this, I did that, whatever had to be done. And I'm a worker, I'm always hyper, it's in my nature, so I had to do something. We used to carry some of the wounded down. You always pitched in where you could. No matter what it was, we still had to carry ammunition. We didn't have seventeen thousand rounds to begin with, it had to be picked up at the beach and carried up. I was told later that we had fired seventeen thousand rounds on Iwo, okay? And I can tell you that the guns sometimes got so hot, we used to take our T-shirts off, or whatever clothes we had, and go down to the ocean and wet them and put them through the barrel, just to cool it off so it wouldn't warp.

We had pack howitzers that could be assembled and carried anywhere. And on this little congested island, you were limited, and this was the first battle where the mountain was just one tunnel after another. We'd set up camouflage nets over the guns and over the ammunition, so the gooks couldn't see where you were located, but they must have known everything.

We were attached to the 25th Marines, and if you look at the battle maps, we didn't advance any. We couldn't, because we had the Quarry, Turkey Knob, the Amphitheater, those were ahead of us. Those were bad points, okay? It took the 25th weeks to get them, so we were right there, fixed with the 25th. And we just kept firing at those things. So even when the battle ended, we were still fixed in one spot, with the range of our guns. We knew they were finally getting past Turkey Knob and such because we had communications, we knew what was going on. We were firing right up till the last day. The island got safer, you know, you could walk around after about the twenty-fifth day and feel like it's got to come to an end. You'd just hoped it would have been sooner than it was. But even after the island was secured, there were still Japs coming out, there were still killings, trouble going on.

You know, war is a different humor. You laugh at something that if it happened here today, you wouldn't laugh at it. We had a fellow from West Virginia named Smokey Stover. He had married a girl who was in the Army before he went across with us, and she used to write him about every two or three weeks, whenever we got mail. She would always enclose a pubic hair in her letter. Old Smokey used to save it. He had this little jar, like a baby food jar, full of these things. He'd been collecting these hairs for years. And when a letter came, we'd all go over and see Smokey's letter.

I think I was there thirty-one days, and they came up and said you're going to leave. And then they brought us out in landing craft to the APAs, and we packed up and left. And what was touching going back, we always had some wounded with us, and when one of them would die, they would bury them at sea. That was very impressive, touching, anyway. They'd have them all wrapped up, there were clergymen there, they slid them down a plank and hold a little service for them. Most APAs had somebody who would die en route.

I wouldn't sell my experience for a million dollars, but neither would I want to do it again. At that time, age twenty-two, it didn't mean anything. I did my job. Fear was not part of the act. But today, knowing what you know, you wouldn't want to do it again. That's the place for young people.

Not all artillery missions were called in by FOs. Light observation planes called some missions, and others, such as those from Cpl. Carmine Abate, were a result of the new technology of DODAR Ranging.

Cpl. Carmine Abate
DODAR Sound Ranger, HQ Battalion, 14th Marines, 4th Marine Division

When you use DODAR, things are different. DODAR means *detec*tion *of direction, azimuth and range.* Duke University had invented these machines that could detect objects through the use of instruments and three sets of two microphones. First you had to survey where you would put the microphones on the ground, find out that coordinate. Then you plot that point on your map, until you had three points. Then you installed the microphones by running two wires from each machine to each microphone, for a total of six wires. When a gun went off—and you always knew where your own lines were so you wouldn't be firing on your own people—and the microphones picked up that sound, they would send it back to the DODAR machine, and you'd get a plus reading, or a further plus reading. Obviously the one farthest would give a bigger angle still. And where those three lines crossed is where the sound theoretically emanated from. And if they didn't cross exactly at the same spot on the map overlay, then you had to triangulate. You drew a line from the midpoint of the longest side to the opposite angle, then found the midpoint of that line. Theoretically, that was the origin of the sound. Sometimes the triangles were very small, so you were really right on. Sometimes the triangle was a little larger, it might be dispersed fire, maybe there was more than one, you know. But they were *there*. And my job was to translate the readings to an azimuth on the map. And when I got that cross, I called artillery and said, Give me one gun, seventy-five, on target area 248 Charlie, fire one round. No sooner than you said it, "Boom!" The round was going. You flicked the machine switch, the machine went back to zero, so that when the round landed, now you plotted that round. I could plot that easily with a slide rule. Wind conditions and so forth, take that all into consideration. And then, depending upon where a round landed, I would say left fifty, or one hundred, meaning yards, fire for effect, because I knew they would be on. Then they'd fire a battery of four guns. And if we didn't hear that sound again, you knew that we got it.

I think I stayed in bed until the first morning we landed. Or that they landed, because we didn't land the first day. We landed on D+2, because there was no room. They hadn't gone any place. They hadn't even made it up to Motoyama Number 2, the second airfield.

We had radios aboard ship and you could hear them ashore, saying what they needed, bring some more ammunition, get these guys off the beach, all this business. You listened to it like it was a radio show. And we all huddled around, listening to what was happening on shore, just waiting to go in. You were kind of anxious to go in and get going. Finally, they told us we were going in, the morning of D+2. We weren't far offshore, you could see boats getting blown out of the water, it was a mess. You could see the shore itself, that's how close we were. Battleships were firing their big sixteen-inch guns, you wouldn't believe the amount of fire they laid on that island. You could see the Marine Air Corps, Navy, Army Air Corps going overhead, strafing the beach, diving right into Mount Suribachi. You could see them, right where we were aboard ship. You'd swear they were going to crash.

Riding in to the beach that day was a funny experience. None of us had been in combat. Didn't have a clue of what it was going to be like. Your heart picked up the pace a little bit, now that you'd heard the radio, you'd heard the action going on. We went in on DUKWs, vehicles that went on water and land. So when we hit the beach, we went up these steel ramps the stevedores had made, steel mesh, so you wouldn't sink into the ash and sand on those terraces. The first thing I remember is seeing my first dead Marine. He was still laying out there, they hadn't had the chance to do a cemetery. There were dead guys on the shore, lined up and covered with ponchos. There was just no room. So we went up maybe thirty yards off the water, and mortar shells started to rain down. We were sitting right on top, there was no hiding, no trees, nothing. There was no cover. Your DUKW was standing right up there like a tank, you know. They pasted us for what seemed like an hour, but it was probably only thirty seconds, thirty-five seconds. I almost didn't realize what they were doing until somebody yelled, "Hit the deck," and we all jumped out of the DUKW. I jumped into a hole that was a bomb crater, me and a kid named Dick Harris. I could feel my heart pounding. I thought to myself, Boy, they're not fooling around here, these are real shells. And now you start to think, This is the *first* day? Oh, Jesus, what are we in for? But pretty soon they called all clear, and ten or fifteen yards away there was a pillbox. Some of our guys had gone in to check it out, and about four Japs ran out and about fifty guys shot them. I don't think they got more than three yards from that pillbox. And all this happened within five, maybe ten minutes, from the time I landed.

From there, we made our headquarters. We had to fill sandbags to shore up where we were going to put these DODAR machines because we knew we were going to stay there, at least for a little while, before we moved up. No place to move anyway. We were right with the infantry, the artillery was right next to us. We started to survey our points on the ground, started to get information, set up for work. That night, we were operating, we were firing.

The first day was a rainy day. I'll never forget it. It rained and drizzled, cold and drizzled, you had that black sand that stuck to you, it stunk of sulfur. And you really didn't notice it too much because you were concerned with staying alive, doing your job. But that first night, you didn't know what to expect. We didn't know what the extent of their aerial bombing would be, whether they had enough planes to bomb us. They did come over, but our flyers were so superior, they knocked them all out. So from the air they didn't hit us at all. What got us was the ground fire, the cannons, the artillery. But otherwise, the first night we were busy setting up and we didn't think too much of it. We expected a counterattack, you know, they always counterattacked at night, so we took turns outside watching, but nothing happened. Every night, though, they fired on us with their artillery. That's when we did most of our business as sound rangers. And a lot of them came close. It wasn't that accurate. They didn't have an exact spot. It was called harassing fire. There was a 240mm gun they used which wasn't that accurate, they launched the shells more than anything else. There were a couple of nights where they must have had some object near our headquarters that they were aiming at that came pretty close to our CP, to the point where part of our sandbags started to fall down outside. Some of the planks and sandbags we put across the top broke through. It landed close enough to have a shudder. Two of our guys were in a foxhole near our CP, because you couldn't put twenty-one in the CP. You just put in the operators. They got up the next morning and the guys, Caranikus and Callahan, looked around their foxhole and there was a shell, a dud, that had landed right in their foxhole. Talk about two scared rabbits, they wouldn't move out of there. Later on we laughed at this incident, but it wasn't funny at the time. If that dud had gone off, we could have lost some of our sound rangers, including those of us in the CP.

The biggest problem we had was keeping the microphones from being destroyed by the Jap artillery, and the wires being cut. I spent several nights outside being the third azimuth. You used an aiming circle that's measured in mils, not degrees. I'd look through it and I'd see where the flash came from and I'd plot that.

One time, during the day, I saw this guy walking, and he looked like an Asian. The Japs used to sneak in and steal water. They didn't want ammo, they needed water. I'm on the other side of this humongous bomb crater, surveying my point, and he's looking at me, I'm looking at him, and I don't know to this day if he was a Jap or an Asian-American serving in our outfit. But I said, Hey, leave well enough alone. He shoots at me, he's fair game. But as long as he's not shooting, not making a problem, I'll let him go.

But compared to the infantry, to the real fighting, ours was not a very perilous task. Just the fact that you were there was perilous, but not like being an infantryman. I give them a lot of credit. I don't know how they withstood it. Unbelievable.

The one situation that meant the most to me was this one time when we were getting this harassing fire from the 240mm cannon that was located around Turkey Knob. We were trying to find it for two or three days, and not having any success. We couldn't understand it, and we were starting to doubt the accuracy of our machines, whether we were doing it right, making a mistake. But after checking it out, everything seemed to be okay. So I said to the lieutenant, there's something wrong here, they're doing something when we're ready to fire that we just can't figure out. I said maybe the way to do it would be to send some timed shells over the area. Not so much to knock out the gun, but to knock out the personnel. That way they couldn't move the gun. And after that, if we fired some smoke, those that are still alive will get confused, and then fire HE, which is a point-detonating shell. We could do this from our seventy-fives, and I put the one-oh-fives on them, too. We fired the first shells by time, but in rapid succession. First timed shell, then smoke, then HE, so everything rained down on them at one time. And the next day, the reconnaissance plane, this little Piper Cub, went up and took pictures, and I didn't get to see the lieutenant until later on and I said,

Lieutenant, how did we do? Did we get that sonofabitch? He smiled this big, broad smile and said, Yeah, we got him, Carmine. What happened was they had it on rails and they were pulling it back into a cave after it fired. I don't know which shell got them, but they were all laying out there, and the gun was torn apart. And I was pleased because the system worked. That was the biggest contribution I made, getting that sucker. Because we were so crowded, nearly every square foot was taken, so no matter where one of these bombs came from, it had to hurt somebody.

After a while, everything just flowed into the others. If you succeeded, that's it, you were moving up. Every day at four o'clock I got a call from headquarters which would tell me where our lines were, when they ceased attacking, or when they withdrew, whatever, so that I wouldn't fire into our lines. And I liked that because at night, even when we didn't have targets or didn't hear the shelling, we knew that they were out there. I would fire rounds where I thought they should go, on my own. I figured, hey, whether I hit them or not, at least the guys in the infantry know there's somebody firing back, instead of them just firing at us. I said, Christ, we got more ammunition than we know what to do with. They piled the ammunition up in back of the guns like cordwood. So I said, Let's use it. What were they going to do, use it when the operation's over? Let's use it now. And they would not dispute it. When I asked headquarters for a gun for a target, they didn't say, You sure? They just did it. Which was good. So I felt a measure of satisfaction, because it didn't do the Japs any good.

We knew the end of the battle was coming when we started getting less fire from the enemy. They had a defensive perimeter line that bisected the island almost in half, where they had their main artillery counterfire. Once we got past Hill 382, then it seemed like it broke their back. There was still a lot of casualties, but it wasn't the intensity of before. I don't remember how we came to get off the island. They just came around, said it was time to go, the 4th Division was leaving. I remember the mood was quiet. Nobody was bragging too much, you were just glad to get out of there. It was still kind of messy around the beach area, they were still taking off dead bodies. There was no jubilation. Everybody was just glad to get the f—— out of here. When we got back to Maui, they gave us a five-day furlough to Oahu, Pearl Harbor. I think we spent the five days in a room, drinking.

11

REGIMENTAL WEAPONS

Not all the big guns were located in the artillery and tanks. Each regiment had an integral weapons company which consisted of 75mm guns on halftracks, and towed 37mm. Originally intended for an antitank role, the nature of the fighting in the Pacific required a change in tactics. Regimental weapons now provided antipersonnel support or antistrongpoint fire.

Cpl. Raymond J. Mik
Gunner, 37mm Antitank Gun, Regimental Weapons Company, 23d Marines, 4th Marine Division

The war happened to come along, and I didn't want to be drafted into the Army, and I wanted to be a Marine, so I enlisted on June 8, 1942. I am always asked why Marines act the way they do, and I say that in boot camp they put you in a tent with a corpsman and a DI. You are told to drop your trousers and bend over a table while a specially qualified Marine Corps physician, armed with a hypodermic syringe about the size of a bicycle pump and fitted with a needle six inches long, injects a substance known as "The United States Marine Corps Serum" into your keester. This needle is then broken off at the flesh line, and thus you are and act like a Marine forever.

We trained at Tent City at Jacksonville, North Carolina, for a while, then we went up the road a-ways where we stayed with a tank company, way up the road, in an area all our own. We first started off with a type of 37mm gun that was mounted on a two-ton truck, which was mostly for fast maneuvers. In combat we would be right up there with the tank and rifle companies. We were supposed to hit tanks and then disappear. The idea was to camouflage ourselves in the woods, hit the tanks, then mount up and get out of there in a hurry. Later on, they came out with the 37mm antitank guns which were pulled by a jeep or a two-ton truck. Once we got into combat, of course, that never happened that way. We had to push those things by hand. You couldn't use jeeps in combat, especially at Iwo. I preferred the 37s, the towed ones, because you weren't exposed that much. You could take the 37 and camouflage it in the woods, take branches and put them around it. The other things were more of a job to camouflage. And, of course, we got involved with the rifle companies, training with them. We found out in combat that they really didn't want us around because we always drew mortar and artillery fire. But at night, on the line, they appreciated us for our buckshot shells.

There were four platoons of 37s in the regimental weapons, and four 75 half-tracks, and there was one platoon and one half-track assigned to each battalion, with one in reserve, and we were called upon to do whatever we had to do. And we had machine guns, .50- and .30-caliber machine guns, along with the 37. I happened to be a gunner. My job was to make sure those guys were in my sights.

We didn't actually see Iwo Jima until the early morning of landing day. We were told to have our breakfast of steak and eggs, and we went topside and saw the island, shaped like an ant hill. Then we got into our amtracs, but I don't believe we had our 37mm guns with us at the time. I think they followed in another boat.

Riding in was a terrible experience. You're out there early in the morning, the smell of diesel is everywhere. Now, when a bus goes by, I still get sick from it, it turns my stomach over. But we circle out there for a couple of hours like all the guys did, then we got the word to form up and go in in the third wave. When we hit the beach, things were wild. Boats were starting to pile up, and the ashes were up to your knees. It was very difficult to move around. I happened to come ashore with a Seabee, an advance man for the Seabees, and he said to me, What do I do? And I said, Well, you can follow me, if you want to do that. So he stayed with me, and when we hit the beach, I said, Let's go, it's too hot here, and when I shook him, he was dead. I saw no blood on the man but he was dead. He must have had a heart attack. But he was about forty-three years old at the time, he was considered old.

I moved away from the beach and moved over the terrace to a crater. And for some reason, the shells just kept going over me and around me, but nothing went in the crater. And I heard later that after our wave, the fourth wave, they didn't let anybody land because the beach was a mess.

I met up with some of the fellows, some of the men who would be killed later. Fellow by the name of Sam Beam, he had the top of his head shot off by a piece of shrapnel. A fellow named Charles Journey who was supposed to be discharged because he was the only son left in the family. So we reorganized around in that area, and John Benkovich, my platoon leader, who I thought the world of, got us all organized, and we found our weapons, although I lost a fifth of booze. Every squad had a fifth of booze and we lost ours at the beach, and I don't know who the hell found it.

That night we dug in at the point of the airfield and waited for a banzai charge that never happened, but that night it rained. And I kept looking back at the ships and saying, Boy, you guys are lucky out there, clean sack, great chow. And all night long, we had the star shells going up, and the next morning we started our push. We pushed that 37 all across the island by hand. We pushed those guns up the hills, where some of the riflemen used to help us, and we had a certain job to do, fire into a cave, a pillbox, whatever. And then we'd dig in at night with the buckshot shells, just in case there was a banzai charge. That was pretty much the pattern throughout the whole island. Fire by day, dig in at night, hope that there wouldn't be much of a banzai charge. You hardly ever saw any Japs, they were all dug in. Simply day-to-day, by operation, move along working with the rifle companies, and we managed to go right across the island.

There were several fellows who had combat nerves, nervous breakdowns. The ones who cried and got it out of their systems were great, but the ones who stared off into space, those were the ones who gave you a lot of trouble. At night, if that happened in the line, you had to be sure that they got off the ones who were screaming. I never reached that point, but I was probably close to losing it.

I do remember the last night we were there, slightly. The yelling, the screaming, the burning flesh, and it was so pitch dark then, it was a real nightmare. And somehow we lost our weapons again, I don't know how. And the next morning we got the word to go down the hill. We went to the cemetery first, like most of the fellows did, to pay our respects to the dead. After that, we went directly aboard ship, and we were glad to get aboard and look at the island, that stinking place, and say, "I made it."

12

PHOTOGRAPHER

The camera is war's backstage pass. If you carried a camera in World War II, you could just about go anywhere, anytime, during a campaign. In the rear areas or base camps and training depots, restrictions still applied. But at the front, matters were far different.

Some photographers, like Sgt. William Genaust, the Marine movie cameraman who accompanied Company E of the 2d Battalion, 28th Marines, to the top of Mount Suribachi, spent a great deal of time in the lines under enemy fire. Genaust himself was killed on 4 March, shot to death inside the mouth of a cave, and his body was entombed when a demolitions team blew the opening to seal in the defenders.

Cpl. Arthur Kiely did not see as much direct action but, like Genaust, he had orders to record all he saw of the battle.

Cpl. Arthur J. Kiely Jr.
Headquarters, Fleet Marine Force (photographer attached to the staff of Lt. Gen. Holland M. Smith)

I was transferred to Headquarters Division of the Fifth Amphibious Corps, and being a photographer they put me into the Public Relations Department. From there I started shooting pictures of any Marine activities that came along. One of them was when the combat photographers and correspondents were being shipped back from Kwajalein Island in the Marshalls. They were in a rough state. They were getting off the ship, and I posed a picture of them. It was quite a picture. Well-known fellows, artists, writers. That was my first assignment.

160

In the meantime, Lt. Gen. Holland M. Smith needed a photographer, and the first few times I went along it was great. He got used to me. He always insisted that I take his pictures for him, you know, his activities with the other Marine groups. When we went to Saipan, I was still with him. Aboard ship, a command ship. It wasn't a troop ship, so I was fortunate there. I was with General Smith all through Saipan, and then we went back to Hawaii, where I was still doing public relations activities. We were in a Quonset hut, where we had our facilities, and we used to go back and forth between Camp Catlin and Pearl Harbor, which was about five miles away. Our Quonset hut was right in the middle of Pearl Harbor, the Marine Barracks area.

That was the latter part of '44. In the beginning of February, the Commanding General's Office put out a directive with a list of names of who was going to go with him to Iwo. My name was on it. From the general all the way down to Corporal Kiely. They told us when to report and all that, on the directive. I still have it.

Now I was aboard another command ship, the *Eldorado*. It had beautiful facilities for photographic work. I was in with a lot of Navy photographers, plenty of equipment, and I worked with them. I slept in the darkroom rather than the sleeping quarters. There was plenty of room in it. We played cards to pass the time, and there was a lot of stuff coming in from the air reconnaissance that was photographing Iwo, before the landing. It was aerial film, we used to process that. I didn't have to, but I just chipped in because the guys were pretty busy. Then, at times, General Smith and his staff would come down and read the maps underneath a lightbox. There's a word for that. Photo interpretation? I didn't know it.

Forrestal, the secretary of the Navy, flew to Eniwetok and we picked him up there. He got pretty chummy with me. He was quite an aficionado of the medicine ball. He used to go on deck and throw it around with part of his staff, and the Marine staff, too.

When we were approaching Iwo, you really couldn't see anything until the morning of D-day. All you could see before was ships, there wasn't any land. But on D-day, there was the island right in front of you. You could hardly see it because of the dust and smoke from the bombing. General Smith was on deck, watching. He practically lived on deck. I didn't hear any comments then, any conversation. But I know he made a comment the night before we hit Iwo Jima. He was walking up and down the deck and he told Admiral Turner,* who was command of the operation as far as the Navy was concerned, that there were going to be a lot of dead Marines tomorrow. But that's all I heard.

On the twenty-third of February, I went in with General Smith, Secretary Forrestal, and Joe Rosenthal, the guy who photographed the famous flag-raising picture. The first flag had already gone up while we were going in, about 10:30 in the morning. And I remember Joe Rosenthal was jumping from one little landing craft to another and he dropped his helmet in the water. I'll never forget that. And when we landed General Smith and his staff and the secretary of the Navy took off in one direction, and General Smith's aide and myself took off in another, to get involved more into the island.

I took a lot of photos. We were walking in areas where there was hardly any action, but you could hear it all around you. You'd be walking along and see dead Japs, dead Marines. I was never scared, not really scared, until the shells hit near you, because I was doing something you had to do. You didn't think about being scared. I didn't, anyway.

General Smith wanted me to take a lot of photos of terrain, and I'd come across a lot of places like the Quarry, just nothing but broken-up stones and rocks. Be hard to get through that stuff, being an infantryman. I took pictures of terrain with dead Marines spread out on it. I took photos of all the commanders, General Erskine, General Schmidt, General Rockey, General Cates, all those fellows. Erskine was probably my favorite, because he gave me hell once on Saipan when he was General Smith's chief of staff. During the bombing, they had killed a carabao in the backyard of his headquarters. It was hot, and I was stripped down to my skivvie shorts, and I was shoveling, trying to bury that carabao. And Erskine asked me what

*Vice Adm. Richmond Kelly Turner, Joint Expeditionary Force Commander at Iwo Jima.

kind of outfit I was in. I said, Marines, sir. He said, Well, you get dressed like a Marine! And there I was in my skivvie shorts. I'll never forget that. But he recognized me on Iwo. He said, Hi, Kiely, what are you doing here?

Once I came back to the *Eldorado,* I processed the pictures, gave an eight-by-ten to the general and a print to Art Kiely, of course. Which is the reason I have this huge album today of the pictures I took in the Pacific. I left Iwo around March 20, I don't remember the exact date. But I didn't go back by ship. I flew to Guam, picked up Admiral Nimitz's personal plane, and flew back to Pearl Harbor.

I was sure proud to be a Marine. I was sure proud to be on Iwo. Most of the operations in World War II are forgotten now, but Iwo is not. It's one of the only things that people keep referring to, even involving Europe. You hear about the Battle of the Bulge, things like that, but Iwo Jima you see on license plates, bumper stickers, things like that. It's still alive today, in our history.

Two 4th Division Marines help a third to an aid station.
Arthur J. Kiely Jr.

Gen. Holland Smith uses a penknife to pick at the firing tube of a
Japanese spigot mortar. *Arthur J. Kiely Jr.*

Equipment piled up on Beach Red 2. *Arthur J. Kiely Jr.*

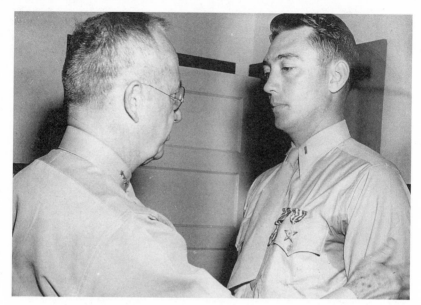

Gen. Holland Smith awarding the Silver Star to Lt. Harold Schrier, leader of the patrol that raised the first flag atop Mount Suribachi; photo was taken in Hawaii after the end of the Iwo Jima campaign. *Arthur J. Kiely Jr.*

Secretary of the Navy James V. Forrestal tosses the medicine ball around with members of his staff aboard the *Eldorado*. *Arthur J. Kiely Jr.*

5th Divison Marines gather before a Japanese emplacement. Marine sitting at right is believed to be Ira Hayes. *Arthur J. Kiely Jr.*

Destroyed DUKW in the 4th Division sector. *Arthur J. Kiely Jr.*

Marines in the 4th Division sector await orders to move into the front line. *Arthur J. Kiely Jr.*

LSMs pass to the south of Mount Suribachi on D-day, 19 February 1945. *Arthur J. Kiely Jr.*

Aboard the *Eldorado,* Gen. Holland M. Smith listens to incoming radio reports of the landing's progress. *Arthur J. Kiely Jr.*

Aboard the *Eldorado* prior to the battle, Gen. Holland M. Smith explains the battle plan for the invasion of Iwo Jima to a group of war correspondents. *Arthur J. Kiely Jr.*

Seamen load .50-caliber machine-gun rounds into cloth belts before the battle. *Arthur J. Kiely Jr.*

APAs follow in line en route to Iwo Jima. *Arthur J. Kiely Jr.*

A wounded Marine is carried up a gangway from a Higgins boat by Navy personnel. *Arthur J. Kiely Jr.*

13

COMMUNICATIONS

Signal Companies linked the Headquarters Battalion of a regimental command to its subordinates. Their main function was to make sure commands and communications were disseminated and received accurately.

The Marines discovered earlier in the war that the one code the Japanese could not break was really not a code at all—the language of the Navajos. These Native Americans trained together and developed a metaphoric code, using Navajo words and phrases, to communicate commands to each other. A phrase could be as simple as "The bear has returned to his cave," meaning that a commander has gone back to his command post. To Japanese ears, spoken in Navajo, the words were gibberish.

Most Navajo code talkers were like PFC Thomas H. Begay, simple men with basic education. Their skills and accomplishments have earned them places of high honor in Marine Corps legend.

PFC Thomas H. Begay, Navajo Code Talker
Signal Company, Headquarters Battalion, 27th Marines, 5th Marine Division

I became Marine because I was unable to work, to get employment during the summer. I went to Federal Munition Depot near Flagstaff, Arizona, and I ask this guy for a job. He look at me and say, You too young, you not old enough to work. Kind of teed me off, then I told him, I show you, I old enough to go to war and fight. Now, Marine Corps, they fighters. They had some kind of prestige. They dignified, you know. There's something about Marine. You see newsreel, they say Marine have landed, this kind of thing. There was already a whole bunch of Navajos, they come home, wear Marine uniform. And the music, "Marine Corps Hymn," that's another thing. It sound so good. And then the uniform is different. The Army, they got uniform like horse blanket.

So I enlist in Marine Corps in September 1943 to be aerial gunner. The Marine recruiter say, Yeah, you small enough, you fit in one of those bubbles, whatever, shoot down Japanese plane. So I join, and he didn't say anything about Navajo code talker. Didn't use those words. Didn't come around, say, Need Navajo for code talkers, there was no such thing then. So I went and had about three physical before they accept me. I had physical in Albuquerque, New Mexico, I had physical over in Santa Fe, then another physical where they have big gymnasium. There was lots of men. What they do is you come in there, you strip to nothing, all you had is little bag for your wallet. You wander around in circle to check station. Everybody was naked, walking around, and the men they check in all the holes, and then they tell me they let me know. Then a few days later the recruiter say, Hey, you leaving. So he put me on the train, in Gallup, New Mexico. He gave me some kind of tickets, meal tickets. I found out later it was government transportation request, about fifty years later I find out what it was. I was in line to eat somewhere between Barstow, California, and Los Angeles, and they were checking every person in the line. I showed this coupon, he say, Hey, you volunteer, you go first, let these 4Fs wait. But he didn't say I could sleep, you know, in sleeping berth. Here I set up all night, all way to Los Angeles, and then this guy say to me next morning, How come you didn't sleep in your berth? I say, What's that? Bed, he say, don't you know what that is? I say, No. So that's the first experience I don't know how to travel. That my first time on train. You see, I from traditional Navajo family, never have contact with all these outside. I rode pickups, buses, things like that. I went to boarding school. That was the best thing to do. If you live out in the remote area, you work seven days a week, thirty days a month, 365 days a year. Going to school you had the free meal, nice bed, you work for it, but it was the best so I rather be in school than herding sheep or something. But in Marine Corps I found out you could ride a train.

Then I graduated with the platoon. I got PFC stripe. So I was ready for aerial gunner school. But I got orders to report to Camp Pendleton. Signal company, radio school. I say, I sign up for aerial gunner, they say, You just take orders.

Here I show up in Camp Pendleton, there whole bunch of Navajos, going to Code School. Those people that went overseas, they have one barracks that got nothing but Navajo code talkers. I happen to know one guy, he got back from Guadalcanal, PFC Wilson H. Price, the only one I knew. The rest, I don't know them.

They start with climbing poles, stringing telephone wire. They teach us this is telephone wire, this is real telephone, this is switchboard, this is radio TBX, this is TBY. They show us semaphore, panels you put on ground for airplane, all that stuff. Then they introduce me to Navajo code talking, so we have to memorize a lot of this code. At then end of the day, they pick up all the notes. They say, You don't take no homework home, and we don't release nothing, no information on Navajo code. They say, You do, we going to court-martial you, if you ever give up information to the enemy, there's spies all over. That's what they told me.

Finish training, it depends on individual progression. I finish in no time. Then I was assigned to 5th Marine Division. They activated around November or December of 1943. Signal Company, Radio Platoon, Headquarters Battalion. They small unit. They gave us the task of developing a code book. Three of us. The first Navajo code talkers, they develop 234 codes. Vocabulary, all the phrase military. All they did is put some words on the board, they told us to develop it. We develop additional 274, so there was 508 that we had to memorize, so we develop handbook for Navajo code talkers assigned to 5th Marine Division. We have at least three code talkers to a regiment, one or two to a battalion. It depends on what kind of assignment they get. If they have to go in, they usually assign one or two code talkers to a battalion, to go with the landing. The reserve, they usually have one or two.

They told us that being a code talker, we can't make mistakes. Has to be perfect. Because if we make a mistake, say the wrong word, could kill a lot of our men. Never be in doubt, make a person spell out the word you need. So we had to work on that, plus learn all the codes.

We had thirty-three code talkers assigned to that division. We make sure we update, make sure we all know what to do, and field training, march, go out in field, set up radio—most of time we're field training. Maybe a little recreation on Saturday and Sunday, but depends. Maybe pull guard, something like that. We have no exception. We do same thing as anybody else, like other Marines.

One day we get orders to load up. We been loading up, unloading, loading. I think we maybe spend seven months altogether on ship. You know, go out, then go land, go Maui, come back. It happen to be that I was always on General Rockey's ship, so we always pull into Pearl Harbor and get liberty from eight to five. No overnight. So we were lucky, radio platoon. We always with the general's ship. Then one day we head out to sea. Waterproof everything, ready for action. They didn't tell us until couple days out they tell us where we going. First we went to Marshall Islands, then from there we went to Marianas, which was Guam. We went by Saipan. They were still fighting. We saw some of the people jumping off the cliffs. Suicide Cliff. We just watched them from the ship. Then we went out one day, head towards Japan. Everybody say we going to hit Tokyo. Some say Kyushu, some say Yokohama. All scuttlebutt. About a few days out of Saipan they tell us we going to hit Iwo Jima. They brought out the map, show where Green Beach, Red Beach 1, Red Beach 2, I don't know the others from 4th Marine Division. Then we get telephone, we practice messages. Other times on transport we clean our weapons, we write letters, always try to maintain radio silence. They always use only blinker. You don't throw cigarette overboard, they say submarine will follow you and torpedo your ship. At night we have blackout. Whole bunch of ships. They got transport, destroyer, you name it, we had all kinds of ships. Then finally on the eighteenth, they say tomorrow we land at Iwo Jima. The nineteenth, they wake us up at two o'clock in the morning. They told us we have the last breakfast. They gave us steak and eggs. It make you feel funny when they tell you that. They weren't bashful about it. Then we all pack our bags, poncho, gas masks, everything's ready. Radio equipment, we make sure it's working and waterproof. But on D-day we had to test them. Top deck and lower deck, we had to test those radios. If it didn't work, we had a radio repairman. Sergeant Rose was his name. Then we test, have radio network set up. Sergeant Manuelito and I set up the first radio network on frequency. All the other code talkers in Higgins boats out there. They check radio while going around in circle. And then, while we were setting up, there's a shell came over. Dong, dong, went across and over, hit like this. Dong, dong, hit the deck, like ricochet. We heard it explode. For some reason it didn't explode in front of us. If it hit straight, we would have been gone. We look and say, What the hell was that?

There was no unnecessary transmission, but we always say something besides test the radio. Where we at and all that. Anglo don't understand, but we communicate where we are, you know, location, in Navajo, while we test radio. But there's always somebody monitoring, he say, Hey, no unnecessary transmission. We say, Testing, testing, I'm so-and-so. We work around the clock.

On D-day, we never seen such a thing. All this dust, smoke, the Navy were bombarding this place. I figure they kill all the Japs. Whatever live on that island was gone. They have planes strafing, they were bombing, there was smoke, I mean the dust was so high. Sometimes you couldn't see it. We figure they all killed off, we just going to land, walk on the beach, set up communication with the ship. That's not what happen after they start landing. That damn place like blew up.

We landed on Beach Red 2 in afternoon on D-day, but when we got there, you don't know what it was. It's the scariest damn thing you ever saw. I got numb, all numb all over my body. No feeling, I was scared as hell, I mean scared. Even though I'm walking, I feel like I'm standing in one place. And that place was like wrecking yard. They had things blown to pieces, it's like traffic jam. There only certain way you go in. There was piles of bodies, and wounded ones, that beach was littered with you name it. The sand was knee-deep, and you had your radio and your rifle and your pack, and we had to dig foxholes and set up radio network. The first thing I do is protect myself from getting shot in foxhole. There's already people digging holes, so you jump from hole to hole to get up to the company CP. It was the scariest damn thing. I grow up that day. I age about two years right on that beach, got my Ph.D. about war.

When we set up, we send messages all over. I think we sent close to eight hundred in the first forty-eight hours. I went to 27th Marines a couple of days after landing. They short of people. One day they had me in outpost to guard for our CP. That's a scary son of a gun, because you don't move at night. If you did, they kill you. We out there between unknown and the CP. You can't stand up to take a crap. You just dig down deeper in your foxhole, go there, then cover it up. Guy who lay other way do same thing. You lie in your own crap. Only move around daylight. They told us to shoot anything that moves, so we have passwords. And every two hours, we trade off, go to sleep. We don't talk. If you say something, they throw hand grenade at you.

When we were up here at the airfield, they raise the flag on Suribachi. We watched it. The first one. And everybody was so happy, you know. And we had a radio network, we know what's going on. It felt so good, we say, We won. I mean it wasn't even over yet, but hey, we won. Them Japs, we kill them all. And this is where there were three Japs came out in middle of our CP. They just jump out of foxhole, start running for these rocks north of Iwo Jima, small rocks above seawater, then we got them to put their hands up. I guess they said ships is coming, they going back to Tokyo, what Nisei interpreter say, you know, Army guy. They took them to this prison somewhere. I understand they have one Navajo guy from 5th Marine Division in there. He wasn't a code talker. They capture him somewhere, and they thought he was a Jap, wearing a Marine uniform. His name was Jim Benally. One of the code talkers, he go over there and say, "Ha-dish-nah-na," and Benally says he's from Crown Point, in Navajo. He was with stretcher bearers.

There was all these ridges up along the coast, kind of like hills, rocks. There were a lot of holes yet, some place the Japs come out. Of course, the other guys usually get them. I was kind of in-between the front lines and the rear. In fact I come back to get supplies one day, stop at my signal company, get hot meal one time only. Usually I was always with the colonel, a full bird colonel, regimental commander, Colonel Wornham [Col. Thomas A. Wornham, CO, 27th Marines, 5th Marine Division]. And there was all kinds of craters, all Japanese bodies. You can smell them, even fresh killed. They smell sort of like fish, mix with rice. It was their food, I think, make them smell that way.

I got off the island on the northwest side. I say, Oh, this is it, you're going home. We all real happy, boy. And one of the big LCMs, the ramp comes down, we just walk on there. And then they took us out to the bigger ship. Just two code talkers walk off there, Milton M. Gishal and I. The others I never saw again. Paul Kinlacheeny was killed, Jimmie Gleason was wounded. I never saw him again until 1953, he died some time later. Milton M. Gishal is still around, lives at Jeddito, Arizona.

So that was our job, as code talkers, to maintain radio and telephone communications. Communication was very important to any kind of battle, they tell us that. Can't make no mistakes. Our messages never been decoded. Navajos make supreme sacrifice. They left their home, volunteer, a lot of them, to do the job.

PFC William Doran was a radio operator with the 25th Marines, serving in the lines under fire with the 2d Battalion. He had seen other campaigns and knew the experience of combat intimately, especially since radiomen, with their transmission packs and antennas, made obvious targets. Doran considers himself very lucky.

PFC William C. Doran
Communications, 2d Battalion, 25th Marines, 4th Division

The reason I joined the Marine Corps was due to the fact that my uncle was in World War I, and his training was going up to the front in France, and they threw him in a hole and made him a machine gunner. And he says, That's where I learned how to shoot a machine gun. So he says, If you're going to go into the service, go in the Marines. At least you'll know how to shoot.

I went to Camp Lejeune for communications school, and at the end of it, I bumped into Johnny Croce. Johnny was a radioman. We started out together in the 4th Division. We were with the 20th Marines, combat engineers, went through three battles together, Roi-Namur, Saipan, and Tinian, and after we finished them, we were called down and given new orders. Well, I was sent to the 25th Marines, and Johnny was sent to the artillery. So Johnny says, You give 'em hell, Bill, I'll be right behind ya. I'm getting ahead of myself, but when we got into Iwo, on the third day, I'm up in the front lines and we got tied into a hand-grenade battle, throwin' grenades back and forth. I jumped into a hole, and who's in there but Johnny Croce. I said, Johnny, what the hell are you doin' here? He said, I'm a forward observer for the artillery. I said, Give 'em hell, kid, I'm right behind ya. The next day, we had some naval gun-fire that landed on our front lines, and Johnny was hit, but fortunately he was just wounded. Johnny is still alive today.

I had to get my own .45, which I got because my mother had written President Roosevelt, saying I wanted a .45. I was not an officer, so I was not allowed to have a .45, but because of doing the work that I did, running the telephone lines, the carbine you had over your shoulder usually fell off when you were bending down, and you were picking it up and throwing it back on your shoulder. You didn't want to tie it on, because you were over the front lines, you might have to use it. So I wanted a .45. She was able to get per-mission from the government to buy a gun at Colt's factory in Hart-ford. The police took it apart and sent it to me, and that's what I had. And on the ship to Iwo I was dum-dumming my .45s. This lieutenant came up and tapped me on the shoulder and said, Son, you're not supposed to dum-dum a .45, that's against the Geneva Convention. I said, Hey, lieutenant, I don't know if you've ever been in combat or not, but after this, if we both get out, we'll have a little discussion about the Geneva Convention and what's right and what's wrong in a war. Well, we never had that discussion.

This always bothered me, because of the fact that you're dealing with a group of men that were never trained to kill, that were all young kids who went in to the service and got trained to kill, to do your job. And there seems to be a difference on how you kill people. Like he was saying about a dum-dum. I've seen people get hit with flamethrowers and I thought that if there was a choice I'd rather get hit with a dum-dum .45 than a flamethrower. You also have the thought that here you are, it's a man-to-man situation, sometimes a woman-to-man. Sometimes the women had hand grenades under their armpits and they'd offer you a baby, and you'd take the baby and they'd raise their hands and blow you or your comrades up. War is not a pleasant thing. There are certain people who have the idea that it's like going to a dinner party or going to a prize fight. The only problem is, when you make a mistake in combat, it could be your last mistake. You don't get a second chance like you do in life. In combat, you'd better be right, and be right all the time.

When we were on the ship going to Iwo, topside, about two or three o'clock in the morning before the landing, and we were talking to a group of three guys. The three knew they were going to get killed. We were up there trying to talk to them, Hey, don't feel like that, don't think like this. Well, within fifteen, twenty minutes after we hit the beach, the three were killed. It's a feeling I've never had. I don't know if I could have gone over the side, having the feeling as strong as these fellows were. It's a scary feeling. You're scared, there's no question about that.

You have to remember that going into a battle like this, you have veterans, and you have new men. You're trying to calm down the new men because they don't know what they're going into, and in the same token, you *have* to talk, because you know what you're going into, you've been there before, and you're trying to get that out, that you're going to be okay, too. A lot of the time, talking is the best thing in the world. It relieves the tension, helps you to relax a little if you can.

Of course, we knew where we were going. They showed you all the maps, the details, and you're getting the constant reports that this is knocked out, that is wiped out, this isn't gonna bother you.

You get your steak and eggs, your battle breakfast. Then you go over the side, start heading in. You got real keyed up, because you could see what was happening, you could see all the gunfire between all the battleships and the cruisers, and all the rockets going in. You know what's coming because you've been there before, you know exactly what you're going into. You want to get out of the boat because I've seen too many get blown up in the water, you want to get on land because you think you're gonna be safe, but you know darned well that once you hit that land, you're gonna be in just as much trouble. It's just the idea, get out of that water, hit that beach. Then once you hit the beach, you got the problem that you know they're gonna try to force you off. They tried to knock us off the beach before we even got our footing. Our colonel was hit, our chaplain was hit, our officers were getting killed. There was no place to go. They were shooting down on us from Mount Suribachi, they had the cliffs on the right-hand side, shooting down on us. But we made our way up.

Our job mainly was to get to the airstrips as fast as possible. Of course, you had to go up this incline from the beach, which was all this black sand, you couldn't get hardly any footing, you're in up over your ankles trying to run up this stuff, and you knew that once you got up to the top, then you had that airstrip that's straight across, and there's no protection there. We tried to get the airstrips within the first twenty-four hours, but of course they pinned us down on that beach and shot us up left and right and you didn't know where to go, you just keep pressing as far as you can. And at the same time, you're trying to dig in as much as you can, but go forward as much as you can. You got artillery coming in on you, you got mortars coming in, they got machine-gun fire, it's just madness, that's all it is. You're just trying to stay alive and go forward.

The Japs, they were good fighters, they had good equipment. We beat them mainly because we overpowered them. They had some terrific sights. When we got up in the hills and took their guns, their artillery pieces could almost pick out a button on a man's pants down on the beach. It was just hand-to-hand, you just had to fight for everything you got. They didn't give up easy. But you still did what you had to do. I don't know what makes you do this. We Americans, we fight because we have to. We were fighting the Japanese, they were different. When they got killed, they'd take as many as they could. We were fighting to kill, but we were trying to fight to stay alive. There's a big difference when you're fighting somebody with that type of a background, where they'll die for the emperor, as they were doing. They were good fighters. They fought hard.

Going into these situations, God knows why I was protected. I went through four invasions, and I had no idea how I was saved from all this. I never got wounded. I've jumped into foxholes and had men on both sides of me get killed, and I come out. I've been with fellows when we go out to run a wire, and we go to the right three times and we'd be all right. The next time, we'd go to the right, and the guy that went to the left where I had just been, he got killed. It's a horrible thing to see. I've seen men burnt. I had to go look at ten guys who were burnt from the top of the head down to the toes and all they are is one great big chunk of blackness. You couldn't even pick out your own father or mother.

A perfect example of how you got no control over what's going to happen, was there was a pillbox at the base of this cliff, a great big concrete pillbox with an opening at one end. We decided we'd set up our communications team in there. We set up our switchboards, we had a radioman in there. There was a little hole, about seven or eight inches, in the top of this pillbox. The whole thing was covered with rice, in bags. We just stayed there and laid there and got our sleep when we could, when we got relief from doing a patrol or running our wire. We tied in with a new group to our place, and we moved on up to the top of the hill. As we got up there, a mortar went right into that little hole and killed all the guys who were in there where we had been for three solid days. Under that rice was Japanese ammo and it just blew that pillbox to kingdom come. So here we were for three days, laying on top of this thing, thinking we were perfectly safe, nothing can happen as long as we're inside, and these guys were only there for fifteen minutes, and that was it.

Same thing when you'd go up to the front, and then go back for supplies. Our officer would try to get fellows who were starting to crack, who'd had too much, and let them go back and get supplies, get away from the front action. You went back by this mortar platoon, guys who were part of our outfit, and they'd have hot coffee there where we had only K-rations and chocolate bits, and you'd sit there and have coffee with them, then take off. For some unknown reason, on this day when we were having a lot of action in our particular sector, and these mortarmen asked us to have coffee, we said, No, we'll take a rain check. We walked by and a shell went in and blew this whole mortar platoon to kingdom come. The only thing we found was a wrist, maybe five by six.

You just . . . I don't know. Why? Why did these things happen? Why did this fellow get killed, and you didn't? This fellow gets wounded, and you don't? There's no rhyme or reason for it, just count your blessings. We've had guys you considered brave, and they'd crack under the strain. Then there was a guy you'd think wouldn't be able to take it, and then he'd have all kinds of guts, unbelievable in combat.

Our greatest fear, for us, anyway, was going out at night, because the Japs would cut our lines, and we'd have to go out and repair them to keep the circle in communication. And sometimes, coming back in, you'd get shot at by your own men, because the replacements coming up at night wouldn't call out the password, they'd just shoot first. We had a lot of exchanges, nice words, because you're gonna throw grenades at your own men. That's just the way it was.

Then there were other times. We had this fellow, Joe Ucha, from Massachusetts, who was the supply sergeant, and Joe had some Japanese flags. We were up at the front, during the day, and it got to the point with some of these snipers where it was almost ridiculous. A guy would shoot at you, but if he didn't hit anybody, you left him alone. You figured, Forget this guy, because if you get rid of him, they'll probably send some guy who's a good shot, and he'll get ya. Well, we were situated where there was this little walk, and we were on one side, and Joe was on the other. The Army had started coming in with their airplanes, and all of a sudden we look up and we see this fellow with no equipment and Army gear on, but no helmet, no rifle, no pack, no nothin'. So one of the guys says, Hey, buddy, what are you doing up here? Oh, he says, I'm looking for some souvenirs. I said, Do you know where you are? He says, Yeah, why? Well, Jesus, the Japs are right here! Oh, he says, they're not mad at us Army guys, they're only mad at you Gyrenes. We couldn't believe this guy, so we said, Hey Joe! Do you have a Japanese flag? Yeah, I do. Well, would you give it to this guy? He says, Sure. So we say, Run over there to see Joe. The minute this guy gets going, the Jap lets loose with about four shots, and *boom,* this guy goes barreling down, back to the airstrip. Never saw him after that.

And then we had this fellow, Franny, and he went through four operations, and after a while you start getting dizzy, I suppose. He says, I think I've had it, I had four of these things, I don't think I wanna go back and train to hit Japan, because we knew that eventually that's what we'd have to do. So we were in a hole and he props his foot up in the air, braced on a rifle, and leaves it up there all night. Japs couldn't even hit his foot. The next day he says, I must have been out of my mind, leaving my foot up there all night. You had funny things like that where you sit back later and say, This is crazy, you know.

It's hard to figure out why a man can go out and do some of these things, and yet be criticized for being a killer, because you're in this type of situation. Yet when a guy's in an airplane, dropping bombs and killing women and children, they're considered heroes. It's a different ballgame. I can never understand that. You see a lot of funny things, and then you wonder how you can be so cruel to each other, and the injustice that people do. You become like an animal. The things that you do, you'd never think of doing here. You're trying to stay alive, and then in the same token you'd go out of your way to help a friend, knowing that you probably would get killed. But you still did it, and not with the idea you were gonna get killed. I did what I did, and I never thought I was gonna get killed.

I wouldn't want anybody to go through and see what I saw. You know, you can read about it, you can hear about it, you can see it in the movies, see it on TV, but you don't know what a punch in the mouth is until you get one. I wouldn't take a million dollars to go through it again. And then we had a lot of good times with the guys, and then you have that comradeship of combat that nobody understands unless you went through it. But it did a lot for me. Made me learn fast, made me grow up, made me appreciate life more so than when I went in. I've enjoyed every single day of my life since I got out of the Marine Corps. I feel very blessed that I lived. I just get up every morning and try to do the best I can.

14

AMPHIBIAN TRACTORS

After the First World War, farsighted Marine officers such as Gen. John A. Lejeune and Lt. Col. Earl "Pete" Ellis realized that any future war would probably pit the United States Navy against Japan in an island campaign in the Pacific. Hoping to avoid anything like the disastrous British landing at Gallipoli, subsequent planners saw the need to develop armored troop transport designs that could carry Marines to do battle with an enemy who would no doubt be defending heavily fortified beaches. Standard Navy motor launches in use for decades were unworkable, so another method had to be developed.

Fortunately, Donald Roebling, the grandson of the builder of the Brooklyn Bridge, designed a tracked amphibious vehicle to use in rescue operations in swamps such as the Everglades, which had been devastated by a hurricane in the early 1930s. After several refinements in the vehicle's flotation, speed, and mobility, Life magazine printed an article about Roebling's invention in 1937. This article came to the attention of Gen. Louis Rittle, then Commander of the Fleet Marine Force, and he passed it on to others like himself who were interested in developing an alternative troop transport. The Navy initially turned down purchasing a test vehicle due to a lack of funds, but the Marine Corps was undaunted and convinced Roebling to design an armored vehicle for military use. Thus the prototype "Alligator" was born.

As the Second World War drew closer, the design was refined and more money was allocated for defense and finally, in 1941, two hundred vehicles designated LVT-1 "Alligator" were delivered to the Marines for training. Many of these vehicles saw action at Guadalcanal, primarily in a supply transport role, but the armored amphibious design was refined and ultimately proved its worth at Tarawa. There, the LVTs, armed with one .50-caliber and two .30-caliber machine guns, could climb over the reef barrier approaching the landing beaches and deposit their troops at the critical points. Troops carried in the Higgins boats—a craft that will be addressed in the next story—had to disembark at the reef barrier and then wade through one thousand yards of bullet-swept surf. Casualties among those men were tremendous.

From that point on, the LVT became the assault landing vehicle of choice for the Marines. The LVT's ability to support the Marines with firepower and supply capabilities once ashore made it valuable beyond its assault capacity, and two more years of experiences at amphibious landings brought other refinements to the LVTs. Gunnery Sgt. Daniel Benwell benefited from those experiences, having already participated in landings in the central Solomons and at Guam. Iwo Jima would be his last campaign.

Gunnery Sgt. Daniel Benwell Sr.
Company C, 3d Amphibian Tractor Battalion

We had secured the island of Guam and now we were preparing for the next campaign, maybe Iwo. That's where we got most of the amtracs called the Buffalo.* We had some Buffalos on Guam, and trained new troops, replacements that we get after each campaign. I was always with Company C of the 3d Amphibious Tractor Battalion, attached to the 3d Division, from the States right on through Samoa, Bougainville, Emaru, and Guam, and then we were attached to the 5th Division for Iwo. I was the maintenance chief and had charge of the headquarters platoon. This meant getting the company combat-ready, teaching the drivers and the mechanics who weren't familiar with the amtracs on how to operate and maintain them. Actually, you might say, I determined what the policy was going to be concerning the maintenance of the amtracs and keeping them in operating condition. All this training happened both on land and sea, of course, the same kind of training as for any other campaign. Now, on Iwo, we didn't have the coral. All our training was mostly the same, you know, preparing for the unexpected on our landings. We would rendezvous, get in a line of departure, and

---

*The LVT-2 was the original "Buffalo," but LVT-3s and -4s had the same moniker. The LVT-4, with its rear ramp, was used most frequently for amphibious troop transport at Iwo Jima.

then go in. There would be a commander with a flag and a radio-man in a small boat. When he would lower the flag, that meant we would form a skirmish line and head in. Each amtrac had a driver and a radio operator, and there would probably be ten tractors in a skirmish line. All our combat training for Iwo happened around Guam when we were attached to the 3d Division, but a lot of us had already seen combat, that's an experience learned nowhere else.

On the LSTs to Iwo we sat around, played cards, shot the bull, and checked the equipment to pass the time. We didn't know for sure we were going to Iwo. I guess, maybe after we got on board, traveled a few days—well, the scuttlebutt was we were going to Iwo because we were told it was going to be a three-day campaign, they expected to secure it in three days. So that's what we prepared for, took provisions for, clothing, what have you, for three days, and you know now how long it lasted. But from the Navy shelling and the Marine Air Corps bombing we knew long before we'd arrived. It was the most I'd ever experienced, preparing the island for us to land. For days before we landed you could see it, it was like lightning in a heavy thundershower, the whole sky was just lit up. Right up until we actually landed, they were bombing and shelling Iwo.

And this one island, they really put it on. In fact, right up until the minute we landed, Marine Corsairs would actually be flying right over us, strafing and bombing the beaches, flying up and down as we were coming in, and then all of a sudden, right as we hit the beaches, all the strafing and bombing and shelling stopped. And everybody keeps their heads down coming in, except for the driver, of course, who's looking through the periscope. Our job was to keep the amtracs running and lay down covering fire, so normally I would ride with the first wave going in. And I had a maintenance tractor, which would come in with the last wave, but it was our responsibility to keep things organized as far as the amtracs were concerned. If we stayed back on the ship with the maintenance tractor, and we had a problem with the equipment, say in the very first wave an amtrac conked out or something, well, we had to be there, to keep things running.

It's hard to describe what it's like going in on a landing, being in combat. It's not a game, but yet it's similar to one, only deadly. It's like you're in competition with these people on shore who have prepared for years for our landing—it's difficult to explain. But now is when all that previous combat experience comes in handy. You know there's going to be lives lost, you know, hey, you can lose your own. You know they'd been shelling this island for I don't know how long, maybe over a month, and you really didn't expect to see that much, because you felt that with all this bombing, with all the shelling that went on, compared to all the other islands, that this would be just a walk-on. But the minute we landed, the minute they stopped shelling and strafing, it seems that the whole island just exploded, especially Mount Suribachi.

So when the amtracs hit the beach, the troops would disembark and immediately the driver would turn around and go back out and pick up more troops. In the meantime, Marines had set up a line of defense ahead of us. As you've seen in the pictures of Iwo, you see Marines digging in on the bank there, and we're not standing there watching. The amtracs would lay down a line of fire with the .30- and .50-caliber machine guns as the Marines disembarked, and then you would turn your amtrac around as more were coming in and going out to pick up more troops. Then of course the maintenance tractor comes in and we set up a maintenance area where we could do repairs on the amtracs as needed. We were shelled at times, and we always had to be on the lookout for land mines, like previous times. I think the Japs used hundred-pound bombs that would arm themselves. They would bury them nose-up and then some sort of acid would eat away a safety device and then it was primed. These bombs would blow the track off and maybe damage the amtrac. Tracks were a problem. If the driver turned too sharp, you could throw a track. And if it wasn't broken, you could walk it back on. We could maneuver in most anything. But the volcanic ash was a problem with the engines and filters. We had to be concerned about the dust constantly.

The troops still hadn't gotten too far off Green Beach when we'd set up the maintenance area. The amtracs would go as far as the front lines, carrying equipment, rations, whatever was needed, but we stayed right in this area from the first day on. We set up a regular maintenance area as we did on every campaign. We had acetylene welders to cut and patch the amtracs, we had a tent up now. We had very few amtracs idle, unless it was blown up completely, and then we would scavenge parts from it. If need be, we would go after one, go wherever we had to get the equipment, bring it back even if it needed to be towed. And we didn't have any Marines to maintain our own security. First of all, we were Marines, okay? We were infantry, that's primarily what you're trained to do. And, if need be, we would bring wounded back and take them up to the ships, because we were amphibious. I tell you one thing I remember. I was quite young and I didn't smoke, but what surprised me was it seemed that every injured Marine wanted a cigarette. They'd be laid out on a stretcher, wounded, but they all had to have a cigarette. But I couldn't be much help. I didn't smoke.

I was responsible for thirty, maybe thirty-five amtracs. We would lose some temporarily, like the one we had to go out and bring in. The only thing wrong with it was they hit a land mine and blew the track off. So three maintenance men and myself went out and repaired the track. Well, we started to return and then found out that during the night some Japs had infiltrated back through the lines which they did at times. They must have hidden in an underground cavity of some sort during the night. That's what Iwo was, full of caves and tunnels and everything. We figured we were in a somewhat secure area because we weren't that far from the front line, and then all of a sudden all hell broke loose. I was on one side of the amtrac when the snipers started firing and I ran around to get on the other side, not realizing they were on both sides of us. I knew the ramp was down on the amtrac [in this case, an LVT-4] and I had to get to the machine guns. So as I ran around one side, big Swede, I'll always remember, he was running around the other and we both came together at the rear of the amtrac. Of course, he was a lot bigger than I was.

As far as firepower and being secure, we had plenty, but we didn't know where the shots were coming from, because the Japs weren't exposed. Fortunately for us, at this same time there were some

Marines just to our front who realized what was going on and so it didn't take that long between us to get rid of them. The amtracs are armed with .30- and .50-caliber machine guns, so we had to be careful for our own troops, you know. But it didn't take long to secure the area and bring back the disabled amtrac.

Now, we weren't front-line troops, but they could use us and our machine guns and tripods to set up a line of defense at night. I know some nights we went out and just set up a defense line with machine guns. Sometimes they used the amtracs' firepower with the .50-calibers and so forth. We were in combat, but we weren't considered front-line troops unless called upon. The amtracs would always be in a defensive position at night, unless we were called to go up to the front lines, and then we would go up as machine-gunners. I myself was armed with a .45 and a carbine, and the maintenance tractor was my command post, my little haven. We all carried the K-Bar, too. Used to sharpen them on our boondockers, hone them razor sharp.

I got up to the airfield, Motoyama 1. I could see it, that is, maybe a hundred yards away. I remember them shooting at some Jap, he must have had a hundred rounds fired at him as he ran like a rabbit. He must have been concealed in something on the airport when the troops got to that area, and I can still see this poor son-of-a-gun running, and like I say, there must have been a hundred shots. I don't know, maybe most of them were missing him. But some didn't.

Fortunately I met up with my brother on Iwo. He was in the Navy on LST 943. I had everybody on my LST looking for LST 943, but we never spotted it until late one afternoon somebody came running up to me and said, Hey, Gunny, your brother's here! And there was his LST almost on our beachhead. Now, mind you, this was great for me because we went with clothing for only three days. Of course, you took some extra underwear and so forth, but, hey, after a week or two you get kind of grubby, you know. And there were no showers, as you can imagine. So I went aboard his LST, took a nice hot shower, changed into Navy gear, and came off his LST looking like a sailor.

It had to be a day or two before my brother landed that they'd landed these—I want to say ramps—strapped to the sides of LSTs, but they weren't really ramps. They were big pontoons [causeways]. You could drive a truck over them when they were tied together. They were going to try to secure these ramps so the boats could come in and unload equipment and then the trucks could come out to carry equipment to the shore, but it didn't work out at all. The tides ran so hard there that they couldn't secure them. Now, my brother's LST had its bow doors open and the ramp down unloading, but the surf was running so swift that they were losing their position. They had a stern anchor out and they pulled the LST off the beach, maneuvered out, then came back at flank speed to beach it. In doing so, they left a sailor on the beach with a flashlight, so they could direct them between all the sunken pontoons. But I guess the sailor, he was kind of worried about somebody taking a pot shot at him, and he wouldn't leave the light on long enough for the captain. So the LST came in at flank speed but got too close and hit one of those pontoons, and the LST sprung its bow door. Now it can't put down the ramp, and that's the only way I can get off. So I had to go to the captain of my brother's LST to get his permission to call the captain of the LST alongside to get his permission to board, then get permission to leave my brother's LST, get a small boat to take me over to the other LST to get on board and walk off that ramp to shore. But it was worth a hot shower and clean clothes.

At the end of the battle I left and came back to Hawaii. But we were on Iwo until the island was secured. I must have missed the dedication of the cemeteries. All I can picture is all of us parading up to an LST, I can't even tell you the ship I came home on. My gear was put on another transport and I never saw my gear again after that, not my souvenirs, or a footlocker I had made in New Zealand for a carton of cigarettes, and my seabag with whatever. But I was lucky I came back.

15

HIGGINS BOATS

The one water craft most frequently associated with World War II amphibious landings is the Higgins boat. This tall-sided, flat-bottomed boat was also called the LCVP (Landing Craft, Vehicle and Personnel) which could carry about twenty fully equipped men, and, like the LVTs, it evolved from a craft designed for very unwarlike intentions.

In the early 1930s, Andrew Higgins was contracted to develop a craft suitable for navigating the difficult bayou country of Louisiana. His solution was a shallow-draft, flat-bottomed boat with a reinforced bow and a tunnel stern that would allow it to be grounded and retracted easily. Higgins's craft came to the attention of the Navy and Marines during the FLEX, or Fleet Exercises, of the late 1930s, when the existing motor launches were repeatedly proven useless for efficient troop landings. In 1937, resulting from the Navy's creation of the Continuing Board for the Development of Landing Boats, Higgins was contracted to supply one "Eureka"-type boat for evaluations during FLEX-4 in 1938. Tests were satisfactory, and five more were ordered for FLEX-5 in 1939, in which the Marines also participated. Again, the tests were satisfactory, but the Marines had only one objection.

The original "Eureka" Higgins boat had an enclosed, blunt bow that was poorly suited for offloading troops and supplies. In April of 1941, Maj. Ernest E. Linsert, secretary of the Equipment Board, showed Higgins a picture of a Japanese Dai-Hatsu 15 Type M landing craft which incorporated a bow ramp, and asked Higgins if he could put such a ramp on his craft. Higgins had a new boat ready for testing in five weeks. This is the craft upon which all designs and development of the LCVP and the LCM (Landing Craft, Mechanized) were based. These two craft would be the two most widely used landing boats of World War II.

The LCVP, successful as it was, had limitations. It was not armored, and although of a shallow draft, the horrifying experience at Tarawa revealed the Higgins boat's inability to deposit troops at critical points. Still, its availability and usefulness of design contributed overwhelmingly to the success of Marine amphibious operations.

In the following story, Albert D'Amico skippered an LCVP in the Iwo Jima campaign. He had also participated at Saipan, then Peleliu, which he said was his most important campaign, and which made him decide that he had had enough of the Higgins boats. An ear infection precluded him from training for underwater demolitions, so he was placed in an outgoing unit, from which he was "shanghaied" for Iwo Jima.

Motor Machinist's Mate Third Class Albert D'Amico, USN
Coxswain, LCVP Glamour Gal *and LST* 399

There was never a dull moment on the way out. We had men from the 5th Division on board, and there was a lot of name-calling, all good-natured. There would be rifle cleaning, and when the officers left, the name-calling would start. "You damn bellhops, you can't clean rifles," we'd say. "What the hell's wrong with you guys?" They called us swabbies, cornballs. We called them bellhops. I had to get personally acquainted with the guys, because I had to deliver them on Iwo.

On February 19, at four in the morning, we were on the deck and the chaplain gave a sermon. I had to get together with these Marines because I was bringing them in. Until then, lots of them didn't know I was a Higgins boat operator when we were kidding each other. But now they respected me more because they knew I was going in with them.

We all got into the small boats and I took them to a rendezvous, and we circled around the command ship, the *Eldorado,* until we got the signal to go in. I was in the first wave. The lieutenant on my boat, he had the 5th Division battle flag, from the 28th Regiment. I went right in to Green Beach. The guys in my boat, they hated going in. Everything always stunk of diesel fuel, and they got seasick, you know, with the boat going up and down, and then after they hit the beach they felt like they had been on a merry-go-round.

Going in, we had no opposition. I thought to myself, Geez, this is a piece of cake! The first Marines I brought in went up to the top of that first terrace, but you could see they had a hell of a job going through that sand. Then I had to go back for another load. I went to whatever ship the *Eldorado* assigned me to, to get more men to bring in. On the second and third waves going in, that's when we caught hell, the Japs started firing at us with mortars and five-inch shells. And our cruisers could zero in on them now and knock them out. But until then they were giving us hell. You've seen pictures of all the wrecks on the beach? Well, I saw a boat take a direct hit, thirty-six Marines plus two sailors. You didn't even see a toothpick in the water. But I kept going, and a shell would land here, a shell would land there, all around you, you didn't know where, you just kept going to the beach. You get hit, you got hit, that's all.

After I unloaded the guys, I had to take on the wounded from the earlier waves and take them out to the hospital ship *Samaritan*. For the two days I was hauling Marines from the APAs, and the ammo, and taking the wounded to the hospital ship, the *Samaritan*. Then they got the bright idea of putting the LSTs right up on the beach instead of bringing the wounded out to the hospital ships. They beached the 807 right on Red Beach, turned it into a hospital ship. But the most severely wounded, I had to bring them from the 807 to the hospital ships until the ship was full, and then it would go to Saipan and come back in a couple of days.

I remember this one Marine who never prayed with us on the LST when we were going in. He used to just sit and swear and say, I don't believe in God, and sharpen his knife and say, I'm gonna kill Japs and everything. And when I went on the island on the second or third trip, this lieutenant comes down with this same guy and says, You take him out to the ship, and he gives me a .45. He says, If he's faking it, shoot him. The guy was shell-shocked. The lieutenant said he lost two good men on account of this guy. So I brought him out to our ship where there was a pontoon lashed alongside and left him off there. I told the corpsman to take care of him, he's shell-shocked. Later I came back to my ship, to the crew's quarters, to go to sleep in my bunk, and there's this same guy, in my bunk. He was dead. He must have fallen off the pontoon, and they picked him out of the water and put him in my bunk. I had to take him out of my bunk and put him below. And he was six-foot-two, dead-weight, and I was only five-seven. And there was another one above me. We had to bury both of them at sea.

I took Jap prisoners off the island, too. One day I took two or three, but they had a Marine with them. I took them out to another LST that was called a prison ship. I would go out to the *Eldorado* and they would tell me what ship to take them to, which I did, and then I came back to the *Eldorado* for more orders, whatever they wanted. If they wanted flamethrowers on the beach, I went to the APAs to pick up flamethrowers and bring them in.

I would also go out to the merchant marine ships to pick up ammo. They were anchored about ten miles out, away from the rest of the fleet, because if they blew up they'd take everything with them. I'd say, Why don't you come in closer? They'd say, No way, we're getting paid twelve dollars an hour out here. I'd buy bottles of whiskey from them, twenty dollars a bottle. I'd hide it, because we weren't supposed to have it, but I got my shots in. I didn't eat much, because a lot of the stuff I saw would just turn your stomach. But I drank a lot, I had my booze and chewing tobacco.

On D+4, in the morning, I went to the *Eldorado* and I got orders to go to this APA, and I had to take these Marines into Green Beach. So I took them off the cargo nets, and while I'm going into the beach, there were these Associated Press boats, these LCVPs. And this lieutenant I was bringing in, he said, Do you mind if this photographer jumps on your boat? He wants to take a picture of Marines leaving your ramp. I says, Sure, so he has me circle around and come in again, and I drop the ramp and let them off. But I didn't know that this photographer turned around and took my picture. You can see the name of my boat, *Glamour Gal,* in the picture.

Believe me, all the time I was out there in the water at Iwo, I froze. I was so used to being out in the South Pacific, where the temperature was 80, 90, 110 in the shade. Iwo was so damned cold, and even with the life jacket and all that gear on me, I still froze. On the Higgins boat, if you hit the side of a wave, it splashes and hits you in the face and goes right down to your feet. So I always had wet feet, for the eight days that I was there.

After we beached my LST on D+5 and got all the gear off, we pulled off and headed off to Guam to pick up troops for the invasion of Okinawa. We left about D+8, I think. All the way to Iwo and back, we had had LCT 1326 lashed to the main deck, and during Okinawa I could see why. The Navy had our flotilla all planned. During the invasion, by Naha, the capital of Okinawa, we launched the LCT by filling up the ballast tanks on our starboard side and making the LST list thirty-five degrees, then cutting the cables.

I really didn't think much of Iwo Jima at the time. I thought I was in a great battle, but it was nothing like Peleliu. I never got over that. Now, if I had been up in the front lines with the Marines like when I was on Peleliu, I would have experienced more. But I was just on the beach, all I got was mortar fire. After Peleliu, I came back concussion-drunk. You know how a boxer gets punch-drunk? I was the same way. After each invasion, my ears were ringing so bad that you couldn't talk to me or give me orders. I'd end up doing something else and the captain would give me hell. During one pass at the beach between the third and fifth waves, the boat crew actually saved my life, in a way, by conferring with the captain, because my ears were ringing and I couldn't drive the small boat while shells were going off. It kind of stiffens you right up, when a shell lands too close and you get hit with the concussion. I had an infection in my ear for thirty-eight years because of it.

Iwo was tough, but I wasn't there long enough to really worry about it. I worried more about the wounded guys I brought out. One would say to me, Hey, you remember those guys you used to bull-crap with on the LST? Well, they were all killed. Right on the second airstrip, on D+3. Most of the men I took in were dead. Only a few of them made it.

16

AMPHIBIANS

The third type of amphibious vehicle was known as the DUKW, which was shaped like a large bathtub with wheels. Like the LCVP, it was a lightly armored, propeller-driven craft in the water and, like the LVT, it could operate on land. It had neither the versatility nor adaptability of the LVT, so it was relegated to an artillery transport role and a resupply role.

Cpl. Stanley Zabicki drove a DUKW in support of the 13th Marines during Iwo Jima, his only campaign.

Cpl. Stanley Zabicki
DUKW Driver, 5th Amphibian Truck Company, 5th Marine Division

I didn't start driving DUKWs until New River. I thought I was going to go with Motor Transport because I was a truck driver in civilian life, and I did drive a truck for a little while. When we were given the DUKWs to drive, well, I just took to them like a duck to water. The colonel used to ride in my DUKW all the time. Every time we were going from the mountains in Hawaii down to Hilo, we would be in the lead DUKW and there was so much shifting gears, going up and down those hills, I'd get so far ahead of them that he'd say, You'd better stop, we gotta wait. And we'd sit and wait—and I'm not exaggerating—for twenty minutes, half an hour, so they could catch up to us, and then we'd continue on. I can remember they sent me and my DUKW to Hilo, and anybody that bought a war bond, I would give them a ride in the DUKW. So that was good duty.

Transport to Iwo was another racket. I mean, there was nothing to it. And I guess the lieutenant, my commanding officer, considered me the best driver there, so whatever we did, he always rode in my DUKW, and I was always the lead DUKW.

Off Iwo, I remember all the shelling they were doing to the island. There were three fighter planes that were making runs at Iwo Jima, just prior to our coming ashore, and the three went down, but only two of them came up. I said, Oop, they got one. And the captain of the particular LST I was on, he was so scared, you wouldn't believe. He didn't want to come close enough for us to get out. He'd have left us five miles out to come in with the DUKWs, but he came in closer.

I can remember driving in, and one of the fellows with me was from Middletown, a mechanic, John Heppinstall. Going in there, he says, God, Zebby, even I'm scared, I'm shaking like a leaf. I says, My foot's shaking so much, I can't keep it on the gas pedal, I got the hand throttle out. A DUKW will do about six miles an hour in the water. Talk about a target. I looked back and I saw a shell land about ten foot in back of me. I says, God, it's a good thing I was just a little bit faster.

When we came ashore, I waited for the other DUKWs. And coming ashore there, Iwo Jima was just a mountain of ashes. There were no sandy beaches, they were ash beaches, you know. Like ashes out of a furnace. And boy, you couldn't get any traction in them. The DUKWs were getting mired down, some tipped over when a wave would flip them over.

What I did to get ashore was there were valves that you could let air out of any of the six tires, or you could just throw the main valve and it would let air out of all the tires to get better traction. Instead of having sixty pounds of air, I can remember going down to six, to finally get traction so I could go through that damned sand. And once I got moving, I threw the valve up so I wouldn't tear the hell out of the tires.

Every one of the DUKWs except mine had a 105- or a 75-mm howitzer in the back. My DUKW happened to be the A-frame DUKW. Which means it had the pipes, the cables, and I would lift what the other DUKWs were carrying. We were connected with the artillery, and so we'd come in with Marines and artillery pieces.

Once we got ashore to unload the weapons, a DUKW would drive underneath my A-frame, and I would pick up the artillery piece with the A-frame, drop it down and unhitch, and the guy would pull out with the DUKW and take it to whatever position he was going to. And then, when they got them all up there, I would have to go up and unload them. I stopped, and they would come right around my back so my A-frame could pick up the 105, and they would pull out, I drop it down and unhitch, and wait for another DUKW to come with another artillery piece.

After the artillery was placed, they were pretty much on their own. They could hit any part of the island they wanted. We would go out to a supply ship and pick up five-gallon cans of water, just fill up your DUKW with them. And you'd bring them in and go to the mess tents or the foxholes or wherever they were going to be cooking. After that, go out and get shells for the howitzers, bring in ammunition. And after it was over, we'd have to go out and bring in all the unexploded shells, grenades and everything, that were lying all over the place, and go out in the water and dump them. And some of these guys got a little crazy with the grenades, pull the pin and toss them in. Somebody was out there with a submarine and boy, they raised hell. And somebody came right out and said, No more of that stuff. Oh, the ammunition that we just dumped into the ocean.

At night, you'd watch shells go overhead. There was one that had to be as big as a fifty-five-gallon drum. It made a swooshing noise, it was rolling through the air, right over the top of us. And then when it hit over by Suribachi, boy, it sure made a big bang.

When the Marines started going up the other end of the island, and they just blocked up all the caves that the Japs were in, they were dug out by the Army that took over. And there was so much rivalry between the branches of the service that whenever the Army started unloading and coming up the hills, oh, did we razz those poor fellows, they walked up there with their heads hanging down. "Oh, the Army's here, we're safe at last!"

There were times when we'd have to bring the wounded out to the hospital ships, and we'd get up alongside and they'd drop the ropes and pick up the stretcher and all. That was kind of risky. I was hoping we wouldn't lose any of them, and we didn't.

It was thirty-some days that we were on Iwo Jima. Then we just loaded on an LSD, a ship that could open its back end and pump in water so it would sink, and then an LCVP could run right in. Then they would close the gate, pump the water out, and work on the LCVP.

I remember getting back to Hawaii, and there were signs that said, "Welcome Home, Marines," and I said, Knock it off, I'm far, far away from home. Don't refer to this place as home. I was insulted by that.

17

ARMORED AMPHIBIANS

Armored amphibians were a special class of LVTs. Earlier landing experience had indicated the need for heavier fire support than the lightly armed LVT transports could provide, so the designers married the 37mm cannon turret from the M3 tank to the hull of the LVT-2. This armament also proved too light, so the 75mm howitzer turret from the M8 was mated instead. More design improvements earned this vehicle the designation of LVT(A)(4), the typical amphibian support vehicle used at Iwo Jima.

Armored amphibians preceded the first landing wave of troops. Their mission was to lay down suppressive fire close on the beach after the naval artillery barrage had lifted, and maintain that fire while the first waves of troops landed. Cpl. Roy V. Benson relates his experience here as a 75mm gunner in support of the 5th Marine Division.

Cpl. Roy V. Benson
Gunner, Company C, 2d Armored Amphibian Battalion

My outfit was designed to give heavier weapons support than had previously been available during invasions. When the troops would be going into the battle, the heavy guns from the Navy ships and the strafing from the carrier planes had to be lifted for the assault. We had 75mm howitzers on those amphibians, as well as other machine guns, and the principle reason for that was we would precede them, we were the first assault wave. And we had the capability of destroying pillboxes and machine-gun nests and other fortifications that otherwise couldn't be destroyed with small arms fire. We trained for that at Camp Lejeune, at Hadnot Point, in North Carolina, and in California.

We trained off the coast of California in heavy surf, with landing craft, so that when we came off the LSTs you felt that you were going into Davy Jones's locker most of the time, and some of them did sink, they were overloaded and got swamped. We also trained at Maui, in Hawaii, before the invasion of Saipan, my first battle. We had training to go over reefs, and it was a slow process going in on those things, because the Japs had all the points targeted, I'm sure, prior to our arrival. They knew when we were going to be there. You didn't worry about swamping so much then, because you were concerned about getting hit more than anything, because as soon as we made that reef at Saipan, they kept bombarding us every inch of the way in with shellfire. No, you didn't worry about swamping. You worried about trying to get ashore.

We were en route to Iwo Jima, I forget how many days it was, maybe seven days, and we were shown a mockup of the island. We were told it would be a three- to five-day battle, and that all the things that they had learned from the preliminary bombardment of other islands would be put into effect here, so there should be a minimum of [Japanese] survivors, which, of course, as you know, was not true. And you talk about being swamped. There was a rumor that after the first wave, which we were, we would get within a certain distance of the shoreline, and they would light the fuel that they had pumped from fuel lines that led out into the water. It would consume us, and then the next wave, same thing. It didn't happen, of course, but you looked behind you as you were going in, I'll tell ya, because you didn't know if there would be this wall of flame after you reached a certain point.

On the way in, my amphib went under the battleship *Washington* and we weren't too far away when they let a salvo go, and it almost lifted us out of the water. You could even feel the heat of the powder charge.

It was a damp, cold day when we went in, and perhaps it was good in that regard. They didn't fire as much when we were going in, until we got close to the shore. My squad happened to be the second squad ashore at Iwo Jima, and I think we had the first flag because we had a little flag on the end of our radio antenna going in. Not that that made any difference, but we always talked about that. And those armored amphibs, as well as any other vehicle, once we hit that black sand, that volcanic ash, we couldn't move in it. Just bogged you right down. So as a result of that, the ones that didn't get hit had to back off the shoreline into the water, and engage targets which we could see, or suspected to see, with our 75mm howitzers. And we were constantly getting shelled and we had to make room for the other guys who were trying to get in.

I remember that very first day, I was gunner on the 75mm, and the commander, Frenchy Alleman, said, You see that guy up there? There was a Jap standing between two rocks, and he had binoculars and a radio. Obviously, he was a forward observer. I took care of him with one shot. A terrible thing to say, but it did the job.

So at the end of the first day, we had to get back into the shore. We went in on Red Beach 1, which was almost at the base of Mount Suribachi. From there we crossed the island after the bulldozers had come through and made roadways, and we did what we had done in other battles, which was prevent any invasions on the flanks near the water on the west side of the island. We worked all the way up the island with the 5th Division. You couldn't see the Japs there. They were all underground, in tunnels and pillboxes, and you had to dig them out. Or burn them out. We fired as artillery, at known and unknown targets, both direct and indirect, depending on the target of opportunity. It was almost routine. Somebody would ask for fire on a target, and we'd fire into it. You couldn't always see the results.

We were fired on several times. I got hit with a shell fragment, in the elbow. And they had one thing that was quite frightening. We used to call them the Midnight Express, the Bubbly-Wubbly. It was like a torpedo that was launched from the northern end of the island, and when it landed it would shake the area all around. We had some come very close to us. No control over it, you can't get out of the way of that. If you're the target, and it's on target, you're done. But it wasn't in our case.

As far as the relations with the immediate squad in my platoon, there was deep friendship, a great trust. You watched out for each other. There was an uncommon camaraderie, a closeness. I would say, from training, it was just something that you did. We didn't have any fellows who were heroic or fearful, there weren't any great emotions about our accomplishments. We just did what we had to do.

We knew clearly when that battle was over. We stayed until the sixteenth of March. We were very glad to get off, go back to Hawaii. We were alive, and we had accomplished what we went there for. We were disappointed that it took as long as it did, but they underestimated what was there. There was a lot of joy to be alive. And we stopped at Guam on the way back, to pick up some men who had been prisoners of the Japanese. They were elated to see us, and we were delighted to be part of what was kicking the pants of the Japanese. I mean, some of these guys had arms about as big around as broomsticks. That made it worthwhile, to know that these guys were free.

18

WOUNDED

Naturally, combat produces casualties. Some—the unlucky—would die, or live without limbs or sight, or worse. Others, also unlucky by being wounded, might consider themselves lucky by receiving a "million-dollar wound"—not serious enough to be life-threatening, but still bad enough to take them out of combat, hopefully for the duration of the war.

In the following story, PFC Stanley Zegarski explains not just the experience of being wounded, but how that wound has affected his life, both physically and emotionally.

PFC Stanley Zegarski
Machine Gunner, G Company, 2d Battalion,
21st Marines, 3d Marine Division

When I was aboard ship, I got to know a sergeant pretty good. And this sergeant says to me—he was an old-timer—he said, Son, remember one thing: "Kill or be killed." It stuck in my mind. I never thought that way. I never thought to "kill or be killed." I went into action, and I thought, Well, we're here to do a job, and we did a job. And now that I sit around, I sit in a chair on the lawn, I think about it. Children say to me, when we have a reunion, kids'll say, Did you ever kill the enemy? And it's a hard question for me to tell them, even though I did. To say, Yes, I did. All I say is, We were fighting. He at me, me at him. I never say, Yes, I killed someone. And I don't think that any of my friends who were in there, in action with me, would say, Yes, we killed them. But we did, we did. We had some terrible fights. I lost a lot of friends. But to this day, after I got hit, I want to know how many of our squad are walking this earth today. I know two of them, three of them, that never came back. But the others, I don't know.

When we were coming near the beach, our coxswain, and our lieutenant, says, Everybody down, and of course we're in water up to our knees, and the coxswain says, Okay, boys, get ready, I'm dropping the ramp. Well, he dropped the ramp and the lieutenant went out, and all of us after him. It just happened that there was four feet of water. We weren't hitting no land. And, of course, I'm tall. And in back of me, it was Peavey or Zilli, they were smaller. I didn't see him, I just reached back and held him and came into the beach.

We must have went about fifty yards. Shells started dropping, and we headed into a shell hole. It rained, and toward night it was getting cold. Soaking wet, cold. There was a burning tank in front of us that the three of us bellied up to. We dug ourselves a hole just to keep warm.

The following morning I recall the lieutenant coming up and saying, Change the colors on your poncho, turn the camouflage inside out. We started and didn't go too far before our rifle platoon was getting smacked around. We went a few yards, but it was steady mortars, rifle fire. Fortunately, the six of us pretty well stayed even, for a while. The question came into my mind—and all of us, who were in our squad—are we afraid? Like I told my wife, I says, Hon, you know, I wasn't scared, I wasn't afraid. Because there was so much happening around us, we didn't think about being scared. All we thought about was go forward, fight. Keep going until someone tells you to stop. And I recall someone told us to stop, and there was sort of a little hill that we dug into. Night came. You could see flares out in the front, maybe 125 yards, and you could see Japs walking to different positions, but we couldn't shoot because that would give away our line.

We'd always hear someone say, Okay, move out, we're moving out, keep going, left, right, straight ahead. And what you were seeing on the sides of you were dead Japanese, dead Americans, but you kept going. Then they said we were on the second airfield. We were going on the left and we hit some of the sulfur mines, hot as hell. When we set up for the night, there was Degrafenried, Dickinson, myself, Zilli, Peavey, and Russell. The gun was set up on a little knoll, all rocks, you couldn't dig anything. Zilli and Peavey were on the right of the gun, Dickinson and I were on the left, and Degrafenried was to our left with Russell. Zilli and Peavey were on watch. They woke us up and said it's our turn to get on the gun to watch. We stood up, and a grenade came. Zilli and Peavey were already in their sleeping position, cuddled up, sort of. This grenade landed in between them. It hit one in the head, the other in the hip. It hit the spare part kit, and an oil can that flew and hit me in the leg. I'm thinking, I'm hit. I reached down, felt the wet, brought my hand back up and smelled it. I thought it was blood. It was oil from the oil can. Not wounded, but it hurt. That night, we were just praying that nothing else would happen. I still don't know if Peavey and Zilli were killed. We never got word about them.

That morning we moved out, and all hell broke loose. We didn't know where the hell we were. They were coming out like ants out of the woodwork. We fought, then it would quiet down. We gained yards here, lost a few yards, but always went forward.

We were all laying in this big shellhole, about three o'clock in the afternoon. We got word that we had to go up front about fifty, one hundred yards to deliver overhead fire the following day. We went about fifty yards and Dickinson put the tripod down, Degrafenried put the gun down, and spare parts and bullets in the cans. I looked up, and in this bunker I saw a flash, a gunflash. I hollered, "Nips!" I ran to the right, jumped in a hole, Russell jumped in with me. As he jumped in, here comes a grenade. He jumped this way, I jumped the other, and here's this Nip with the rifle, looking at me. I had my carbine, I dropped down like this and came up and he whacked me, and as I was going down, "poom-poom-poom," I nailed him. Then I dropped.

I crawled back in the hole and when I looked back I saw Lieutenant Mulvey and Lieutenant Dausch coming towards me. I hollered to them, "Down, Nips!" So they got down behind some rocks. They hollered for a corpsman for me. And what I heard—I don't

know how true it is—Russell hollered, "Ski is hit." One of the lieutenants said, Get the gun out, and Degrafenried went over to pick
the gun up off the tripod. He got hit right in the head. Over the gun
he laid.

Anyway, the corpsmen came, and the stretcher-bearers carried me
down out of the way from where the fighting was. I laid there three,
four hours. I didn't bleed much. Everything settled in here, collapsed
my lung eventually. When they moved me, they were taking me back
and mortar shells started dropping. They jumped in a big hole, and
of course they just laid me down in the open.

I got to the airstrip, and they were going to evacuate me by plane.
But the doctor looked at me and said, No, he's a chest case, we can't
take him up because of the oxygen, and the air pressure. So they put
me on a jeep. They put me in the top (it was covered) and while they
were driving—it was not a nice, paved road, you know—I got my
arms up to hold a bar across the top of the jeep to keep my back up.
When I got to the beach, they put me on a Higgins boat. Water was
underneath me, and the bouncing. They got me to the ship, hoisted
me up, took me down into the cafeteria, and I was laying on a table.
Finally a doctor or someone came down and took me upstairs, next
deck up. I was in line to be operated on, and the doctor came and
said, No, we got more serious cases than him. They put me in a sack,
on oxygen. I went like that until we hit Saipan, where I was in a hospital when they went in with a syringe and pulled out a hell of a lot
of blood. The day before Easter, they were going to operate on me,
and they gave me blood. Easter Sunday morning came and the nurse
came up and said, Stan, we can't operate on you because Okinawa
was hit and they're bringing in casualties, so we're moving you out.
They took me down on a plane, a C-47, on the top stretcher. The
guy below me was hit in the arm and he had a cast, and where was
his elbow? In my back! I'm trying to get over on my side, and I can't
get over on my side, I don't know how many hours. We landed in the
Johnson Islands, then Hawaii, where they operated on me. After
being there maybe a month, I got on board a ship, an LST, they got
us all on the vehicle deck, stretchers and all. One man comes up to

me and says, Hey, how ya feelin? I says, I'm draining, soaking wet from all the pus. He says, C'mon, I'll fix ya up. You know those first-aid boxes they have on ships? He opens it up, takes out a little vial. What am I, going on nineteen? He says, Here, stick it in your leg and squeeze it, you'll sleep all night. Jesus, I'm a dummy, I still don't know much about dope. Oh, it was beautiful, slept all night. Next morning, I'm dying again. So a corpsman comes around and took me up to the sick bay and changed all the bandages. I got into California, the hospital there, then Portsmouth Naval Hospital, for quite a long time, until they discharged me.

There's a few things, like I said before. Were you scared? I'll repeat it again. There was no time for it. There was too much going on to be afraid. We were probably scared, but it was never on our minds. It was too much. Bullets, shells. Seeing men crying. Seeing men walking off with tags on them, they were maybe shell-shocked, frightened. Fighting? Yes, we fought. We fought hard. And then, after this, after all of this, after getting discharged, many times I think, the men, I'd like to know if they're still alive, or dead. It hurts. And to think, the future generations should be proud of the servicemen—not just Marines, but Army, Navy, Women's Auxiliary, everything—and they should be thankful the war wasn't in this country. We fought like hell. We were determined we were going to take that island one way or the other.

PFC William A. Bain

Gunnery Sgt. Daniel Benwell

2d Lt. Angelo Bertelli *(right)* at Camp Lejeune with fellow service-men, 28 July 1944.

Platoon Sgt. James Boyle

Sgt. Alfred F. Cialfi

Motor Machinist's Mate 3d
Class Albert D'Amico

PFC Edwin Des Rosiers

Cpl. Donald Dixon

PFC Bernard Dobbins

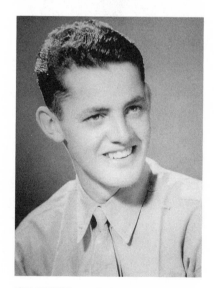

PFC William C. Doran

Cpl. George Gentile

PFC James Falcone

Cpl. Arthur Kiely

PFC Robert Lanehart

Cpl. Raymond Mik

Pvt. Liberato G. Riccio

Lt. (jg) Evelyn Schretenthaler

PFC Fred Schribert

Sgt. William J. Smith

Capt. Lawrence Snowden

PFC Robert W. Stewart

19

MEDICAL PERSONNEL

Unlike the Army, whose medical personnel were derived from its own ranks, Marine medical personnel were supplied by the Navy. Many performed their duties on board the hospital ships, but the most important were those at the first points of care—in the front lines, or in the beach evacuation stations. All areas on the island were subject at many times to heavy enemy fire, and acts of heroism and self-sacrifice were common. Casualties among doctors and corpsmen totaled 738, with 197 killed.

The corpsmen knew their Marine charges intimately. These men first received medical training in naval hospitals, but then moved on to Marine bases to finish their instruction as corpsmen. They trained under the same conditions as the men they would treat, who would come to revere their "Doc."

Pharmacist's Mate Second Class Stanley E. Dabrowski
Corpsman, Company C, 5th Medical Battalion,
28th Marines, 5th Marine Division

Before we went off on leave, we were allowed to apply for whatever school we wanted. I always had an interest in medicine so I decided the Hospital Corps was for me. I filled out an application for that. When I got back from leave I went to what we called the OGU, Outgoing Unit, for processing, and lo and behold I was selected and sent to the Hospital Corps school at the Naval Hospital at Portsmouth, Virginia. It was a six- or eight-week course that emphasized the basics. After that, I reported for duty at the U.S. Naval Hospital in Charleston, South Carolina, where I was assigned to the contagious ward.

And having learned something of medicine, I said, This is not for me. I was always gowned, masked, and rubber-gloved, and even had disposable sandals. There were many cases of tuberculosis and other diseases. I was very unhappy with that and decided that this was not what I went into the Navy for. I went to see the chief pharmacist's mate in personnel and asked, Chief, do you think you could do something for me? He said, Of course I could, son, don't worry about it. If you want a transfer, I can get you a transfer. He was a very nice man and very obliging until I realized that my name was on the list for Fleet Marine Forces and that I was to report to Camp Lejeune, North Carolina, to Field Medical Service School. Of course, I had no idea what Fleet Marine Forces were. *Fleet* Marine. This must be sea duty. It was, but not the kind I expected. Thus started my introduction to the U.S. Marine Corps.

We got off the bus at Camp Lejeune and I looked around and said, Gee, there's no Navy here. It's all Marine Corps green. Everything is USMC, USMC. Standing there on the asphalt was this Marine corporal with a Smokey the Bear hat and his duty belt, starched shirt with the creases right down here, very neat. "All right you guys, fall in." He impressed me tremendously and was our DI throughout our training.

After training at Camp Lejeune, we were assigned to Company C of the 5th Medical Battalion of the 5th Marine Division at Camp Pendleton, California. And as a medical company in a medical battalion, C Company was assigned to an infantry regiment, the 28th Marines. We were the pool of corpsmen that would staff the battalion aid stations or regimental aid stations. And parts of the company would also staff division or regimental hospitals. I was assigned to a thirteen-man medical collecting team. Our job was selecting casualties that needed attention first. We were to transfer them to better facilities as soon as possible. We had four stretcher teams assigned to us. The corpsmen were to do the histories, tagging, and administering first aid. The training was fantastic and everyone knew exactly how we were going to do all these things. We did it repeatedly until we could do it in our sleep. We had both Marine Corps and Navy personnel conducting training. We had ensigns and pharmacists who were warrant officers, not pharmacist's mates. They were in the Hospital Corps. We were also trained by senior Hospital Corps personnel who were part of the training battalion. They were training us to do the things they had already become proficient in. Many of them were combat veterans from previous engagements like Guadalcanal, Tulagi, Bougainville, even Peleliu.

We were assigned to our infantry units. A medical company consisted of about ninety-eight corpsmen and six physicians, three surgeons, two internists, a dentist, and an administrative warrant officer. We had five chief pharmacist's mates assigned to the medical company. And then down the line, there were a few pharmacist's mates first class, pharmacist's mates second class, and a lot of HAs, hospital apprentices.

On September 19, we went overseas. I remember very well the ship we went on. It was a Liberty ship manned by a civilian crew, SS *John B. Floyd.* I honestly don't recall if we had an escort or not. We went directly to Hilo on the big island of Hawaii.

One thing always stood out in our minds. We were assigned to the 1st Battalion of the 28th Marines. Every time we went on these so-called field problems, there was always a hill involved. One battalion would turn to the right, another battalion would go straight across, and another battalion would assault the hill. It wasn't until we saw the first picture of Iwo Jima on our way there that it dawned on us why. That hill was Mount Suribachi.

We were off Iwo Jima on the eve of the eighteenth but everything was black. We didn't see the island. Reveille was about 0300. We had the typical breakfast of steak and eggs but not many people ate an awful lot because your heart was up here in your throat. We had no idea what to expect.

We got down to the tank deck and got aboard our vehicles, the LVTs. Their engines were already running and in spite of huge fans, there were an awful lot of fumes. People started getting sick. When they realized what was happening they shut down some of the engines. But they had to be sure these vehicles would start up and go.

Fourteen men plus equipment fit into our LVT. We were taking medical equipment. They had a three-man crew, the coxswain* and two machine-gunners manning .50-calibers.

We got off at 0800, just drove off the ramp into the sea. We bobbed around while they formed the assault waves. This was very important. You had to get in line. On paper it was a beautiful thing and if you had been up in the air it must have been a thrilling sight. But as soon as we got on that beach everything fell apart. It was just mass confusion. The thing I noticed immediately was the tremendous amount of noise, concussion, small arms fire, explosions of artillery and mortar shells. As we were coming into the beach, we were under a rolling barrage of the sixteen-inch guns of the battleships. You could just feel those shells going over your head. Units were scattered and casualties began mounting immediately. My unit landed in the third assault wave at 0907 on Green Beach, right under Suribachi.

I had a carbine and a .45. Unlike the Army in Europe, we were armed. That was because of our experience on Guadalcanal. At that time corpsmen still wore Red Cross brassards on their arms and a red cross on their helmets. They were the first ones to be knocked off. The snipers were looking for key personnel. In the Marine Corps, nobody wore any kind of insignia on their helmets or clothes. At Guadalcanal many corpsmen were killed almost immediately. Even in subsequent campaigns corpsmen would be singled out simply because they looked different from others because of the equipment they carried. We carried a medical kit on each shoulder suspended from a shoulder yoke. In the left pouch we carried all our battle dressings, sulfa powder, burn dressings. In the right pouch we carried morphine syrettes, tags, iodine pencils, ammonia inhalants, hemostats and scalpels and other assorted equipment. I didn't like it at all because they marked us as corpsmen. It was like a lieutenant or a captain carrying a map case as opposed to an infantryman who had only had a rifle and a canteen on his belt. Because of this, we were told to carry sidearms, not as offensive weapons but for self-protection.

The beach was very narrow because the winds and the waves had terraced the volcanic ash. There were two or three terraces. Just try-

---

*More accurately, the driver. An LVT is not a boat.

ing to crawl up this thing was like trying to crawl through buckwheat in a bin. But we had to do it in order to make headway. Casualties were mounting all over the place. I lost a very dear friend right there on the beach, Stan Sanders. He was sewed through by machine-gun bullets. It was the most shocking thing you could experience. Here you were talking to the man just a few minutes ago, and now his eyes were glazed over and he was dead. It was a devastating experience. Everyone was saying, "Move, move, move." And then from everywhere were these pleas, "Corpsman, corpsman!" Casualties mounted tremendously. Japanese artillery, mortar, and rocket fire resulted in exceedingly severe traumatic wounds and traumatic amputations with extensive blood loss and severe shock.

My first casualty was a sergeant with a sucking chest wound. He had taken a machine-gun bullet right through the lungs. One of the paramount things we had trained for were sucking chest wounds. You had to do something immediately or else the man would drown in his own blood. We had to close off the wound so he would not get air through it. You had to ram this big battle dressing into the wound and compress it as much as possible and tie it off. Give him a shot of morphine, write out a tag, and mark him. You had to put a big *M* on his forehead to indicate that he had already been given morphine. And then someone would have to drag him off the beach. I could not do this, I had to advance with my unit.

As it was, we had to catch up with our units. The Marines were trained to move, to push to reach an objective. They just went and we had to go along with them. My battalion was assaulting across the island into the narrow neck and we were catching all our fire from Suribachi. The people who were entrenched up there could see all over the island.

By this time there was some semblance of order. We didn't have an official aid station as such. We chose the deepest shell hole we could find and started taking care of the severely wounded as they were brought in. Distances from the front line to the battalion aid station were very short due to the difficult terrain and confined battle area. Evacuation of wounded was extremely hazardous. The stretcher-bearers were under constant fire. The LVTs and Weasels were the only vehicles that could be used to evacuate the severe casualties.

The first night on Iwo was a nightmare. We were getting artillery and mortar fire from the mountain, from the other side of the island, and a lot of small arms fire as well. The first day had been a bright, sunny day, but the second day it started to rain and it was very miserable. We had spent most of our training in the tropics, but Iwo Jima was in the temperate zone and temperatures at night would fall down to forty or fifty degrees. It was cold, wet, and miserable. All we had were our combat jackets and combat utilities, and one blanket. I didn't use the blanket because we spent most of the night sorting, treating, and evacuating the wounded.

Things slowed down because we had ceased advancing and were in defensive positions. But there was constant harassing fire. We were still under the mountain. It seemed that all night long our ships were covering the island with star shells to illuminate everything and keep the enemy down. You could become mesmerized watching them explode and come down slowly on little parachutes. When they went out it was like pulling a chain; everything got black again.

The battalion aid stations were never very far away from the front line or, at the beginning, from the beach. So evacuating casualties was a short trip. But when we started experiencing heavy casualties, it was almost impossible to comprehend. Because of the heavy artillery and mortar fire there were a lot of traumatic injuries, traumatic amputations. The first thing you had to do was assess the casualty. "What do I do first?" Almost certainly, they had immediately gone into shock.

Combating shock and hemorrhage were the first priorities. We used tourniquets and hemostats. There were so many cases where there were traumatic amputations. No arm, or both legs. And then there were abdominal injuries, torn-out intestinal tracts. Often I was beside myself trying to decide what to do with these people. And surprisingly, sometimes these young men would be covered by a poncho and lying on a stretcher. And I'd say, Hey, Mac, how are you doing? Pretty good, doc. What's the problem? Oh, my left arm got it. So you'd lift the poncho and you'd see a stump. My God, you'd think, he's still lucid and he still can talk. First, I had to tourniquet it, give him morphine. We had these huge battle dressings about the size of an 8½-by-11 page of paper with ties on them. You would sprinkle sulfa powder on the stump, which would almost immediately be washed out by the oozing blood. But you did it nevertheless. And then you'd put the dressing on as tightly as possible. These men, the resolve they had. You'd tag them, get their name and number off their dogtags. You'd put the man's unit down if you could find out what it was because they always took statistics down at the end of the day as to killed and wounded and what units they were from. Our fight was preserving life. You did all this automatically. It was just so natural to do these things even though you were never, never, never primed for the things you saw. The injuries to these men were traumatic, so were the experiences. Concussion resulted in a great number of casualties, hearing loss, confusion, and shock. Many men had to be evacuated suffering from combat fatigue. Along with agonizing terror, gruesome sights and trauma, it was enough to try anyone's resolve, like going through the gates of hell.

Nevertheless, we did what we had to do and then we got the stretcher teams to get them down to the beach as soon as possible. At that time the regimental aid station was not set up to take care of them. Things were too fluid. The beach was the best place to send them so they could be evacuated offshore.

I believe there were three hospital ships, the *Samaritan*, AH-10, *Bountiful*, AH-9, and the *Solace*, AH-5. They were way off the beach. These cases needed immediate attention. We had hospital LSTs lying two thousand yards offshore. The wounded always went back on Higgins boats or LVTs. But on that first day there was no way Higgins boats could get ashore because of the tremendous amount of wreckage.

The first LST to land on Iwo Jima did so on the twenty-first, I think. The only way we could get the wounded off the beach was with the LVTs. With these we could get them to the APAs which were equipped with sick bays. It wasn't until later on in the campaign that the hospital ships could come in close to the shore.

After the twenty-third the battalion had a few days rest when we got a little reprieve to resupply, collect the wounded, and get some food. We started again toward the north part of the island. We were right beneath Suribachi. We had bisected the island, and the 4th Division was already pushing north from their sector. By this time two regiments of the 3d Division had been brought in due to the tremendous number of casualties both the 4th and 5th Divisions had suffered by that time. They ran into some very fierce opposition and it got to a point where it was inch by inch, foot by foot, rather than yards at a time. The terrain above the airfields was very pocked with caves, pillboxes, labyrinths of tunnels, and such a crossfire that it was a murderous situation. You can read this in the historic accounts of the battle, and one that will stand out in my mind forever. This is where our regiment was pinned down by murderous fire. The most terrifying and devastating aspect of combat was the mortar barrages. They came straight down on you due to their trajectory and when they registered you were in for a terrible beating. In both instances when I was hit it was due to mortar fire.

Of course, as corpsmen, we advanced with our troops. On the third of March I was administering a unit of serum albumen to a very severely wounded Marine in a shellhole, where we had some semblance of safety. I was about six inches above ground with my hand holding the bottle, which is a bit smaller than a Coke can. I caught a piece of hot shrapnel which shattered the bottle and almost took the tip of my finger off. The shock of all that flipped me over while at the same time I lost my helmet and another chunk of shrapnel grazed my scalp. Neither wound was severe enough to take me out of commission. But I did have a helluva headache and one big bandage on my finger. And I just continued my duties. Later on, I was showered with the blast from a phosphorus round and was hit in the left knee. Phosphorous, unless you get it out, will continue burning. Again, I was lucky enough not to have gotten a wound that put me out of commission. However, I did have the latter wound attended by a surgeon back on the beach. These were my only encounters with wounds. My most traumatic experiences on Iwo Jima occurred in the Hill 362 sector. I was about to get out of a shell hole when I was knocked back down by a mortar round that hit my shoulder pack but did not detonate. It was a dud. It was agonizing terror to try to get out of that hole. To this day I shudder when I think of it. There were other close calls, but this one is etched in my memory forever.

We made trips almost constantly evacuating the wounded. By the time we had advanced further the battalion aid station was in full operation. Understand that it was always mobile. As the troops moved up, we had to follow, otherwise there would be too big a gap between the line companies and medical help. We evacuated the wounded with the LVTs. You couldn't use trucks, there were no roads. The LVTs could go anywhere just like a tank. And we used another little vehicle we called the Weasel, a small tracked vehicle about the size of a jeep. You could do anything with this little thing. We could get two severe casualties on a Weasel.

When we had to do it by hand, our stretcher teams were under constant fire. And the stretcher teams were always singled out by the snipers. Frequently, you would hear these things, "pft, pft." It didn't register after a while but you were being shot at. In one instance, I had a wounded man not fifty feet away. Some of the Marines told me that he had been there for about a half hour. "Hey Doc, go out there and bring him back in." He wasn't moaning, he wasn't doing anything, but you could see movement. So I figured I would go out and take a look at him. I started across this area and right behind me someone said, Hey, Doc, where the hell do you think you're going? I said, I've got a man out there I have to bring in. He said, The hell you are. You're in the middle of a minefield. *Freeze.*

Talk about traumatic experiences. Usually, the engineers would indicate an access path with tape or white streamers. They would probe for the mines with a bayonet and clear the area. Apparently, this hadn't been done yet and I hadn't realized it. I was halfway through so I continued and got my man.

My commanding officer, Jens W. Larsen, was a man fifty-six years of age and very much like a father to all of us. He was not military at all. He volunteered for the Navy. He was a great surgeon. By this time the division hospitals had been established on the beach or close to the beach. The division hospital was staffed by about fifteen physicians and about seventy-five corpsmen. There were admitting tents, ward tents, surgical tents, three or four operating rooms going constantly. I also saw the first hospital plane come in from Guam or Saipan on the third or fourth of March. It had a big red cross on it. We were told to deliver a group of severely wounded to the airfield for air evacuation. The first Navy nurse came on this plane, Ens. Jane Kendeigh, Flight Nurse. In that batch of supplies they brought were cases and cases of whole blood. This blood had just been donated on the West Coast days before. I remember taking a case of this refrigerated blood and putting it aboard a Weasel and taking it back to the battalion aid station. The surgeons began using it immediately. You could see the tremendous response with whole blood as opposed to plasma. You would get color, pink lips again rather than purple. It was fantastically lifesaving and there's no question that the whole blood saved many, many more lives than the plasma or albumen.

Then we began getting air evacuation, and that was very important, too. During the battle, better than twenty-five hundred Marines, very severe casualties, were airlifted to the Marianas. The planes were able to accommodate three tiers of stretchers. And I understand that they never lost a patient en route to those hospitals. Of course, most of the evacuation was done by hospital ships. They would come in closer to the beach during the day to pick up casualties. Once they were loaded they would steam back to the Marianas. At night they were fifteen to twenty miles offshore, fully illuminated. Hospital LSTs played an important part during the early phases of the battle, receiving casualties and distributing them to APAs and hospital ships.

We left on the twenty-sixth of March. And that was a tragic day for C Company. The island was secured and the company had been reunited. The 147th Army infantry regiment had come in as garrison troops and taken over from the Marine Corps. The 3d Marine Division was going to stay behind, the 4th Marine Division was already gone. We were already on the beach and getting ready to board the USS *Cape Johnson*, APA 172. And then one more of our boys was hit by a sniper, right through the temple. By this time, of course, no one wanted to wear his helmet anymore so we weren't wearing them. It happened right there on the beach. Guy Siler was his name.

We didn't know where the sniper was hiding. No one knew. Even after the island was secured and the Marine Corps left, the Army garrison forces killed about six thousand more Japanese. That place was just honeycombed with caves. If you could have looked at Iwo in profile it would have looked like an anthill. Naval gunfire didn't knock out very much. These people just went below decks.

What was left of our division went back to Camp Tarawa on the big island of Hawaii. From April to mid-May we were left to regroup mentally and physically. And we were getting our replacements of raw, young people. Mind you, we were ourselves eighteen- and nineteen-year-old combat veterans. We were old salts. These kids who were joining our division had dungarees that hadn't even been washed once. And they looked at us with great awe. After all, we had been on Iwo Jima.

That month and a half was like R&R with good food and fresh milk which we hadn't seen in months, fresh fruit, a sandwich this thick, a hot steak dinner. Once we got to Hawaii we got new equipment and supplies. Many of those who had been hospitalized came back to duty. I remember the first casualty on Iwo that I took care of on the beach, the sergeant I told you about? One day we were sitting around when I heard a voice in the background say, I'm looking for Doc Dabrowski. Dabrowski, where are you? I recognized him immediately. He gave me this big bear hug and said, Doc, I just wanted to thank you for saving my life. Now that one thing was worth Iwo Jima to me. It just does something to you.

Also among the medical personnel provided by the Navy were the flight nurses, like Lt. Evelyn Schretenthaler, who flew as crew members of evacuation R4Ds out of the Marianas. Out of 16,186 casualties evacuated from Iwo Jima, 2,449 were airlifted. Not one died in flight.

Lt. (j.g.) Evelyn Schretenthaler
Flight Nurse, U.S. Navy Nurse Corps

It was in the days when you became a nurse, or a teacher, or you married. Well, I wanted to be a nurse. So I entered Trinity Hospital, Jamestown, North Dakota, a Catholic institution, and spent three years to become a registered nurse. When the war broke out, I was a student. I had three brothers who were all going in the military, one after the other. One had just finished college, the other two were in college, so I joined the Navy as soon as I finished. I was glad I was able to serve, because I had three brothers who would eventually all go overseas, and all in the air. I had a brother who would be a Navy pilot, one who would be a paratrooper, and one who would be in the glider infantry. And people would say, Oh, you're going in the service? And I'd say I have three brothers in, somebody has to take care of them if they were injured. And I felt like I was doing my duty. I wasn't out there for the glory. I was out there to help.

I went to Great Lakes for six months, to the surgical ward, then I was transferred to Brooklyn, New York, the Brooklyn Hospital, the Navy Yard. And I did dietary work, which was very interesting, because the Navy didn't have dietitians, they used nurses at that time. From there I became a flight nurse. The Navy decided they needed flight nurses for the evacuation in the Pacific, so if you were interested you had to sign your name, how much did you weigh, and could you swim. Well I weighed 122 pounds, and I could swim, so I signed my name. There were two hundred of us, but they took only one. I was the one they took. I had the right age, the right background. And I was thin enough. This sounds ridiculous, but it was true. They wanted you tall, thin, pleasant, and with a good record. And I had that.

They flew me to Alameda, California. There were twenty-four of us from all over the country who had all been Navy nurses for at least a year. We were all about the same age, twenty-three, twenty-four, twenty-five. And they gave us six weeks of intensive training, of caring for patients at an altitude, in planes that weren't pressurized. How to draw blood, a lot of first aid. They also wanted to be sure you knew how to swim, which was rather silly because if one of those planes went down with a load of patients, they always said, Forget it. You wouldn't be able to save your neck, let alone any of the patients. But we were disciplined young people. We had to be. During the war, they didn't take any goof-offs. Anybody who goofed off, well, you just weren't in the military. They couldn't take the chance. The Navy didn't take just anyone to be a Navy nurse. You had to be able to handle it. At Great Lakes, you know, I took care of fifty patients. You worked hard, you had a lot of responsibility.

Then they flew us to Hawaii, a sixteen-hour flight. They didn't ever tell us where we were going, so when we reached Hawaii, they split us up. Twelve of us were sent on to Guam. They still didn't tell us where we were going. The put us in a hospital tent there, with the nurses from One-Eleven. About two days later, we were taking planes out to Iwo Jima. And they still didn't tell us where we were going.

It was eerie, flying in that first time. We'd leave about midnight, we'd land about seven in the morning. We landed on the strip as soon as it was secured. They wouldn't allow us to go in when it was dark, there was too much shooting. We could see ships out in the bay, we could see the shelling from all the ships off shore. You could hear the gunfire, and the shelling. You could see people in fatigues, you know, the men, the Marines. And it was chilly, and it was gray, and it was bleak. I remember seeing a truck loaded with Japanese, probably marines, and they were big fellows. I always thought of Japanese as being small, but these were the big ones. They had captured them, they were taking them some place. And you wondered, What am I doing here, how did I get here? And you'd see these young men who were so badly injured and it made me wonder what it was all about. But then you were so busy trying to take care of them and make them as comfortable as possible you just didn't think about it.

First we would check around to be sure it was safe to get off the plane, and then we would go into tents or caves* to try to screen the

*More likely, concrete blockhouses or bunkers taken from the Japanese. Many caves were interconnected in the massive underground defenses which the Japanese had dug in the months prior to the invasion, and might still have contained enemy soldiers.

patients that we thought would be safe to fly, because it would be seven or eight hours and we flew at about seven thousand feet. We would talk to the Navy doctor who took care of the Marines. He would give us a rundown of what they had and what they wanted to go out. And he left it up to us to make the decision of who we thought we could take. They were all on stretchers, they would be stacked about three or four high on the plane. These were cargo planes, R4Ds, and they were cold. When we'd land on Guam, it was like an oven, but when you were in the air, it was quite chilly. Well, my first flight I had this young man with a hole in his back. We got up to seven thousand and he started to hemorrhage. I asked the pilot if he could go down, and he did go down to about three thousand. Of course, then it got very rough and everyone became ill. I gave him plasma and put a pressure dressing on, and kept my fingers crossed until we landed. After that first trip, I learned that you tried not to take anyone who was in big danger of bleeding. We also learned that with brain cases and chest cases, the pressure would make a difference. Those were things you learned, because we were just not experienced. It was a new field. They had had corpsmen before who had done a tremendous job, but they had never used nurses. They had used us on board ship, and at fleet hospitals, but never in the air. This was a first for the Navy. You see, if you were a flight nurse, up in a plane, there was no phone, no doctor. You were responsible for all of the casualties. And if something went wrong, well, you couldn't land. You were over the water. So it was up to you. But when you're young, you're confident. I was confident I would do the best I could.

We carried about twenty-eight patients. There was one nurse, one corpsman, the pilot, copilot, and a mechanic. And I always laughed because everybody had a firearm but the nurse. I don't know what I was supposed to do.

We gave plasma and pain medication. We had a lot of dressings, and that's about all we really needed. We tried to feed the patients. We brought in dehydrated food from Guam, like dehydrated eggs, canned butter, and water, and bitter, bitter coffee. But the young Marines were so glad to get off of Iwo Jima. They never complained, all they asked for was a drink of water. Of course, they were in battle clothes that they had probably hit the beach with, and heaven only knows how long they had worn these clothes. They were so exhausted, and they were so very young. I remember them being seventeen, many of them seventeen. Some of them we flew back to die. I felt very protective of them, because they had been through so much. And I felt like, is this necessary, should these young men be so brutalized? And they were such brave young men. And it always bothered me that they told us if the plane went down, you're not going to save anyone, you're not going to save yourself. It always bothered me that all those young fellows would go down. It really used to upset me. But you had to forget about it, there just wasn't anything you could do. You were so busy, you just couldn't think too much. And they would try to have conversations with you. They were cute, real cute. They'd say, "Oh, I haven't seen a white woman in three years!" And they probably hadn't. They'd just look at you, "I haven't seen a white woman in three years." Some of them had been out there that long, I suppose.

Of course, they were all hospitalized once we got to Guam. Some of them I'm sure would go back to duty, but a lot of them were so badly injured that you knew they would not ever go back. And eventually they would try to get them back to the States, you know, close to where their family was.

In between flights, we worked at the hospital, because the ships were bringing in casualties. Sometimes I think we worked twenty hours straight, with no relief, because there were so many casualties. We would screen and stabilize the patients, maybe they couldn't go back to duty, maybe they needed further work, so we might fly them in to Hawaii. We'd fly into Kwajalein, where we'd have a crew change, and the next crew would take them into Hawaii. And they'd be screened again and maybe flown back to the States, to San Francisco. Some who were really badly hurt, say a quadriplegic, they might be flown somewhere to be close to their families. And some were so bad that they couldn't be moved. Of course, some of them passed away. Then we'd head back from San Francisco to Guam. That was quite a flight.

I made about three or four trips into Iwo. There were twelve of us, and there was only one nurse on a plane, so we were busy. One of our planes had been hit by a sniper, and it had to turn around and come back. They gave them a different plane and changed the load. No one was injured, thank heaven. That was the reason they wouldn't let us come in at dark, because it was dangerous. Luckily we never lost any patients coming out of Iwo, which I thought was terrific.

Some corpsmen served on board the hospital ships or evac transports. While Hospital Apprentice First Class Emile LaReau was not subject to the intense combat conditions of his counterparts in the front lines, his duties contributed immensely to the recovery of the men he tended.

Hospital Apprentice First Class Emile LaReau
On board the APA USS President Jackson

I was a corpsman on board ship, doing all hospital work. I remember, going by Iwo Jima on the day of the invasion, the captain saying over the loudspeaker that we were traveling past the island to fool the Japanese. Then we were to circle back. The captain said that while we were at an island called Chichi Jima.

During the start of the invasion, my job as a corpsman was probably the quietest day I ever had in the service. The ships anchored out maybe three or four miles. We could see the beach, we could probably see some armored vehicles, but we couldn't see much, so we couldn't hear any of the noise, the shooting going on or anything. My job was just handing down sandwiches to the crews that kept coming to the ship to load and unload all the vehicles and supplies we had. It was an all-day affair, until such a point as we started getting casualties on board ship. Then I was assigned to a compartment where casualties were coming in.

The wounded were treated on the beach, then brought on board ship, and the doctors on board decided whether they were life-threatening cases or not. If they were life-threatening, they were put right in the sick bay, because chances were they would need an operation for stomach wounds and all that. Those they thought weren't life-threatening came to my compartment.

I had fifty-one or fifty-two, between me and another corpsman. Then the compartment next to me, they had 250. The difference was that my compartment was all bed patients. One man got up twice and passed out on us twice. The rest of them never got up the entire trip. The compartment next to me, they were ambulatory, they could walk around and take care of themselves.

My compartment was right next to the chow hall. And in order to feed these fifty-one patients, we knew we couldn't possible carry fifty-one mess trays. So the patients from the other compartment, whenever they came through to go to chow, we asked them to bring back a tray for somebody in one of the beds. They were very good, all these wounded. They could walk, they could help themselves.

I think I had about three or four hours sleep each night. I remember one of the patients saying to me, When do you sleep? We never see you sleep. That's because I slept between the time that they went to sleep and when they actually woke up.

We did a lot of things. For instance, when the patients had to go to the bathroom, we used plasma cans. The plasma bottles came inside containers that looked like tennis-ball cans. We took the bottles out and then put tape around the edge of the cans, and the patients used these as ducts to urinate in. We'd collect all the cans and dump them into a bedpan, and unfortunately I'd have to walk through the other department to empty them out.

I always had four or five things on my mind. There was never a time when you had nothing on your mind. I'd walk by somebody and he'd ask, Can I have a duct? Then somebody'd say, Corpsman, can you get me a glass of water? Okay, I'll be right back. Then, on the way back someone would say, I have pain. I used to carry two packs of four morphine syrettes in my pocket. Finally I'd get to the man who wanted the water, then somebody else would ask for a duct, somebody needed a bedpan, somebody was uncomfortable and needed moving around. I can't remember all the things we did, but those were mainly the things we did. Basically, we just tried to keep everybody comfortable, because they were wounded quite badly, even though they weren't life-threatening.

There was one in my department who did die. We notified the doctor and they moved him to sick bay, but the man did pass away. That was a misjudgment they made, putting him with us instead of in sick bay. He might have passed away anyway, who knows?

We had pretty severe cases. One man was missing his hand. When the doctor took care of him, the doc said, Have you seen this before? The man said yes, he had. I guess the doc wanted to warn him. Another man was burned. Another was on his back with broken legs. They were all bedridden, they couldn't get up. They were pretty badly wounded, but I'm pretty sure all the men in my department survived the war. Except for one.

One time I had to go to the sick bay to get something, and as I passed through the corridor at the end of sick bay, there was a fellow on the left who had his leg missing. And he said to me, Corpsman, could you clean me up? He was lying in his bunk and there was still a lot of sand from the beach and everything else. He had just gotten treatment on the beach and hadn't had anything further that I know. I couldn't really pass him up. I got a washcloth and cleaned him up the best I could at the time. Then I turned to my right and there was another man with the exact same thing, a leg missing. I said, You want me to clean you up, too? He said, No, that's okay. He must have known I was in a hurry and didn't have time. So I got what I needed and went back to my compartment.

When the patients were coming in, there was this fellow who was wounded and he had a twin brother, and they were together. When the other wounded came back, they told him that his brother was killed on the beach. I remember this fellow went to all the patients in my department, and I guess it was something to do to pass the time, so he wouldn't think too much about his brother, but he wrote V-mail letters for all the guys who were lying around wounded. He wrote I don't know how many letters. We were off Iwo Jima for fifteen days, and that's what he did for all the time he was there, writing V-mail letters.

There was this young doctor on board, and I think he had seen campaigns before. He couldn't bring himself to go in again, even though I felt he was one of the beach party, the men who went in and actually took care of the wounded on the beach. I think he was supposed to go in but I think it was meant to be that he stayed behind, because for three straight days the three doctors on our ship worked around the clock, trying to save lives. And we worked in our department, trying to make the patients comfortable. But these doctors must have been so tired when they got through. This young doctor took care of all the patients in my compartment, and I don't know for how many long hours, because I don't remember any other doctor taking care of these patients. He'd treat their wounds. We'd carry a man in on a stretcher, the doctor would give them a shot of sodium pentothol and have them count backwards until they fell asleep, then he'd fix up their wounds and we'd carry them back. And this one time we carried in a fellow and when we went to carry the stretcher back, this doctor who was no bigger than me, about five-foot-five or so, he wouldn't let me carry the stretcher back. He said, No, I got it. Like I say, I think he was meant to be there, because he did so much good work on board ship.

After the fifteen days at Iwo Jima, we went back to a neutral base. I forget what island we went back to. They set up these portable hospitals on every island we captured. We brought them all back and landed all the casualties. Then we got word that we were going back to the States for repairs and everybody was pretty happy about that. We missed Okinawa, and I was in Portland, Oregon, at Swan Island, when the war ended. It was great. I remember I didn't have liberty. I had duty in the sick bay, and me and this other fellow jumped ship that night and went to town. We went to the Kaiser shipyards and put on our blues or maybe our whites at the shipyard and left our dungarees in a locker. The fellow who was taking care of the shipyard was glad to see it, he just said, Yeah, leave your clothes here. We never did pick our clothes up. Our dungarees are still there. So we had a good time. The war was over.

20

ARMY ANTIAIRCRAFT ARTILLERY

Not all units on Iwo Jima were Marines or Navy. Shortly after the landings, Army antiaircraft artillery units arrived to protect the airspace above the invasion beaches, and after the Marines departed, the antiaircraft batteries stayed to protect the airfields and the reveted P-51s and P-61s from Japanese attack. The Army 147th Infantry Regiment arrived to maintain the security of the island, which was still subjected to the occasional sniper who had survived in the tunnel complex that honeycombed the island. These units, and the Army Air Corps personnel, occupied Iwo Jima through the end of the war.

PFC Julius A. Ruskin
B Battery, 506th Antiaircraft Artillery Gun Battalion, U.S. Army

My Army experience is something I'll never forget as long as I live. Particularly if you've been in combat, and if you were on Iwo Jima. It was hell on earth, beyond description. Although our unit was artillery, and we were in a fixed position, we did not see a lot of combat, but we did partake of it, and we lost some personnel.

We were being trained for combat in Europe. However, the European theater of operations was under control at the time that we finished our training, and we were a very well-trained, high-shooting unit. We ended up at a Marine base in San Diego, where we had amphibious training under Marine auspices. At that time, we were going to become part of the Fifth Amphibious Corps, even though we were Army, so we had to take orders from the Marines. We went into a period of extensive amphibious training. From San Diego we went to San Luis Obispo for a short while, where we had the ocean salt air over here, mountains over there, and, oh, the broads. The place was unbelievable. Hey, when you're young and healthy, what more do you want? Then we went to Camp Cooke, then Seattle, Fort Lewis, and then we shipped out for Hawaii. We got off the boat and went immediately into jungle survival training for two weeks. It was a rainforest, and you talk about misery. My God, unbelievable. We lived in mud, we ate in mud, we slept in mud. But after that we went to Schoefield Barracks for a couple of weeks, and from there to Aiea, not far from the Naval Air Station. We were in back of a sugarcane plantation where every six weeks they'd burn it down and a new crop would come up. We trained and trained again, and from there we went to Red Clay Hill, a staging area. At that time, it was suggested that we get tattoos of our serial numbers put on our arms. I didn't, but some did, and it's just as well.

We finally got ready to ship out. We didn't load our LSTs at the regular port, which would have been Barber's Point. We loaded right next to the barroom we used to get bombed in. There were three LSTs standing there. LST 86 was mine, the second took the other half of the battalion, and the third had Marine Buffaloes loaded aboard, which were going to be in the first wave to hit the beach. And all these young Marines are running around yelling, Oh boy, oh boy, I'm gonna be in the first wave! I thought to myself, God help you.

No one told us where we were going until we had been at sea three or four hours, and then the commander of our battalion, Lt. Col. Donald M. White, called us all together and told us it was Iwo Jima and it would be a piece of cake, it was not too heavily fortified, and the Navy would blow it apart, all we had to do was walk in and protect it against any air raids. He said any questions? I said, Yes, I have one. How far back is it to Hawaii?

We stopped at Kwajalein and Eniwetok, and we loaded food and water on Guam. Then we got hit with a storm and some of the guys got murdered with the weather, they didn't want to go back downstairs, and anyway some were sick from the moment they got on the LST to the moment they got off, four weeks later. And we had some adventures. We were in a convoy of about a hundred ships, and we were on the right outside line. On the other side of the convoy, coming from another area, was a carrier called the *Bismarck Sea*. It got torpedoed* and lost 250 men, and they lost the ship. We were not torpedoed. I guess that made us veterans.

It took us about four or five weeks to get to Iwo, a long, long trip. We were supposed to land on D+2, however, we couldn't. There was a terrible battle going on. Our battery commander, Burl M. Hermanson, and one of the sergeants went in to see our area by the map, and they came back that evening all shook up, they had never seen such carnage, just the most terrible experience in all their lives. So we were sitting out about three miles offshore, and it was terrible. It was raining, there were waves, and you can't land an LST and take off equipment in that weather, particularly in the coffee-grounds that constituted a beach. Then we got some kamikazes. One yellow SOB flew right over my head, I could look him right in the eye. The lieutenant yelled, Take cover, take cover, but it was mealtime, we were all standing on the deck with our mess kits. On a steel deck, where are you going to go for cover? Put your mess kit over your head? If we had been hit, we would have blown up, because we had fifty drums of aviation gas in our bow. The ship next in line in back of us was the *Keokuk*, a minelayer, and a kamikaze hit its bridge and killed seventeen sailors. A disaster. They were all in the wheelhouse at the time.**

The next day was cloudy and foggy, and about three in the afternoon, three TBFs appeared out of the mist. They did not have their IFFs on, and we couldn't take any chances. They were fired on and three were shot down. One parachute came out. It was sad, a tragedy.***

*This is incorrect. The *Bismarck Sea* was kamikazied in the late afternoon of D+1 and sunk, during an attack that Ruskin relates in the following paragraph. So far as is recorded, no ships were sunk en route to Iwo Jima.

**Also damaged in this attack was the carrier *Saratoga*, and the escort carrier *Lunga Point*. Besides the *Keokuk*, the LST 447, bearing 3d Tank Battalion armor, was badly damaged but still able to unload. The escort carrier *Bismarck Sea*, as stated earlier, was sunk.

***I could not verify this claim.

On D+3, they cleared away the debris so we could land on D+4.*
We went ashore and set up. I went in as a forward artillery observer.
Any time we got an alert, I would have to get my battery commander scope and get with the truck that was at our disposal for our
team of three or four. With all the fancy equipment that they had,
they still couldn't tell if they had a hit. The only person who could
tell was me. We had telephone communication with the battery commander, and we were roughly one mile in front of the battery at all
times.

After we went ashore, I was in a beach party, walking backwards
to our area about a mile or so from Suribachi. Some officer mentioned the fact that this could be a mined area, and there was a different pattern of mines. He needed a volunteer to go in and check,
and we had one. His name was Alexis Wobert, young fellow about
nineteen or twenty years old. He found a stick and he went in and
poked around. There was nothing. It was a flat area, below the main
airstrip, so we deployed our batteries into a diamond shape. There
was one in front, one on each edge, and one to the rear, with headquarters in the middle. I was in Baker Battery, in the front tip.

There was also a small island off Iwo called Kama Rock, and I
had to go out to my station to see if they were making hits in the
right places, because we had received mortar fire from it. We leveled
the island, and we had no more trouble. Otherwise, we didn't have
too many firing assignments because the Japanese were short of airplanes, thank God.

We were getting crummy and crusty because of the lack of water.
We got two canteens a day, that was it. You had to drink, clean, and
worry about two canteens because that was all you got. There were
hot springs on the island, and some guys were taking showers with
this sulfur water, and they got terrible rashes. They couldn't even
wash clothes in it because the clothes would fall apart after a while.
So we would go down to the beach, ten men. Five at a time took all

---

*Ruskin is one day off. Two 90mm batteries of the 506th landed on D+5, the
others following two days later.

the stuff out of their pockets, went in the water and did the best they could with the hard Army soap to get their clothes clean, and five stood guard. And we'd get mortar fire. One time we were doing this and a Marine rocket truck pulled up and let loose with those 3.8 rockets or whatever they are [actually 4.5-inch]. There was no more mortar fire after that. They said they were waiting for those guys. But it's a pretty bad experience, trying to get clean but you're gonna get killed.

The first night we were there, my buddy Lindsay Baker, a strong farm boy from Kentucky, dug a foxhole. I had other duties. We got a pallet and put it over the top. That night, the ammo dump blew about ten o'clock,* and we were about three hundred yards away and we started getting fragments. If we didn't have that pallet, it would have been a disaster. To this day, when I see fireworks at the Fourth of July, it's very reminiscent of that incident. Our first sergeant was named Earl Spicer, from Alabama, a regular Army guy. He crawled all around the area that night to see if everybody was all right. I thought that was the mark of a brave man, a nice guy.

In spite of seeing all the horror and carnage, no one cracked. We were a lot of young people who had never conceived of any such thing in their lives, even with our training. Nobody cracked. The Marines had these jeep ambulances which could carry one or two wounded, and they'd come though our area to get to the main road. Sure enough, you'd see these wounded, some with no legs, some with no arms, heads all shattered. It was terrible. We got some fire, sniper fire, and we lost one or two people, and a few wounded. We weren't infantry, we were artillerymen, and there's a big difference in our training and equipment. We were not trained to fight an infantry war.

I had a friend in the Seabees, Abe Tapper, a tinsmith. Somebody had found a copper plate about three feet by three feet, and they gave it to Abe. Now Abe had a delicious sense of humor. With his shears, he cut it into the shape of the tablet of the Ten Commandments, and he didn't know any more Hebrew than the man in the moon, but he scribbled something on there that looked pretty legitimate,

---

*This was the 5th Marine Division ammo dump which blew up on D+9, four days after Ruskin landed, at 2:15 A.M.

and he threw some acid on it to give it that old, old look. Then he took it down to the beach and buried it with just the tip of it sticking out. Sure enough, somebody found it. Look, look! The Jews were here five thousand years ago! That made a big laugh for everyone.

I had another experience that was deeply moving. There were quite a few Jewish soldiers on the island, and sometime around March 10, March 15, they had a Passover service at night. About two hundred of us were there. They had a long table set up—I don't know where they got it—and they had big searchlights that lit up the area. Fool-hardy. The battle was still raging at this time, there were guards walking around with submachine guns. So we had a quick service, ten or fifteen minutes. They brought in the Jewish chaplain from Saipan who said a quick prayer and we each got a tot of wine, and that was it, they said amen and good-bye. And away we went. But at the time of this deep horror of Iwo Jima, you could still have the conviction of your faith, and to me that was absolutely terrific. To this day I think about that very often.

After things had quieted down considerably, we got the word that we were going to invade Honshu, for the invasion of Japan. It's pretty cold up there, and A Battery was being outfitted already. Getting new guns, all the equipment that they needed. But somebody on the *Enola Gay* pressed a button, and the war was over. The Japanese got the message and they quit. But between the end of the battle and then, life on Iwo was very different. We had night baseball fields, we had night theaters, the main roads were paved, and on the day the war ended, they had just finished installing a pipeline from the docks to the airfield so they wouldn't have to bring up the gasoline by truck.

I gotta tell you, there was a lot of screaming and hollering on that island. Oh my God, some congressman came down to visit, I thought they were going to lynch him, the poor guy, because we weren't going home. We had only one comedian come to visit us, all that time. Charlie Ruggles, I remember that distinctly. He's the only one who ever came to Iwo. It's like we were in outer space somewhere. Otherwise, we had wonderful volleyball teams, softball teams. You had your choice, you could play on either. And I was an umpire in some of the softball games. But, what were they going to do, close-order drill you? There was no purpose to it. Everybody knew they were going home. I had quite a lot of points, I was able to get out.

During this time, I was on special duty with the Seabee outfit for a while. It was a stevedore outfit, and there were about thirty of us Army guys. And somewhere during the time the supplies left the ship until the time they got to the PX, about 30 percent would turn up missing. And the island commander thought it would be a good idea to stop this. We used to work twelve hours a day, seven days a week, boy, we had a ball. And we cut it down. About 10 percent. There were some scandals, of course. Liquor was missing. Hey, I didn't know anything about it, you know? But everybody was a little tipsy. And Seabees drink beer, what can I tell you? There was a lot of gambling. If you won, you couldn't hide money. You could send home only 150 dollars above your pay. If you put it in a tin can and buried it in the sand, the money burned, deteriorated, because of the acidic nature of the ground.

I didn't leave the island until November of 1945, on an LCI. We were supposed to go to Saipan but we had a storm. Took us almost three days, a real backbreaker storm. We hit Saipan, they put us into twenty-man groups who were going to the same areas. I left there on a carrier.

The guys I served with, and I still see some of them, we're closer than brothers, all of us. We hug and kiss and cry when we meet each other. At reunions, when we go to the restaurant, we take over the place, we go crazy. It's a wonderful, tremendous experience. Combat brings you closer together than anything, beyond the pale of human imagination, to live through all this.

Cpl. Donald Dixon
Range Setter, Automatic Weapons Battalion,
483d Antiaircraft Artillery, Separate Battalion

We loaded our group, which consisted of thirty-two 40mm guns and thirty-two quadruple-mounted machine guns on swiveling bases. And we just went and went and went, played pussycat for a while, you stay at sea longer than you have to. Then one morning we woke up and there was an island out there that they were just shelling the hell out of. For two days they shelled it out, then the Marines started going in. It was like watching a movie. You're so far away, you can't see people getting hit or anything, but you see the spurts and the smoke and the flame and the battlewagons are in back of you, shooting over your head. The goddamned shells are going over and you can hear them.

On the twenty-second, we hit the beach. The boat I was on got damaged somehow, and I don't know if they couldn't unload it or they didn't have room for it or what, but the beachmaster came down and told us to please get the hell off the beach. So we backed off, but we couldn't go nowhere because one of the props was gone, and we just drifted all night and into the morning. Then an oceangoing tug came out and hooked on and took us down to the base of Suribachi, where we were lashed to another ship. A few days later, two oceangoing tugs came and got on both sides of the LST and rammed it into the beach. The bow doors opened and two bulldozers came down and hooked on cables and held the ship there while we unloaded.

We lived underground. First you built your bunker, then you made a tunnel that didn't go directly in. Like me, I had a carbine that I'd picked up. We had gone up to the area where all the rifles of the guys who got killed were put in a big pile, and we got carbines to have besides our M-1s. We used to have one in the latrine, one here, one there, so no matter where you went, you could grab one. I had one hanging right over my head, looped into the top of the bunker, so if anyone came in at night, you could just reach up and grab it. I never had to, thank God. But the idea was you never went into anyone's tent without hollering. Like one night, I took a couple years off a fellow's life. He had the bad habit of rolling his socks up over his pants to keep sand out, but it made him look just like he was wearing Japanese puttees. And he started to come in one night, and all you could see was his shoes and white socks. I didn't fire, but I kept saying, You better answer, and he said, Byrd, Byrd, tell him it's me, tell him it's Whitey! But it wasn't his voice, you know, because he was scared. And Byrd said, That's Whitey! I said, For Christ's sake, take a look at him! He's standing out there, and all you can see is him from the calves down. So he got out of that habit.

What we took with us was what we had on our back. Everything else went back to Saipan while the ship was being repaired for the next six or seven weeks. I remember writing my mother and telling her, Ma, the extra clothes finally got here and I took off the ones I had on and I shot them as they ran over the sand dune. One guy took his shoes off after almost two weeks. We almost killed him.

But that's the way it was. We ate rations for four weeks, but we were lucky. On Ulithi, we had access to beer. Not necessarily legal, but when we left we still had quite a bit, so we traded it to the Seabees for tuna fish and fruit cocktail, which we then had to get aboard ship. The tuna fish we packed in all the spare gun barrels. The fruit cocktail we put in the director box. It took four guys to carry the director box up on the deck, it took four guys to carry up the gun barrels, which anybody would have known something was wrong, but nobody really cared. We were all laughing that if the Japs came over, we'd knock them down with tunafish cans.

The first encounter we had with Japanese on Iwo was when we were down at the base of Suribachi. We were there two days and these two Marines drove up in a truck to get a pile of lumber that was off on the side. All of a sudden, they started running like hell back to their truck, because they didn't have their arms with them, which we didn't know at that time why, but then they started hollering, "Japs!" These two Japs were hiding under the lumber pile. Now, this just gives you an idea of the Japanese thinking. Instead of coming out fighting and trying to kill Americans, or just give up, they blew themselves up with hand grenades and got meat all over the place. They'd rather die than give up.

One night, I was sitting in my foxhole and I don't know what made me turn around, and there was a goddamned Jap standing there. He's not looking at me, he's looking at one of the other holes. That bayonet he had on his rifle looked nineteen feet long. So I took a rifle, and it didn't work. I don't know whose it was. So I took mine, and in the meantime, whoever was on guard woke one of the other guys up. The Jap saw him and dropped his hand grenade, but he didn't pull the pin, so it didn't go off. Then he turned and ran directly at me. He never knew I was there. I got a round off and I hit him in the shoulder, and down he went. I pulled the trigger again, but nothing happened. That sand used to clog your rifle, you know? So I got the other three guys up and said, Hey, there's a Jap lying out there, shoot him or get him with your bayonets if he comes up, I'm gonna clean my rifle. But the Jap was gone. The next day, the guys down below said they captured a Jap who got hit in the shoulder. Must be the same guy.

Another night, I heard a bunch of guys walking by. The next morning I was talking to these two Marines. I said, You guys go up to the front all the time now, even at night. He said, What do you mean? I said I was on guard duty last night from two to four, I heard four or five of you right over there. He says, You should have shot 'em. After ten o'clock, anything that moves, shoot it. We don't move after ten o'clock. I said, Well, what about the jeeps? He said, That's different. That's for the wounded. But nobody walks after ten o'clock. So I had let a patrol of Japs walk by.

Water, there was no water on the island. You took 140 gallons or so on the island with you, and the biggest part of that was for the gun barrels. You couldn't use seawater because of the corrosive effects of the salt. The gun barrels came first, you came second. You get into a fight, you fired 120 rounds a minute, which kind of warmed up the gun barrel. Every two or three minutes, you changed the gun barrels. They were easy to change, even though they weighed 198 pounds apiece. Two guys could do it easy, you just twist them off, put the new one in and put the old one into a special trough to clean it and cool it off. Took about twenty gallons. For yourself, you got a quart a day, and that was it. Later the Seabees put up a distillation unit and made fresh water, but at that time, what you had was all you had.

We used to see the planes come in damaged. We'd laugh at the propaganda we used to get. Just three hits from one of our guns would bring down any plane, they told us. Then we'd see them big B-29s come in with holes in the wings that you could drive a car through, half the tail missing, one motor gone, and they *still* came in and landed. Or if they couldn't land, we'd count the guys as they bailed out, eleven guys per plane. Sometimes they'd set the plane on automatic pilot and then jump out and let the plane fly out to sea and crash. One time one didn't crash, it just kept circling the island, and they had to send a fighter plane up to shoot it down.

We moved up to an area that was like a big hole in the ground, a big open-pit mine. We saw a Jap there one day, and it was so startling that nobody shot him. There was a chasm, and he came out and he stretched like he just got up in the morning, and everybody was so flabbergasted that they just looked at him. He was pretty far away, it would have taken a good shot to get him, but nobody moved. Then everybody broke for their weapons, but by that time, he'd gone back in again.

From there, they said, Well, now you've got to move up. We went up to the extreme left side of the island and moved in next to the 5th Division's pioneers. Their officers were cut right into the back of our gun emplacement. Very nice fellows. You talk about personalities, there was a Marine there who used to come up at night and he'd leave his personal belongings with us, to send to his family. Then he'd go out looking for Japs. His sister had been a nurse on Bataan, or Corregidor, and the Japs had gotten her and tortured her. It was a personal vendetta. The front lines were about four hundred yards away, and he'd go up at night and come back just before dawn, pick up his stuff and go back down. We said, Well, why don't you leave this stuff with one of your buddies? He said if they find out, they'd stop him. I don't know where the guy is now, but he got off the island.

We had another Marine come up one day, and I thought he was the greatest guy on earth. He stayed with us for two days, and every time a mortar came, he'd know about it. Don't worry about this one, it's gonna fall over there. Or that one's coming close. He could tell, he must have had a lot of experience. He taught us a lot. Afterwards, when I was telling somebody about him, they says to me, He was f——ing off, he should have been with his outfit. And I thought he was doing us a great turn. He was just taking two days off from the battle. So, you know, people crack under the strain all the time.

You know about the last battle? When four hundred Japs came out late in March [26 March, 5:15 A.M.] and raided the airfield tents? That was stopped right at our gun position. I've read articles that said the 5th Marines assisted the antiaircraft crews. Well, they assisted us, all right, there's no doubt about it. Without them, we would have stayed in our gun positions and had a fight. But that morning, Sergeant Byrd and Private Smith went out and saved two Air Corps guys that got hit at a shellhole and carried them back to our position. They both got the Bronze Star for that. And the Marines came after the last Japs, but they had no ammo. Or they each had a clip. But we had our ammo dump for us. So we passed out two cases of grenades, I don't know how many rounds of .30-caliber in bandoleers. These guys were all set to get off the island that morning when all hell broke loose. They had nothing, only their rifles with one clip. So they came up and we passed out everything we had, and the fight ended right down the road from us where these four Japs were in some underbrush, and a bunch of Marines were going to go in after them. Then this Army guy came down with his squad and told them stay out of there. They said, These Japs started it, we're gonna finish it. The Army guy said, You guys got a ship waiting out there for you, what are you, crazy? We don't want nobody else to get killed, we'll take care of it, I got help on the way. Then you heard this "clunk-clunk-clunk-clunk" and here comes a tank. Squirt, and that was the end of the Japs, you know, with a flamethrower. So that was the end of the last resistance.

We did have one more attempted air raid. We got a green alert, there were fifty Jap planes coming. But they never got there, the Navy must have took care of them. So every time I see the Navy guys, I say, Thank God for you guys, there were fifty of them coming, only a couple got through. The two that made it, the 509th knocked one down with the second shot from a 90mm. According to the Marine officers who were with us, we got the other one. But who the hell knows?

Then things quieted down. We went with the GR [Graves Registration] team, looking through caves. The Japs had openings where they could shoot out of, then move to another, shoot out of that. They had steps going down to a big kitchen with a huge copper kettle for cooking rice. You'd go in and down and around to a big chamber, and we found sixteen dead Japs in there, and there were eight passageways going off of it. So we got the hell out of there. We figured that some of them came out under the airfield. And Kuribayashi's cave was supposed to be three or four decks deep. Nobody ever found him. I don't think anybody ever found his cave.

After the battle was over, they came in and built the airfield and put in a ballfield and big-leaguers used to come in and play, things like that. All the gun positions on the island were poured cement. At first we had sandbags, but the ash would eat the bags and your positions would collapse. Must have been like acid in it, you know. The same thing if you dug down to sleep in it, the ground would be hot. You sat up, you were cold, but if you laid down, you'd wake up wet from sweat. Just certain spots, not all over the island, that the ground was hot. I heard of people warming cans of food by setting them in the ground. I never saw it, but I heard about it. We used to think, What the hell, with all this firing going on, what if that goddamn volcano explodes? We'll never get off of here. And one day, when the ammo dump went up, we thought it was the big bomb that somebody said they were keeping up on the airfield, a special bomb. Not the atom bomb, we didn't know anything about that, but all they had up there was a spare plane. They didn't have a spare bomb, just a spare plane, so in case the one from Tinian that was carrying the bomb had trouble, it could land at Iwo and transfer the bomb, I guess.

We had a Jap dog, and a Jap goat, to get to the lighter side of things. And we had a replacement from Oklahoma who could cook goat. And he kept the goat and fattened him up, but one day the goat got in and ate a bar of GI soap. Nobody would eat the goat. And he also was a bootlegger, used to make the bootleg stuff on Iwo. He had a little keg he carried with him all over the South Pacific, and he'd get all kinds of fruit and everything else, and he'd put it in that little keg and bury it. We said, How do you know when it's ready? He said he had a cloth on the top, and he'd catch a fly and put it on top of the cloth. If the fly dies, it's ready.

One time they had all these big wheels come out from Washington, the Secretary, the Treasurer and all that stuff, and they pulled all the guns out of the positions and moved them above the landing beaches. Then they flew all these radio-controlled planes at us and we shot them down. Just exhibition. The war was going to be over soon, anyway. And after they dropped the A-bomb, but before the war was over, we had our carpenters start making cartons. They crated everything up, all stenciled with what was in each box, and we were all set for the invasion of Japan. Then they signed that document on the *Missouri* in Tokyo Bay, and all that stuff was loaded on trucks, driven to the top of Suribachi, and dumped in. Truckload after truckload. We saw ships out in the harbor swing their booms out over the water, and there goes a jeep. Swing out the boom, there goes another jeep. Watching them drop jeeps into the ocean. They needed the ships to get the people back, you know? We were laughing like hell. John Swanson measured all them boxes, each one had to be so long and so deep and everything else, and now they're all in the center of Suribachi. And that was the end of that.

21

WHY IWO?

There has been occasional debate about the validity of invading Iwo Jima, especially in the face of the revisionism that assumes that because the bombing of Hiroshima and Nagasaki was so horrible, and their destruction so complete, there would have been no reason to invade Iwo Jima at all. The Japanese surely would have surrendered anyway. But the fact is that at the time of Iwo Jima's invasion, no one but the very highest people in the U.S. government, and a few select scientists and researchers, even knew the atomic bomb existed, let alone was so close to completion. The revisionists forget that the decisions recorded in history must be viewed within the context of the time in which those decisions occurred.

At that time in the war, military planners expected the war with Japan to continue well into 1948, possibly beyond. The war would still be conventional, and the invasion of the Japanese home islands would still require the use of invasion forces whose tactics had been practiced and perfected. These planners also saw the need for continued bombing of Japanese industrial and military installations in preparation for this final invasion. The earlier capture of the Marianas would now allow B-29s to fly a reasonable distance to Japan, destroy these targets, and give them a chance of making it back to their bases. The planners also knew, given the ferocity of previous battles, that the Japanese would defend their home islands tenaciously from any attack. And defend they did; the B-29s flying out of Guam and Tinian suffered terrible damage, and many did not survive the return flight. The planners knew that effective fighter cover for the bomber forces was essential to the success of the preparation for the home islands invasion. Geographically, Iwo Jima was situated perfectly for the task.

Psychologically, too, Iwo Jima was important. The planners knew that the

Volcano Islands, the third and southernmost group of islands in the Bonins, were under the direct control of the Tokyo Prefecture, and they hoped that their loss would be a severe blow to the morale of the Empire. In whatever way, taking Iwo Jima might just help shorten the war, conventionally. And conventional means were the only means available at that time.

The following two stories reflect two opinions, the tactical and the visceral, for taking Iwo Jima.

T.Sgt. Robert M. Painter
Radio Operator, 314th Wing, 29th Bomb Group,
6th Bomb Squadron, 20th USAAF

To begin with, I was quite a patriot, I guess. I looked at all these guys going off to war, I felt kind of left out. I was married at the time, and my wife didn't think much of the idea, but I told her I had an opportunity to get into the cadets. I had a lot of fun, even though I took the cadet exams twice, because I got in a little bit late, and they were making it hard for you to qualify as a pilot, since there were so many by then. So I finally washed out and became a radio operator of a B-29 after going to radio school in Sioux Falls. It was a tough indoctrination all the way through. So we finally had OTU training in Clovis, New Mexico, and in early 1945 we picked up our airplane, a B-29, at Harrington, Kansas, and flew it to California, and then to Guam after stopping over at Hickam Field in Honolulu.

When we got to Guam, the first thing they did to us for indoctrination, they showed us *The Battle of Iwo Jima,* a movie taken by the Navy as an official record. They wanted to impress on us what that little eight-square-mile island meant to us. Before that we were losing a lot of aircraft because it was a pretty long haul up to the Empire and back. Fifteen-hour flight, over three thousand miles round-trip. The B-29 was designed to fly these long-range missions, but unfortunately we couldn't always get back, because we'd run out of gas, or shot up, things like that. We'd be ditching outside of Guam because we couldn't quite make it. We lost all kinds of aircraft. So the island of Iwo Jima became our refueling depot, and thank God for the Marines. And that film really made an impression on all of us when we got there. I don't know if any civilians have ever seen this film, but it was brutal. The Marines lost more men in that battle than any other in World War II.

We got to Guam on the first of June, but we flew only three missions between then and the end of the war, because the war was practically over. Which was enough, believe me. Our last mission was in August, the fourteenth, as a matter of fact, and the war was over on the fifteenth. The takeoff that day was delayed three different times because they didn't know if the war was going to be over or not. Finally, the general said, Let's go, we gotta put an end to this somehow. We took off and all the radio operators were instructed to keep constant watch on the radio so in case something happened, we could turn around and come back, but nobody got any messages about turning around. We kept on going and bombed the hell out of Kumagaya.

We were in the back third of the Kumagaya mission. It was low-level bombing, about ten thousand feet. The B-29 was designed to bomb from above twenty thousand feet, but the air currents above Japan were so difficult and high that the bombs weren't landing where they were supposed to. So they settled on low-level bombing, in night raids, and our mission was a night raid.

The place was all lighted up. If you're back in the formation like we were, it was quite a rough ride. The thermals from the firebombs hit up against the bottom of the aircraft and everything. You're bouncing all around, and ten thousand feet really isn't very high.

By the time we were coming back, the engineer called the captain and said we were running low on fuel, I think we'd better stop at Iwo. On a previous mission, the engineer told the captain that he thought we could make it back to Guam, and we did, and when the captain pulled off the runway into the first hardstand, the ground crew ran out and dipped the tanks and there was less than four hundred gallons of gas left. It takes four hundred gallons of gas just to get the damned airplane off the ground. So in regular flight time that gas wouldn't have lasted very long, and we certainly wouldn't have made it all the way back if we'd had only that much gas left halfway between Guam and Tokyo, which is where Iwo Jima lay.

I couldn't believe how small Iwo Jima was when we landed. I mean, they had just about enough room for a runway to get a plane off. But by this time, Iwo was a regular gas station. They had a taxiway that was all fuel pumps. We had to gas up our own planes and everything. But thank God for the Marines, to get us a place to gas up so we could get back. If we didn't have Iwo, we would have had to ditch before we got to Guam. We had a guy in the next Quonset who, because of an earlier mission, was gone for six months, riding around on a submarine that had picked him up in Tokyo Bay. And some other guys had flown twenty, thirty missions, they had to go through this every day.

When we landed back at Guam on the fifteenth of August after that Kumagaya raid, the war was over, they'd called off the fighting. I got the message on the radio just as we were coming in for a landing, and oh, jeez, that night all hell broke loose. We all got our .45s out and we were shooting them up in the air. Then the colonel came along and said, Hey, none of that, so he confiscated all the firearms. We didn't need those anymore. Bullets were flying all over the place, he says, we got enough men killed already. It was quite a celebration. So if we hadn't landed at Iwo to gas up, we wouldn't have made it back in time for the end of the war, if we'd have made it at all.

PFC Leo F. Kotch
Machine Gunner, H&S Battery, C Company,
3d Battalion, 12th Marines, 3d Marine Division

Going in was the most horrible sight I've ever seen. I never realized because we could not see the destruction that was on this island, it was so small. We looked around when we came in—bodies floating, bodies on the beach that weren't even picked up yet. It was horrifying. It's only my opinion, but I think it's the most horrible thing for a man to go into a war. In the first place, we never believed that we would see some of the things that we have seen. We're not used to it. We're not that type of people. I don't know how I ever did it. I don't know how I've ever taken it. I know that I'm not ashamed to say that I knelt down and I cried like a baby, with a friend of mine, and said,

Louis, look at this, what could we do? Why did the good Lord allow us to be all right, and look around us? There must have been a reason. Outside of being dirty, sweaty, stinky, nothing happened to us. We were lucky, and the man next to us wasn't. It's a horrible feeling.

You say to yourself, Look at what we've fought for, and what all our men have died for, and the wounded. All the men that are gonna go home, but they're gonna be missing this, this, and this? How do you explain to them that this little piece of land was worth it? Then we found out, when we seen a crippled bomber, a B-29, come in and crash on this airfield they had, and they made it, and you could see the pilot and crew members coming out of this crash. It's unbelievable. Then you say, Maybe it was worth it, all of it. Then we could see, all above us, in the few days afterward, we could see our bombers going towards Japan, or Okinawa, or wherever they were going. And the fighters we had, after we secured the island, that they could land and refuel and help them bombers go out that way. It's a good experience. Sometimes you say, It was worth it.

I myself hope that what I said tonight, even if you don't use any of it, I feel a little better that I have spoken to somebody about it. Never in fifty years have I spoken about my experience in battle. To anybody. You can ask my wife. I've been with other Marines but I never said to them, Oh, yeah, I was this, I was that. I just wanted to forget. I done what I wanted to do, I figured what else could I do? I did my patriotic duty. But why reminisce over something, or try to be something that I'm not? A hero? I was never a hero. I never had a big rank. I was a PFC, I was happy. But you want to prove yourself strong, go into battle. Then see how strong you are. See how much your perseverance can go. See how much you can walk. You gotta pay for your price of being happy. There's gotta be a little sorrow.

22

THE GREATER MEANING

"Remember Pearl Harbor!"
"Because Somebody Talked . . ."
"Why We Fight"
"Buy War Bonds"
"Was This Trip Necessary?"

*Anyone who remembers the war years also remembers slogans like these.
The posters and matchbooks and home-embroidered tapestries they adorned
were meant to motivate everyone to do their part, to "Kick 'em in the Axis,"
get the war won, and get the boys home.*

*Slogans such as these are also superficial. They never completely explain
exactly why someone joined the Marines, or the Women Ordinance Workers,
or the USO, or why they grew Victory Gardens, collected scrap metal, canned
their own preserves, reduced their coffee and sugar use, bought war bonds.
Humans are complex beings and need more than a slogan to sustain them in
their endeavors. To large and small degrees, like Pvt. Joseph Kropf in this final
story, most people needed a greater philosophical justification for the acts they
would need to perform to win the war.*

Pvt. Joseph H. Kropf
Rifleman, FMF-Pac, and Company F, 2d Battalion, 9th Marines, 3d Division

I was thirty, I had friends who were in the service, who were drafted,
and one of them was a pilot who flew up to Alaska, and his plane
crashed and he was killed. And I had another who was killed in
action. This all started to make me almost feel sad, but I also wanted

to do something about it. I was working in a plant, and like the rest of the civilians who were working, we all seemed interested in keeping out of the draft, or how much money we were making, all the material things that made no sense to me, no reasoning. And as time progressed, I almost felt I was coming into the same mold as they were. So I quit my job, on purpose, to get into 1A. People were hounding me to get a job, and even the girl at the draft board, who I knew very well, was almost begging me to go back to work, and I refused. I stayed the time to where I got my 1A notice, and I almost felt that I had accomplished something, and my mind was at ease. I hated to leave my family, my wife and two children, but one night I said, When this is over, through the grace of God, and I come home, my children will never have to answer to anybody. They can always say their daddy was in the service and don't have to feel that I didn't do my part in it.

There is not any person on this planet, when you have to march past the reviewing stand, and the band is playing, and you're stepping out there, who will tell you there's any other feeling like being a Marine. Between the music and the gratification, and the things you had to take, the degradation and everything else from the DIs, when you're marching like that it's all forgotten. And when a man gets that kind of training in the Marine Corps, and when you're pinned down like I was on Iwo, sticking it out with my ankles and all my training helped me out and maybe saved my life. And in their wisdom, I think they did this for camaraderie with the men in your platoon. I think mentally and morally you got closer together. At Parris Island, everybody was by himself, trying to make it. But at Camp Lejeune, you got closer. You think about it afterwards and say, My God, they had a reason for everything they did. As you get into combat, you realize it more, what they instilled in you as a human being and also as each person depending on the other person. I don't think that in combat or at any time afterwards that anybody ever became self-reliant.

On the beach, you didn't have too much of a guard up. There was a perimeter where you had men on two-hour watches, but you didn't guard foxhole to foxhole on the beach. But it wasn't all that secure, because one day I was going down to the Higgins boats and a friend of mine from my hometown was there, a lieutenant in charge of the boats, and he had some eggs. Nobody had any eggs or anything else, so I came back and gave them to the fellas. Then I had to go to the latrine, which was about forty yards on up closer to the airfield, and I heard the screaming demon, one of the Jap mortars that was almost as big as a man. It whistled over and landed in a foxhole in the area where I just was. Took everybody out. I'll never forget that. What is fate? What is timing? You don't know. And that wasn't the first time it happened on that island. Do you have a guardian angel? Where does the fear come in? You're like a person who has disengaged himself from the real you, and you go through these things at the time. You're so busy, and things are happening so fast, you're disconnected from the fear. You think about it afterwards and everybody says everybody gets scared, you're a damned fool if you haven't got real fear in combat. It's afterwards that you're trembling, but at the time the mind has a different way of taking care of you. That was one time I was really shaken up, because it was the first time I had real casualties to look forward to.

I was told, years ago, by a friend of mine who was a pallbearer and used to work for the undertaker, he said, If you ever can't look at a body, touch it right away. Don't just keep looking at it, looking at it, just touch it, you'll be all right. I always remembered that. But it was sad, you know, the first time picking up your own men. It leaves part of the mark afterwards. It's more of "What is war?" Now you've really seen it. It's not a photograph, it's not a movie. It's hell. And you're wondering, Why? We go back to what I said about people trying to get away from the draft and all that, and all these things here. You realize it afterward, you wonder if you're all alone, what am I doing here, you feel like there's a world that you came from and that world is where people are going to bed nice and getting up nice, and you wonder, What am I doing here? You're in between saying, Should I have?, and then you say, No. Your mind is battling back and forth, Should I have left my children or not, especially if they send a picture or something like that. You see, you can't live in that world, at home. Don't ever live in that world. You've got to live in the world of "This is my job." And you wonder what the enemy is thinking. They're probably saying the same thing you are.

In one of the pockets, we were going like hell. We had advanced in a hurry, to get ahead. There was a Nip there that wasn't dead, so my lieutenant says, Get him. So I had to bayonet him. And that's not a nice feeling. You know how you have to bayonet. It's cruel, and you see the blood gushing out, and you see the eyes. That's when you say, That could be me. Then you have to say, Here, what's the bayonet code? To kill, or be killed, or the lust to kill? That's the bayonet code? The lust to kill, never get that. Never get the lust to kill. I will say, Yes, kill or be killed, but never get the lust to kill. Once you've bayoneted a person, you will never get the lust to kill.

I had a friend of mine who died for that reason. We were stuck in a pocket. This man, in training, I wouldn't go across the street with him. The biggest goof-off you ever saw. We got stuck in a pocket, and one of the lieutenants was stuck up ahead, wounded. This guy goes up, not waiting for us, and he must have taken five or six Nips, just firing, firing, firing. We were behind him, trying to get to him. He got killed. This is what I remember as the lust to kill. I don't think I'm made of that. But I can't say. Maybe I'd do the same thing.

Then, of course, at the end they called up and we got shipped out. That was the saddest thing. You would go to the burial ground and see the men buried there, and you get on the ship and you are one bitter person. You don't even like the Guy Upstairs. Then we pulled in to Guam and got off the boat by going down the ropes again, and got in formation. Then I looked, and there were the Guamanian women, who had suffered under the Japs two months before, bayoneted and everything else, buried them alive. They were holding their babies, and I looked one of them in the eyes, and there was such gratitude. They looked at us, "Thank you." Because they knew the Nips wouldn't come back. That was the moment that I knew this was worth it. Until that time, question, question. It erased all the bitterness. Wasn't it wonderful, at that time, that moment, that you were blessed to look into a person and say, "This is the reason." The

Man Upstairs gave you this to show you that's why you did all that. It's a wonderful feeling to have that peace, quiet.

There are certain threads that hold your reasons for why you did things, why you left your family. There were a lot of people who said to my wife, Grace, just who does he think he is? And she may have said that one time. She used to write and say she was worried about me. I said, Grace, you're the one who's taking the beating. I know where I am. You don't. I know where you are. You're the one who's carried the burden, not me. Which is true. A lot of people don't know what a family goes through, every night, worrying, when they hear about a battle and read the paper and all that. They don't get enough credit. I said, If I come home with a medal, you wear it.

I would never again go to visit someone whose son was killed. Never. I went to this kid's house in Columbus, and I walked up that path and I saw the old man coming because they knew about me. I saw it in their eyes—and they didn't mean it—"Why isn't my son walking up here?" They cannot hide that. And I said, I made a mistake.

But what brings me back from all this is now my children and grandchildren see what happened, and they seem closer to me, as though to say, Daddy, we understand more than we did before. And that's a relief. It's mixed with pride, they're very proud, and they're more mature about what war's all about, why people have to leave and all that. I still have moments where I think about whether there is a millionth of a second in your mind, when you see somebody get killed, when you say, I'm glad it's not me. And then the guilt comes. Is that survival as we have been programmed to keep, and yet it makes us feel guilty for thinking, I'm safe? For thinking of yourself? Then you say, What are you thinking? There's no psychiatrist who can explain what happens in these moments. Suppose I'd turned around and ran? I'd have been killed by my own men. I'd be a coward. What moves you on? Is it fear, is it patriotism? You don't know. Where did all this stuff start with, Camp Lejeune, the camaraderie? The closeness? You're all one. See? That's why you don't run. Not because you think somebody's going to shoot you in the back. Because you are all one unit, and you're moving. In battle, I think the regular mind takes a vacation, and all the training you've had takes over. It's only when you look back and say, Jesus, I don't remember half of this stuff that was going on then and there, not until later on. And I suppose it's the spirit, too, of saying, This is right, this is decent. There is something more that we can't explain on this planet right now, that carries you through.

SOURCES AND
SUGGESTED READING

I have avoided the traditional end-chapter use of notes because I did not want to interrupt the reader's sense of the "storytelling" nature of an interview by forcing a clarifying glance at a short string of words several pages later. Personally, I have always found this practice irritating, so I have avoided inflicting it upon the reader. And also, nearly all footnotes can be attributed to the single source which I consider to be the Bible of the campaign—*Iwo Jima: Amphibious Epic*, the Marine Corps monograph by Lt. Col. Whitman S. Bartley, USMC, published in 1954 by the Historical Branch, G-3 Division, Headquarters, U.S. Marine Corps. Whenever possible, all actions and instances that the veterans described were checked against this source, and clarifications were included where required.

I have used as back-up sources other books that have a great deal to do with the Marines and the Pacific War as they relate to Iwo Jima. They are listed below. I recommend them highly to anyone interested in the Marines and Iwo Jima.

Alexander, Col. Joseph H. *Closing In: Marines in the Seizure of Iwo Jima.* World War II Commemorative Series. Washington, D.C.: Marine Corps Historical Center, 1994.

Averill, Gerald P. *Mustang: A Combat Marine.* Novato, Calif.: Presidio Press, 1987.

Berry, Henry. *Semper Fi, Mac: Living Memories of the United States Marines in World War II.* New York: Arbor House, 1982.

Isely, Jeter A., and Philip A. Crowl. *The U.S. Marines and Amphibious War.* Princeton: Princeton University Press, 1951.

Levin, Dan. *From the Battlefield.* Annapolis, Md.: Naval Institute Press, 1995.

Millett, Alan R. *Semper Fidelis: The History of the United States Marine Corps.* New York: Macmillan, 1980.

Newcomb, Richard F. *Iwo Jima.* New York: Holt, Rinehart and Winston, 1965.

Ross, Bill D. *Iwo Jima: Legacy of Valor.* New York: Vanguard, 1985.

Smith, Gen. Holland M., USMC (Ret.), and Percy Finch. *Coral and Brass.* New York: Scribner's, 1948.

Vedder, James S. *Surgeon on Iwo.* Novato, Calif.: Presidio Press, 1984.

Wheeler, Richard. *The Bloody Battle for Suribachi.* Annapolis, Md.: Naval Institute Press, 1965.

———. *Iwo.* Annapolis, Md.: Naval Institute Press, 1980.

ABOUT THE AUTHOR

A native of East Hartford, Connecticut, Lynn Kessler gained his first impressions of military life as a cadet at Howe Military School in Indiana. Kessler earned a bachelor's degree in English literature in 1979, and a masters degree in business communications in 1987, both from the University of Hartford. Currently he is support coordinator for key accounts at Konica Business Technologies in Windsor, Connecticut.

The author's other works include *Honor and Glory,* a historical novel, and, with Donald M. Winar, *Painting Realistic Military Figures.* Kessler is at work on his second novel, and also writes articles for domestic and foreign magazines. He is an associate life member of the Iwo Jima Survivors Association of Newington, Connecticut.

Edmond B. Bart, a Marine Corps Reserve aviator, lives in Franconia, New Hampshire, with his wife, Lynn. He is a life member of the Marine Corps Association, the U.S. Naval Institute, and the Tailhook Association, and is an associate life member of the Iwo Jima Survivors Association of Newington, Connecticut.

The Naval Institute Press is the book-publishing arm of the U.S. Naval Institute, a private, nonprofit, membership society for sea service professionals and others who share an interest in naval and maritime affairs. Established in 1873 at the U.S. Naval Academy in Annapolis, Maryland, where its offices remain today, the Naval Institute has members worldwide.

Members of the Naval Institute support the education programs of the society and receive the influential monthly magazine *Proceedings* and discounts on fine nautical prints and on ship and aircraft photos. They also have access to the transcripts of the Institute's Oral History Program and get discounted admission to any of the Institute-sponsored seminars offered around the country.

The Naval Institute also publishes *Naval History* magazine. This colorful bimonthly is filled with entertaining and thought-provoking articles, first-person reminiscences, and dramatic art and photography. Members receive a discount on *Naval History* subscriptions.

The Naval Institute's book-publishing program, begun in 1898 with basic guides to naval practices, has broadened its scope in recent years to include books of more general interest. Now the Naval Institute Press publishes about one hundred titles each year, ranging from how-to books on boating and navigation to battle histories, biographies, ship and aircraft guides, and novels. Institute members receive discounts of 20 to 50 percent on the Press's more than eight hundred books in print.

Full-time students are eligible for special half-price membership rates. Life memberships are also available.

For a free catalog describing Naval Institute Press books currently available, and for further information about subscribing to *Naval History* magazine or about joining the U.S. Naval Institute, please write to:

Membership Department
U.S. Naval Institute
291 Wood Road
Annapolis, MD 21402-5034
Telephone: (800) 233-8764
Fax: (410) 269-7940
Web address: www.usni.org